T0178725

Parallel Scientific Computing

Series Editor
Serge Petiton

Parallel Scientific Computing

Frédéric Magoulès
François-Xavier Roux
Guillaume Houzeaux

WILEY

Cover photo generated by Guillermo Marin, Barcelona SuperComputing Center (Spain).

© ISTE Ltd 2016

The rights of Frédéric Magoulès, François-Xavier Roux and Guillaume Houzeaux to be identified as the authors of this work have been asserted by them in accordance with the Copyright, Designs and Patents Act 1988.

Library of Congress Control Number: 2015955799

British Library Cataloguing-in-Publication Data
A CIP record for this book is available from the British Library
ISBN 978-1-84821-581-8

Contents

Preface

Scientific computing has become an invaluable tool in many diverse fields, such as physics, engineering, mechanics, biology, finance and manufacturing. For example, through the use of efficient algorithms adapted to today's computers, we can simulate, without physically testing costly mock-ups, the deformation of a roof under the weight of snow, the acoustics of a concert hall or the airflow around the wings of an aircraft.

The goal of this book is to explain and illustrate, using concrete examples, the recent techniques of scientific computing for the numerical simulation of large-size problems, using systems modeled by partial differential equations. The different methods of formation and solving of large linear systems are presented. Recent numerical methods and related algorithms are studied in detail. Implementation and programming techniques are discussed for direct and preconditioned iterative methods, as well as for domain decomposition methods. Programming techniques based on message-passing and loop parallelization are illustrated by using examples that employ MPI and OpenMP.

The main objective of this book is to examine numerical techniques applied to parallel computing for machines with a very large number of processors and distributed memory. Knowledge of numerical analysis, and basic computer science concepts are required for optimal understanding. Though the functioning of scientific computers is described, this book will not go beyond what is useful for writing efficient programs. The underlying idea is to show, in a reasonably complete manner, recent numerical methods used in scientific computing, with an emphasis on their adaptation to parallel computing. We present a number of examples of parallel algorithms, which are more or less standard in scientific computing. Most of these examples are drawn from problems arising from the implementation of the finite element method.

We follow a didactic approach and gradually introduce mathematical and computing concepts where appropriate, and whenever the need arises to enhance understanding. And we present, as examples, the introduction of new architectural characteristics of computers, and current management issues of parallelism due to the increasing complexity of applications. This book is designed to be an introduction to the issues of parallel computing for users of scientific computers, and is not meant as a reference work on parallel computing in terms of information technology (IT).

This book is intended primarily for Master's students of applied mathematics, as well as of computational mechanics, and more generally to students in all fields of engineering who are concerned with high-performance computing. It may also interest any engineer faced with the numerical simulation of large-scale problems from systems modeled by partial differential equations, as well as more generally, the solving of large linear systems.

Portions of this book have been used, for a number of years by the authors, in lectures on scientific computing at Wuhan University of Science and Technology (China), Université Pierre et Marie Curie (France), Université Henri Poincaré (France), Conservatoire National des Arts et Métiers (France), École Centrale des Arts et Manufactures (France), École Normale Supérieure de Cachan (France), École Supérieure des Sciences et Technologies de l'Ingénieur de Nancy (France), Institut des Sciences de l'Ingénieur de Toulon et du Var (France), University Duisburg-Essen (Germany), Chuo University (Japan), Doshisha University (Japan), Keio University (Japan), University of Electro Communications (Japan) and the Partnership for Advanced

Computing in Europe (PRACE) Training Course at Barcelona Supercomputing Center (Spain).

Frédéric Magoulès
École Centrale des Arts et Manufactures (École Centrale Paris), France
University of Pécs, Hungary

François-Xavier Roux
Université Pierre et Marie Curie, France
ONERA, France

Guillaume Houzeaux
Barcelona Supercomputing Center, Spain
October 2015

Introduction

Recent advances in computer architectures (clock frequency, cache, memory hierarchy, multi-core, etc.) have led to the development of today's scientific computers with millions of cores, which often carry out more than 10^{15} floating-point operations per second (flops). For comparison, this figure would correspond to more operations in 1 second than the world's population could make in 2 days, with our estimation based on one floating-point operation per second per person. Twice a year, the TOP500 establishes the list of the most powerful (declared) supercomputers in the world, in terms of flops. Currently, the first rank supercomputer, Tianhe-2 in China, is composed of more than 3 million cores and has a maximum performance of almost 34 petaflops. Nowadays, the limitation in the increase of computational power is the electrical power needed to run these systems. The power of the aforementioned supercomputer is 17,808 kW, which corresponds to the consumption of an average European city of 80,000 inhabitants. The development of more ecological supercomputers is thus a challenge and is now a high priority area of research. But, it is not only necessary to develop lower power computers... but also to develop efficient algorithms that take full benefit of these architectures.

This book is an introduction to high-performance computing (HPC). Its purpose is to present some numerical methods, using scientific supercomputers, for solving engineering problems that cannot be treated by using classical computers. Current issues of HPC are successively addressed: data parallelism, vectorization, message-passing, parallel formation of matrices, parallelization of the product of matrices, direct and iterative parallel methods for solving large linear systems, etc.

The presentation of these methods is brought to life by the systematic use of the programming environments of MPI and OpenMP, for which the main commands are gradually introduced. All algorithms presented here are in the form of pseudo-codes. This allows the readers to quickly visualize the properties of these algorithms, in particular, the sequence of operations, dependencies among data, etc. The resolution of various problems, often drawn from concrete applications, is the subject of numerous examples and problem-solving exercises. At the end of this book, an appendix presents more advanced concepts and provides bibliographic data, which enables readers to deepen their acquired knowledge.

For this purpose, the book can be divided into four parts.

The first part, introduced in Chapter 1, discusses the architecture of scientific computers, different types of parallelism and the memory architecture of these computers. Chapter 2 presents programming models, performance criteria and data parallelism. Then in Chapter 3, we provide a concrete example of the product of matrices to illustrate the parallelization process, temporal and spatial locality of data.

The second part provides a concise complementary numerical matrix analysis. Chapter 4 recalls some basic notions of linear algebra and the properties of matrices, and also explains the notation used later in this book. Chapter 5 focuses particularly on sparse matrices in the context of the finite element, finite difference and finite volume methods, and more specifically on their origins and parallel formation. Chapter 6 outlines the main methods of solving linear systems. The implementations of these methods are detailed in the sections which follow.

The third part examines methods for solving large linear systems. Chapter 7 presents the principles of direct methods (LU, Cholesky, Gauss–Jordan and Crout's factorization), which leads to Chapters 8 and 9 that focus, respectively, on the parallelization of LU methods for dense matrices, and then sparse matrices.

The fourth part treats iterative methods for solving large linear systems by using Krylov methods. A quick review of Krylov subspaces and the construction of Arnoldi algorithms are detailed in Chapter 10. Chapter 11 presents the Krylov methods with complete orthogonalization for symmetric positive definite matrices. Chapter 12 examines exact orthogonalization methods for general matrices, followed by Chapter 13 that considers biorthogonalization methods for non-symmetric matrices. The parallelization techniques of the Krylov methods are discussed and detailed in Chapter 14. Preconditioning techniques and hybrid methods, such as those used in domain decomposition, are briefly described in Chapter 15.

Computer Architectures

This chapter does not claim to be a course in computer programming. Only those architectural features which are not obvious to the user, i.e. those that imperatively need to be taken into account for coding which achieves the optimal performance of scientific computers, are presented here. Therefore, we will not be going into the details of hardware and software technologies of computer systems, but will only explain those principles and notions that are indispensable to learn.

1.1. Different types of parallelism

1.1.1. *Overlap, concurrency and parallelism*

The objective of numerical simulation is to approximate, as closely as possible, physical reality, through the use of discrete models. The richer the model, and the more parameters it takes into account, the greater the amount of computational power. The function of supercomputers is to permit the execution of a large number of calculations in a sufficiently short time, so that the simulation tool can be exploited as part of a design process, or in forecasting.

The natural criterion of performance for a supercomputer is based on the speed of calculations, or the number of arithmetic operations achievable per second. These arithmetic operations – addition, subtraction, multiplication or division – involve data, either real or complex, which are represented by floating point numbers. A floating point number is a real number that is represented by two integers, a mantissa and an exponent. Since computers work in base 2, the value of a real number, represented in floating point representation, is equal to the mantissa or signific and multiplied by 2 times the power of the exponent. The precision of a real number is then limited by the length of the mantissa. The unit used to measure calculation speeds is the "flops" (floating point operations per second). As the frequencies of current microprocessors have increased, the following terms are commonly employed: Mflops, or a million operations per second (Mega = 10^6); Gflops, or a billion operations per second (Giga = 10^9); Tflops, which is a trillion operations per second (Tera = 10^{12}); and even Pflops, or a quadrillion operations per second (Peta = 10^{15}). Speeds are dependent upon the technologies used for components and depend on the frequencies of the microprocessors. Up until the early 2000s, there were enormous improvements in the integration of semi-conductor circuits due to manufacturing processes and novel engraving techniques. These technological advances have permitted the frequency of microprocessors to double, on average, every 18 months. This observation is known as Moore's law. In the past few years, after that amazing acceleration in speeds, the frequencies are now blocked at a few GHz. Increasing frequencies beyond these levels has provoked serious problems of overheating that lead to excessive power consumption, and technical constraints have also been raised when trying to evacuate the heat.

At the beginning of the 1980s, the fastest scientific computers clocked in around 100 MHz and the maximum speeds were roughly 100 Mflops. A little more than 20 years later, the frequencies are a few GHz, and the maximum speeds are on the order of a few Tflops. To put this into perspective, the speeds due to the evolution of the basic electronic components have been increased by a factor in the order of tens, yet computing power has increased by a factor bordering on hundreds of thousands. In his book *Physics Of The Future*, Michio Kaku observes that: "Today, your cell phone has more computer power than all of NASA back in 1969, when it placed two astronauts on the moon." How is this possible? The explanation lies in the evolution of computer architectures, and more precisely in the use of parallelization methods. The most natural way to overcome the speed limits linked to the frequencies of processors is to duplicate the arithmetic logic units: the speed is twice as fast if two adders are used, rather than one, if the functional units can be made to work simultaneously. The ongoing improvements in semi-conductor technology no longer lead to increases in frequencies. However, recent advances allow for greater integration, which in turn permits us to add a larger number of functional units on the same chip, which can even go as far as to completely duplicate the core of the processor. Pushing this logic further, it is also possible to multiply the number of processors in the same machine. Computer architecture with functional units, or where multiple processors are capable of functioning simultaneously to execute an application, is referred to as "parallel". The term "parallel computer" generally refers to a machine that has multiple processors. It is this type of system that the following sections of this work will primarily focus on.

But even before developing parallel architectures, manufacturers have always been concerned about making the best use of computing power, and in particular trying to avoid idle states as much as possible. This entails the recovery of execution times used for the various coding instructions. To more rapidly perform a set of operations successively using separate components, such as the memory, data bus, arithmetic logic units (ALUs), it is possible to begin the execution of a complex instruction before the previous instruction has been completed. This is called instruction "overlap".

More generally, it is sometimes possible to perform distinct operations simultaneously, accessing the main or secondary memory on the one hand, while carrying out arithmetical operations in the processor, on the other hand. This is referred to as "concurrency" . This type of technique has been used for a long time in all systems that are able to process several tasks at the same time using timesharing. The global output of the system is optimized, without necessarily accelerating the execution time of each separate task.

When the question is of accelerating the execution of a single program, the subject of this book, things become more complicated. We have to produce instruction packets that are susceptible to benefit from concurrency. This requires not only tailoring the hardware, but also adapting the software. So, parallelization is a type of concurrent operations in cases where certain parts of the processor, or even the complete machine, have been duplicated so that instructions, or instruction packets, often very similar, can be simultaneously executed.

1.1.2. *Temporal and spatial parallelism for arithmetic logic units*

The parallelism introduced in the preceding section is also referred to as spatial parallelism. To increase processing output, we can duplicate the work; for example, with three units we can triple the output.

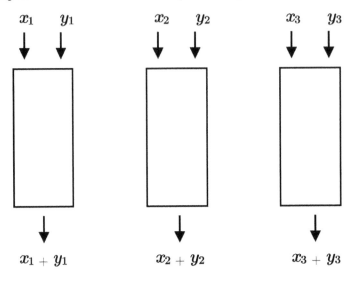

Figure 1.1. *Spatial parallelism: multiplication of units*

There is also what is called temporal parallelism, which relies on the overlap of synchronized successive similar instructions. The model for this is the assembly line. The principle consists of dividing up assembly tasks into a series of successive operations, with a similar duration. If the chain has three levels, when the operations of the first level are completed, the object being assembled is then passed onto the second level where immediately the operations of the first level for a new object are begun, and so forth. Thus, if the total time of fabrication of each object consists of three cycles, a new finished object is completed every three cycles of the chain. Schematically, this is as fast as having three full workshops running simultaneously. This way of functioning allows us, on the one hand, to avoid duplication of all the tools, and on the other hand, also assures a more continuous flow at the procurement level of the assembly line. This type of processing for the functional units of a computer is referred to as "pipelining". This term comes from the fact that a pipeline is in fact a form of transportation chain, unlike independent forms of transportation using trucks, trains or boats.

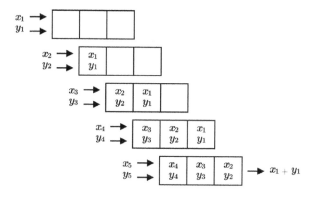

Figure 1.2. *Temporal parallelism: pipeline of additions*

To illustrate how pipeline processing works, let us consider the example of the addition of floating point numbers. This operation takes place in three stages. The first step consists of comparing the exponents, so that the mantissas can be aligned; the second step involves adding up the mantissas; and third to normalize the result by truncating or shifting the mantissa. More specifically, we will take an example written in base 10, just to show how this works. In our example, let us assume the mantissa has four digits. To add 1234×10^{-4} and -6543×10^{-5}, we notice that $-4 - (-5) = 1$. Thus, we have to shift the second mantissa one cell to the right. This is exactly how we treat two operands that we would like to add, when we write one over the other and we align the position of the decimal points. Returning to our example, we then calculate the addition of the mantissas: $1234 + (-0654) = 0580$. And finally, the normalization of the result consists of again shifting the mantissa, but this time back one cell to the left, and reducing the exponent by 1, which gives the final result of 5800×10^{-5}. As an aside, we can note that, in the same way that the precision of the decimal representation of a real number is limited by the size of the mantissa, operations are performed by using an approximation due to this truncation, even if we momentarily expand the size of the mantissa to limit round-off errors. In fact, what is the right extension to five digits of 1234×10^{1}: 12340, 12345 or 12350?

The potential improvements in performance obtained by using pipeline architectures are limited by the size of elementary operations that we can execute in just one clock cycle, like the addition of two signed integers. It would not serve any purpose to split tasks up more than that. We will find both temporal and spatial parallelism used simultaneously in scientific computers that employ pipeline architectures, which is to say that they use multiple pipelined units.

1.1.3. *Parallelism and memory*

A vision of performance based solely on the speed of the execution of arithmetic operations leaves out one important element – the data.

In a scientific code, in general, the most important part of calculation resides in the resolution phase of discretized problems, which necessitate algebraic operations on arrays in one or more dimensions. An emblematic operation of this sort of calculation is the linear combination of vectors:

> **for** $i = 1$ **to** n
> $\qquad y(i) = y(i) + \alpha \times x(i)$
> **end for**

At each iteration of the loop, it is necessary to carry out an addition and a multiplication, to recuperate the data $x(i)$ and then the data $y(i)$, from the memory, and then finally update the result $y(i)$. The data α which are the same for each iteration can be conserved in the internal buffer memory cells of the processor, the registers, for the duration of the execution of the loop. Finally, the memory needs to be accessed 3 times, twice in read mode and once in write mode, for these two arithmetical operations. Therefore, nothing is gained by multiplying the number of arithmetic units, nor processors, if the "bandwidth" of the memory is not also increased. If we want to increase the speed of calculation, it is to be able to treat models with more parameters. So, the memory should be of a sufficiently large size to contain all the data, and simultaneously be fast enough to supply all the available arithmetic logic units. To carry this out, the memory would need to function at a faster rate than the processors, which is obviously unrealistic because both the processors and the memory use the same semi-conductor technology.

Therefore, what is most important for the realization of high-performance scientific computers is, in reality, the architecture of the memory.

1.2. Memory architecture

As we just saw, computing power is in large part dependent on the duplication of functional units, which treat the data stored in the memory. Naturally, this raises the question about how to best supply data to the logic units, so as to obtain optimal performance.

1.2.1. *Interleaved multi-bank memory*

To simultaneously increase the size and bandwidth of the memory, the obvious solution consists of duplicating memory units. Doing this evidently increases the size of the memory, however, access time for a particular piece of data always remains the same. So that the global access times can be increased, as in the case of accessing a series of data from an array, it is necessary for the different memory units to function simultaneously in parallel. The different elements of the array, which occupy successive memory addresses, must be allocated to the different memory units, or banks. The memory is thus referred to as interleaved.

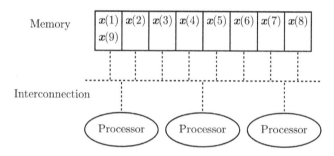

Figure 1.3. *Interleaved multi-bank memory*

Let us assume that an array x is allocated to eight memory banks, as is illustrated in Figure 1.3. Access time to one bank would normally be eight clock cycles, yet after an initialization phase, the interleaved multi-bank memory is capable of providing a new value $x(i)$ with each cycle, because each bank is called upon only once during the eight cycles.

In reality, the access time to a bank is of the order of a few tens of cycles. To best supply in a satisfactory manner a few tens of processors, each with its own arithmetic unit, a few hundred or even a few thousand banks would be required. The memory controller and the interconnection network between the banks and all the processors would then become very complex and consequently very costly to implement.

This solution is only found in specialized scientific supercomputers known as "vector supercomputers". The term "vector" indicates that these computers, in order to facilitate the administration of the system and to improve performance, feature a set of instructions which do not cover just one datum, but a full series of data in an array, known as a vector. The processors generally have vector registers, which are capable of temporarily storing these vectors.

This solution is not "scalable", in the sense that system performance does not increase in a linear manner, according to the number of processors. In fact, to effectively put into place an increase in the number of processors, it is necessary to raise the memory bandwidth, which means increasing the number of banks. If not, the processors will not be correctly supplied and the total computing speed will not increase just because more processors have been added. Moreover, if the number of processors and the number of banks are multiplied by a factor p, the complexity of interconnection between the memory and processors will increase by a factor of p^2. At a certain point, the state of the technology imposes a barrier on the maximal size of systems that are feasible.

1.2.2. *Memory hierarchy*

It is altogether possible to produce memory units with short access times, but which have a reduced capacity. Specifically, increasing the number and density of circuits allows us to add memory on the same chip as the processor. This memory can have an access time of one cycle, however, its size is limited. Nevertheless, the time unit to access large capacity memory can be reduced by putting access procedures into place, which address contiguous blocks of data.

Between a memory of a large size and the processor, there is "cache", which is rapid, and serves the purpose of temporary storage for data used by the processor. In order to optimize the bandwidth between the memory and cache, the transfers are carried out using small blocks of data called "cache lines".

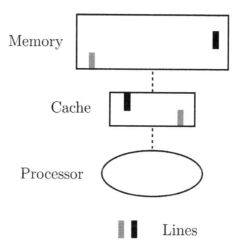

Lines

Figure 1.4. *Cache memory*

The lines transferred to the cache are only temporary copies of memory lines. The system manages the list of lines that are present in the cache. When the processor needs data, there are two possibilities:

– Either the line of data is already in the cache, in which case that is favorable, because the access time to the data would be that of the cache.

– Or, the line is not in the cache and therefore it must be sent from the memory. But before doing this, space in the cache needs to be freed up, so a former cache-line is sent back to the memory first. The cache line being sent back is preferably the one that had the longest inactive period, and is thus considered to be the least useful. Figure 1.5 illustrates this mechanism.

With this type of operation, a new potential problem crops up – the access times to the memory become non-uniform. The organization of the data structures in the code and their use patterns will strongly influence the smooth functioning of the memory system, which reduces both efficiency and performance levels.

First, the system relies on transfer mechanisms, by block or line, of data stored in the memory toward the cache, which is supposed to enhance the data flow rate. Each time data are accessed in memory, the entire line that contains the data is recopied to the cache, before the data are finally transmitted to the processor. If only these data are subsequently used, it is evident that the transfer procedure is more costly than unitary access directly to the memory. However, if other data that are part of the memory line are used by the processor, either in the same instruction or in instructions that immediately follow, then the mechanism proves to be beneficial. Therefore, the use of "spatial locality of data" would be encouraged to access contiguous data in memory.

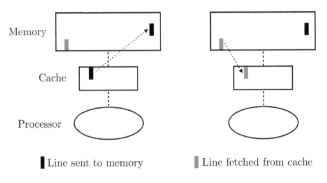

Figure 1.5. *Management of the cache memory*

Yet, if the processor is using data from the same line repeatedly in a short period, the data will stay in the cache line and provide for quick access. Therefore, we should try to group, in a short time frame, successive access to the same datum, which favors the use of "temporal locality of data".

In effect, it is the cache memory of the processor that loads it. To assure a supply to separate processors, separate caches are also needed.

As we can see, both caches share the same central memory. If both caches need to simultaneously access it, access times will be longer. Moreover, this can also produce the phenomenon of a conflict of access to the memory lines. In fact, if a line is stored in the cache, the processor that uses it could modify the data values. If another processor wants to access the same line, the updated content needs to be written to the central memory first. At any given point in time, a line can only be used in write mode by a single processor. So, at each instant, the main memory needs access to a list of the lines stored in the different caches in order to be able to recover the requested line, even when it is not stored directly by the processor in use.

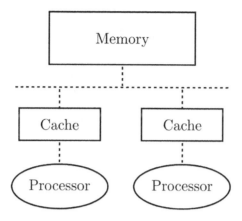

Figure 1.6. *Parallel architecture with cache memories*

When the processor needs data, there are thus three possibilities:

– the line that contains the data is already in the processor cache;

– the line that contains the data is no longer in the cache, but can be accessed from the main memory;

– the line resides in the cache of another processor, and thus will need to be written to the main memory, erased from the list of lines in the initial processor cache and then recopied to the new processor cache that requests the data, as illustrated in Figure 1.7.

The worst situation is one in which numerous processors try to simultaneously use the same lines in write mode, which can cause an incessant back and forth among the different caches. For the system to function efficiently in parallel, when there are a large number of processors, it is not only necessary to rely on temporal and spatial locality of data, but also necessary to avoid conflicts of access, by trying to have the different processors work on only distinct data blocks.

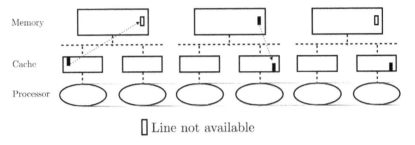

☐ Line not available

Figure 1.7. *Management of multiple caches*

This type of architecture is not really scalable. The number of processors that share the same main memory cannot be multiplied infinitely, because inevitably the transfers among them and the various caches will finally contradict one another. To increase the number of processors, it has become necessary to add different levels of intermediate caches in order to relieve the main memory. This has led to a true hierarchy of memory.

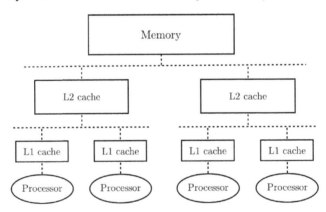

Figure 1.8. *Hierarchy of the caches*

This architectural solution is widely used in systems of intermediate power, referred to as Symmetric MultiProcessor (SMP) computers, where all the processors have the same modes and capacities of access to the global shared memory.

Different cache levels, which are necessarily larger and larger, are thus slower and slower. Scalability is still far from perfect – in order to multiply the number of processors, it is also necessary to increase the number of caches, and the result is that the system becomes increasingly complex. Here again, technology imposes its own limitations on the feasibility of alternative systems. And furthermore, the costs of access conflicts rise sharply, such that in reality, performance does not increase linearly with the addition of more processors.

1.2.3. *Distributed memory*

A major bottleneck, in terms of access to data in the system, will exist as long as there is a main memory that is shared by all the processors. Whatever solution is retained, whether multi-bank memory with one level, or hierarchical memory, it is the memory system located above the processor and its integrated memory, cache or vector registers, which is complex and thus expensive to put into place.

In order to avoid this problem, it is sufficient to simply eliminate shared memory. Each processor, or group of processors, will have its own memory, to which it alone will have access. The different computer nodes nevertheless will need to communicate so that when needed, data can pass from one memory to another. To achieve this, each node will be linked to the others through a communication network. This kind of parallel architecture is referred to as "distributed memory" computing.

This type of architecture is, of course, highly scalable. In addition, *a priori*, it does not require specific technologies; the computer nodes can be standard simple processors, but more often they use multi-processors. And the communication network can also use classical technologies.

This architectural concept, called "cluster computing", is one of the most cost-effective in terms of performance, and is composed of multiple commercial off-the-shelf computers connected by a standard network. But this type of architecture can also be found in more powerful systems, composed of a very large number of networked processors, and is referred to as massive parallel computer, or supercomputer. However, for this type of system, a more efficient specialized technology is used for their networks, and therefore the system is also more costly.

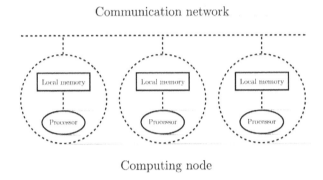

Figure 1.9. *Distributed memory computer*

The use of such systems requires perfect temporal and spatial data localities. In fact, it is the computer coding that completely controls the management of distributed memory. In short, getting rid of the complex side of the hardware and basic software creates a new major constraint in the development of application codes. The rest of this chapter will largely be devoted to the presentation of algorithmic methods that can be efficiently used for this type of architecture.

1.3. Hybrid architecture

1.3.1. *Graphics-type accelerators*

The increase in the number of transistors integrated on the same chip has led to the manufacture of specialized processors, such as graphics processing units (GPUs), in order to multiply the number of arithmetic units. In fact, each GPU is a co-processor, constituted of a number of elementary processors (core), each of which has a control unit that drives a series of identical arithmetical units. Each elementary processor employs spatial parallelism, made to work in single instruction multiple data (SIMD) mode, which signifies that all the arithmetical units simultaneously carry out the same instruction stream, over a large data set.

The term "SIMD" differs from multiple instruction multiple data (MIMD), which is employed by multiprocessors, or multicore processors where each processor can execute unique instructions which differ from the other processors in an asynchronous manner.

This classification of computer architecture is slightly outdated and does not take into account the essential question of how the memory is organized.

When it comes to GPUs, to load all the elementary processors adequately, on the one hand, there is the global multi-bank memory that can transfer a number of data simultaneously, if they are stored in a regular manner and are correctly aligned. And on the other hand, there are the different levels of local memory and registers at the level of the elementary processors.

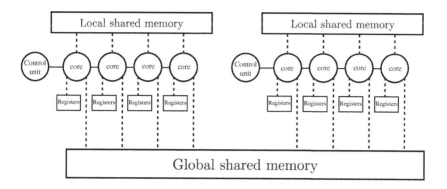

Figure 1.10. *GPU architecture*

Looked at from the point of view of logic, this type of system is similar to a vector processor computer except that the computer parallelism is spatial rather than being temporal. Also, the bandwidth of global memory is much slower than that of a vector processor, which explains the need for the local memories that can load data at the same time as the main memory. Management of the different levels of memory can be completely taken in hand by the programmer, though this does complicate the software design and is also problematic for the temporal and spatial locality of data, as it is with SMP computers. GPUs can thus be seen as multi-vector processors with hierarchical memory. Thus, in this book, their programming will not be discussed separately. Their programming uses specific languages (e.g. CUDA), for which a given instruction is carried out simultaneously on all the arithmetic logic units of a group of elementary processors.

1.3.2. *Hybrid computers*

The large-scale scientific computers exploit all the ideas put forward previously, and therefore possess hybrid architectures. At the highest level, these are computers with distributed memory, for which the computing nodes are themselves SMP computers that use numerous multicore processors, and for which the number of cores tends to increase. Pure vectorial-parallel architecture no longer exists. However, the pipelined units and the multi-bank interleaved memories are base components that are always present in all the systems. In particular, each node features one or more accelerators such as GPU.

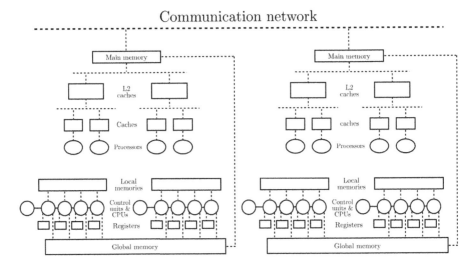

Figure 1.11. *Hybrid computer*

To efficiently employ computers in which the number of cores can vary from tens-of-thousands to hundreds-of-thousands, the elementary processors require coding instructions with different levels of parallelism that efficiently manage both the temporal and spatial localities of data at all levels.

2

Parallelization and Programming Models

In this chapter, we discuss commonly-used performance criteria in the domain of parallel computing, such as the degree of parallelism, efficiency, load balancing of tasks, granularity and scalability. The concept of parallelism of data, and that of dependencies between variables, which is broached afterward, is illustrated using concrete examples. Notably, certain of these examples are explained within the OpenMP programming environment. The specific case of vector computing is also illustrated. Parallelism, using message passing, is also discussed and illustrated by means of the message-passing interface (MPI) library.

2.1. Parallelization

Parallelization of numerical simulation codes, which is to say their tailoring to parallel computing architecture, is an absolute imperative to achieve high-performance computing. One of the major uses of execution time, in the scientific codes, is that spent on the resolution of large linear systems. This part of programming is generally the most difficult to parallelize. The development of efficient parallel algorithms to resolve linear systems, on parallel computers that employ a large number of processors, is thus a fundamental issue in scientific computing.

On a shared memory computer, we could be satisfied with parallel calculations executed in the program's loops. Nevertheless, the existence of different cache levels requires first-rate temporal and spatial locality of data to attain high performance levels. In other words, it is not sufficient that the different block operations can be performed simultaneously on separate processors. It is also necessary that each of these block operations addresses a set of data that can reside in the cache of the processor that treats them. Therefore, we are not far from distributed memory management.

On a distributed memory system, temporal and spatial locality of data is not just a guarantee of performance, but becomes a condition, *sine qua non*, in order to be able to simultaneously use the different computing nodes. In fact, each of these nodes executes a specific process and can only access data stored in its local memory. To implement parallel processing, a program, therefore, must be divided into independent processes, where each program uses its own data. When the different programs need to mutually communicate data, these exchanges are made through a network. The programming model is thus totally different; there is not one code with computing zones processed in parallel, but as many programs as there are processors. And these manage local computing, as well as the data exchanges with other processors. This is accomplished by the use of message-passing libraries. In practice, however, the source codes of the different processes are generally identical. A separate instance is where the code associated with data will be executed on each of the processors. This programming mode is referred to as single program multiple data (SPMD), a subcategory of the multiple instruction multiple data (MIMD) mode, which is that where different processes actually run different codes.

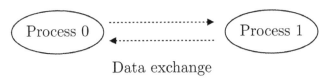

Data exchange

Figure 2.1. *Message passing*

A program written for a message-passing environment can also be executed on a shared memory computer by using the operating system's multi-tasking abilities. Message-passing will thus be achieved by using simple copies in the memory. More importantly, a code designed for distributed systems necessarily assures the temporal and spatial locality of data, which guarantees good performance on hierarchical memory computers with multi-level caches.

Very large computer systems employ hybrid distributed-shared memory architectures: each computer node is a multi-processor with shared memory, and the different nodes are linked using a communications network. This permits programming that uses message passing, either with distributed processes by nodes that use multiple processors to realize local computation, or with distributed processes using physical processors.

For existing codes, the parallelization on distributed systems means, in practice, to first think in terms of the data being used so as to achieve high temporal and spatial locality. Localizing and then distributing data permits the parallelization of computation linked to the different data blocks. This cannot always be feasible using conventional methods. Therefore, it is also necessary to develop alternative parallel algorithms for certain parts of the code, and in particular for resolution methods of linear systems.

Nowadays, scientific codes usually exploit shared memory and distributed memory parallelisms. The parallel performance of MPI-based finite element code, for instance, depends greatly upon the initial balancing achieved by the mesh partitioner, which can be very bad. This is particularly the case of complex geometries like the ones encountered in biomechanics problems. In addition, the rebalancing at runtime is usually very difficult to program in such distributed memory environments. To mitigate these effects, shared memory paradigms such as OpenMP enable us to reduce the number of MPI processes, and achieve a dynamic load balance at the node level. In addition, the presence of accelerators such as general purpose GPUs (GPGPUs) can be used to accelerate the computations even more.

2.2. Performance criteria

2.2.1. *Degree of parallelism*

To achieve a high level of performance, the degree of parallelism must be sufficiently elevated to permit the use of all the processors.

DEFINITION 2.1 (Degree of parallelism).– *The degree of parallelism of a program refers to the number of tasks that can be executed simultaneously.*

The conventional way of considering the question of the parallelization of scientific codes consists of evaluating the parts that can be parallelized and those parts which cannot. This is expressed as the parallelized execution time (T_p) and the sequential execution time (T_s), as parts of the total time of execution (T), i.e. $T = T_p + T_s$. This leads to a formula called Amdahl's law, which is used to determine the minimum execution time on a parallel computer with np processors, if we assume that the parallelizable part of the code is perfectly divided among the different processors so that the parallel execution does not entail additional costs:

$$T_{np} = T_s + \frac{T_p}{np}$$

The ratio between the execution time on one processor and on np processors T/T_{np} represents the speedup due to parallelization. If α is the part of parallelizable execution time, equal to T_p/T, the speedup, within the framework of Amdahl's law, is:

$$A_{np} = \frac{T}{T_{np}} = \frac{1}{(1 - \alpha) + \frac{\alpha}{np}}$$

The ideal speedup on np processors is obviously np.

DEFINITION 2.2 (Parallel efficiency).– *Efficiency is the relationship between achievable speedup and maximum speedup, $E_{np} = S_{np}/np$. Efficiency is expressed as a number ranging from 0 to 1.*

In the framework of Amdahl's law, efficiency is calculated using the formula:

$$E_{np} = \frac{1}{(1 - \alpha)np + \alpha}$$

What do these formulas signify? Let us suppose that a code is 99% parallelizable, which appears to be more than respectable. The execution on a computer consisting of 99 processors would give a speedup equal to 50, or an efficiency of 50%. The weak part of the code, the 1% that is not parallelizable, thus represents half the global execution time on the 99 processors, squandering 50% of the available resources. Furthermore, if np becomes very large, the maximum speedup will always stay limited by:

$$\lim_{np \to +\infty} \frac{1}{(1 - \alpha) + \frac{\alpha}{np}} = \frac{1}{(1 - \alpha)}$$

i.e. in our example, that is 100 times. So, on computers with a very large number of processors, the code needs to be totally parallelized.

2.2.2. *Load balancing*

The preceding simple model assumes that the execution times of the parallelizable parts of the code are perfectly divided among the different processors. But in fact, if a task requires an execution time that is longer than the others, that task will determine the minimal parallel execution time. The second criterion of efficiency, therefore, concerns the regularity in terms of execution time for different tasks, or "load balancing". In the case of a small number of processors, the balance can be obtained by dividing the workload into a significantly higher number of tasks. Each processor will be allocated a certain number of tasks so as to assure overall balance. The parallel execution is said to be in "static mode" . Sometimes, there are cases where the type and complexity of calculations depend on data values, and the duration of each task is difficult to exactly evaluate beforehand. In this case, the different parallel processes will execute the tasks progressively, as space is freed up; each process that has completed a task will next treat the first one (in the global list of tasks) that has not as yet been executed, until all the tasks are completed. This mode is referred to as "dynamic mode".

It will be even more effective to assure load balancing, when there is a large number of tasks, to rank them in order of decreasing size. It is easier to fill the gaps with many small elements than with a few large elements.

When there are a large number of processors, it is generally illusory to think that we can retain a sufficient degree of parallelism to allow for this mode of functioning. Thus, the distribution of tasks is most often static, with each processor assigned one task.

2.2.3. *Granularity*

Finally, the execution of tasks in parallel mode results in additional costs that reduce efficiency. On a shared memory computer, these cost overruns are minimal, and are linked to the system functions that activate the different processors and manage the synchronization among processors, for example with the dynamic memory allocations of tasks. On distributed memory systems, the problem lies with the data transfers among different processors that induce further delays when executing a program in parallel mode. To not lower efficiency, it is, therefore, important that transfer times stay short in comparison to time spent in computation.

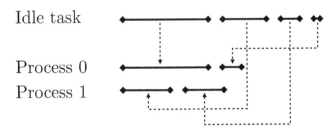

Figure 2.2. *Parallel execution in dynamic mode*

DEFINITION 2.3 (Granularity).– *Granularity refers to the relation between the number of arithmetic calculations executed by a task, and the number of send–receive data messages needed by that task.*

In reality, the important parameter is the ratio of computation time to that of communication time. The computational time depends on the number of arithmetic operations and on the speed of the processor, which is itself reliant on the throughput of internal memory. Transfer time depends on the speed of the transmission of data from one local memory to another via the communication network. For reasons related to hardware and software, the internal communications are inevitably more rapid than external communications, and so it follows that computation time is naturally superior to that of transfer speeds. The execution of tasks on a parallel system with distributed memory thus has all the more need to be finer when the processors are fast and the network slow.

The granularity of tasks for execution on a parallel system with distributed memory thus have to be relatively small in regard to code size and execution time when the processors are fast and the network slow.

2.2.4. *Scalability*

We have seen how the ideal parallel computing code is that which permits us to divide the workload into a high number of balanced tasks with fine grain, or high granularity. To succeed at meeting all the criteria simultaneously is obviously a challenge. *A priori*, the higher the number of tasks, the lower the granularity. A method, or an algorithm, is said to be scalable if efficiency does not decrease with the number of processors. To establish this so-called "strong scalability", we execute the same calculation while increasing the number of processors, and measure the decrease in runtime.

DEFINITION 2.4 (Strong scalability).– *The strong scalability of an algorithm measures its efficiency as the number of cores increases, while maintaining the size of the problem.*

In other words, we can hope that if we have np cores, the computation time is np times faster than if we only have one core. We can then define the efficiency of the strong scalability. Let us define $t_{np}(dofs)$ as the time necessary to carry out an algorithm whose size is *dofs* (e.g. number of nodes of the mesh) on np cores.

DEFINITION 2.5 (Strong scalability efficiency).– *The efficiency of the strong scalability is defined as:*

$$\text{Strong scalability efficiency} = \frac{t_1(\text{dofs})}{np \times t_{np}(\text{dofs})}$$

An algorithm with an efficiency of value 1 thus enables us to perform the work np times faster using np cores than with only one $(t_{np}(dofs) = t_1(dofs)/np)$.

This mode of evaluation is not the only one used to characterize parallel algorithms. The increase in the number of cores used to perform a simulation should not only be considered to run problems faster but also to run bigger problems (e.g. with a smaller mesh size), while trying to control the overall duration of the simulation. Thereof, the definition of "weak scalability":

DEFINITION 2.6 (Weak scalability).– *The weak scalability of an algorithm measures its efficiency as the number of cores increases, while increasing the size of the problem at the same rate.*

In order to illustrate this definition, let us consider the solution of an iterative method for solving an algebraic system. If we use np cores, we hope that multiplying the number of equations by a factor np, the overall CPU time will remain constant. Just as before, we can define the efficiency of the weak scalability as well.

DEFINITION 2.7 (Weak scalability efficiency).– *The efficiency of the weak scalability is defined as:*

$$\text{Weak scalability efficiency} = \frac{t_1(\text{dofs})}{t_{np}(np \times \text{dofs})}$$

To summarize, an algorithm with strong scalability enables us to solve a fixed size problem faster and faster as the number of cores increases. A good weak scalability enables us to increase the size of the problem, while maintaining the overall CPU time of the execution.

Weak scalability is the aim of the researchers working on iterative methods and preconditioners, as we will see at the end of this book. In general, strong scalability is not difficult to achieve in scientific codes. Weak scalability is much harder to reach as it involves not only computer science aspects (by reducing the weight of the communications, i.e. controlling the granularity), but also mathematical aspects so that the number of iterations to reach convergence of the iterative method does not increase too much with the number of equations.

Figure 2.3 illustrates these two concepts. The z-axis is the execution time, and the horizontal axes represent the number of CPUs (np) and the number of degrees of freedom (dofs). The broken line represents the time of a strongly scalable algorithm. If 10^4 cores are used, the time is divided by a factor 10^4. However, if the number of dofs (equations) is increased, this time increases (in a way depending on the method considered). It is the typical case of Krylov method with a simple diagonal preconditioner, whose conditioning degrades while decreasing the mesh size. However, using a weakly scalable algorithm, the time remains constant as the number of cores and size of the problem are increased at the same rate.

Unfortunately, there is no infinitely scalable method. The objective is to maintain a good scalability for the range of numbers of processors available to the user at a given moment. However, it is very important to support research on novel weak scalable methods to face the new scientific challenges and the ever increasing number of cores. Recently, new paradigms to solve linear systems, such as Monte Carlo, chaotic or asynchronous iterative solvers, have been proposed as alternatives to Krylov methods and classical preconditioners, whose limitations are well known.

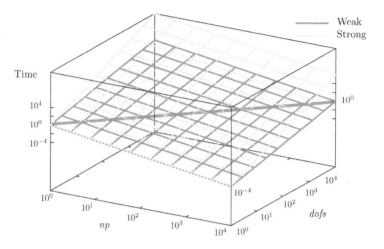

Figure 2.3. *Strong and weak scalabilities. For a color version of the figure, see www.iste.co.uk/magoules/computing.zip*

2.3. Data parallelism

2.3.1. *Loop tasks*

A shared memory computer can be programmed like a machine that is capable of simultaneously executing various arithmetic operations. The source of parallelism lies in the number of data to treat, thus the name, "data parallelism". In practice, at the level of numerical codes, repetitive computation treating large numbers of data appears as program loops operating on arrays. That is why this type of parallelism is also referred to as "loop parallelism".

In this programming model, there is a single computation code, which is executed on one single node. When the code performs the loop tasks, for example the linear combination of vectors previously seen, the different processors share the work, in partitioning the entire set of iterations. This partitioning can be static. For example, in the case of the linear combination on np processors, the k processor will execute:

$$\textbf{for} \ \ i = (k - 1)/np + 1 \ \ \textbf{to} \ \ k \times np$$
$$y(i) = y(i) + \alpha \times x(i)$$
$$\textbf{end for}$$

Dynamic load balance, useful if the cost of each iteration is not constant (for example, because of a conditional instruction), relies on the division of the entire set of iterations into chunks of decreasing length. The number of chunks clearly needs to be greater than the number of processors that treats them in dynamic load balancing mode.

2.3.2. *Dependencies*

Not all loops can be parallelized. In fact, parallel execution signifies that the different iterations will be carried out in an order depending on the number of processors and the mode of load balance – whether static or dynamic – which is, in fact, virtually random due to the fact that the processors are never perfectly synchronous.

DEFINITION 2.8 (Parallelizable loop).– *A loop is said to be parallelizable if a random permutation of iterations does not change its result.*

The order in which two instructions, or a series of instructions, are executed can affect the result only when some of the data to which they apply are shared. Thus, there is dependence. More precisely, an instruction, or a series of instructions, has a certain number of input data, which lies to the right of the equal sign, and an output that is found to the left. For an instruction, or a series of instructions $Inst$, these two groups are referred to, respectively, as $In(Inst)$ and $Out(Inst)$.

DEFINITION 2.9 (Data dependence).– *Two instructions, or a series of instructions, $Inst_A$ and $Inst_B$, have a "data dependence" when:*

$$Out(Inst_A) \cap In(Inst_B) \neq \emptyset$$

EXAMPLE 2.1.–

$$Inst_A : x = y + z \ Inst_B : w = \alpha \times x$$

DEFINITION 2.10 (Output dependence).– *Two instructions, or series of instructions, $Inst_A$ and $Inst_B$, have an "output dependence" when:*

$$Out(Inst_A) \cap Out(Inst_B) \neq \emptyset$$

EXAMPLE 2.2.–

$$Inst_A : x = y + z \quad Inst_B : x = \alpha \times w$$

We can see that the order in which two instructions, or a series of instructions, are performed has data dependencies when the output impacts the data values at the end of processing. However, two instructions can very well use the same input data, as long as they do not modify them, and then the order in which the instructions are executed will not have an influence on the result. Consequently, "input dependence" does not exist.

EXAMPLE 2.3.–

$$Inst_A : x = y + z \quad Inst_B : w = \alpha \times y$$

Due to the random order of execution in parallel, of different loop iterations, we can state the following theorem:

THEOREM 2.1.– A loop is parallelizable if and only two instructions, or a series of instructions, associated with different iterations do not have any input dependence, nor output dependence.

2.3.3. *Examples of dependence*

Dependencies can exist at any time the same array appears on the left and right of the equal sign when the indices are functions of the iteration number.

```
for  i = i₁  to  i₂
    x(i) = x(i + k) + α × y(i)
end  for
```

Here, the question of dependence is expressed in a very simple manner:

$$\exists? i \neq j, i_1 \leq i \leq i_2, i_1 \leq j \leq i_2 / i + k = j$$

To determine if a dependence exists, we must first look at the values of i_1, i_2 and k: if the absolute value of k is greater than $i_1 - i_2$, there cannot be any dependence. Otherwise, there is dependence from the moment that k is not equal to 0.

Two different types of dependence arise. The first, qualified as "backward dependence", corresponds to a recurrence, with $k < 0$.

> **for** $i = i_1$ **to** i_2
> $\quad x(i) = x(i - 1) + \alpha \times y(i)$
> **end for**

A simple rewriting of the loop will never permit us to avoid the dependence. It is absolutely imperative to carry out the calculation of the iteration $i - 1$ to recuperate the value of $x(i - 1)$ before moving on to iteration i.

The second type of dependence corresponds to the case where $k > 0$, which is qualified as "forward dependence".

> **for** $i = i_1$ **to** i_2
> $\quad x(i) = x(i + 1) + \alpha \times y(i)$
> **end for**

In this case, the value of $x(i + 1)$ used for the iteration i is the initial value, not yet modified. If we change the order of execution, there is the risk of modifying $x(i + 1)$ before calculating $x(i)$ which evidently alters the result. To avoid this, it is sufficient to conserve the initial value of the array x.

> **for** $i = i_1$ **to** i_2
> $\quad w(i) = x(i + 1)$
> **end for**
> **for** $i = i_1$ **to** i_2
> $\quad x(i) = w(i) + \alpha \times y(i)$
> **end for**

Now, each of these two loops is parallelizable.

Dependence can also occur because of the utilization of a temporary variable during the course of iterations.

```
for  i = i₁  to  i₂
    s = x(i) + y(i)
    x(i) = x(i) + s
    y(i) = y(i) − s
end for
```

The s variable is present among both the input and output data of each loop instance. Consequently, there is dependence. Clearly, it is not possible to simultaneously carry out two iterations that use and modify the same data s. However, in this case, the value of s used during an iteration depends only on the calculations executed during the course of the same iteration. In other words, the different instances of s can be arranged in an array.

```
for  i = i₁  to  i₂
    s(i) = x(i) + y(i)
    x(i) = x(i) + s(i)
    y(i) = y(i) − s(i)
end for
```

This loop shows no more dependence.

If the temporary variable is calculated in the body of the loop before being used, there is not really a problem. However, if the variable is used before being updated, there is a real dependence.

```
for  i = i₁  to  i₂
    x(i) = x(i) + s
    s = x(i) + y(i)
    y(i) = y(i) − s
end for
```

In this case, arranging the different instances of s in an array clearly shows a backward dependence. The calculation is thus recurrent.

```
for  i = i₁  to  i₂
    x(i) = x(i) + s(i − 1)
    s(i) = x(i) + y(i)
    y(i) = y(i) − s(i)
end for
```

2.3.4. *Reduction operations*

A particular case of dependence associated with a modified variable at each iteration is that of reduction operations that consist of executing successive addition and multiplication operations on the elements of an array.

$$s = 0$$
for $i = 1$ **to** n
    $s = s + x(i)$
end for

The s variable is both input and output data for each instance of the loop. Therefore, there are input and output dependencies at all the iterations. Manifestly, the loop is not parallelizable. However, due to the associativity of addition, the loop can be clearly partitioned into a number of loops that process partial sums. Let us suppose that n is divisible by np:

$$s = 0$$
for $j = 1$ **to** np
    for $i = (j - 1) \times n/np + 1$ **to** $j \times n/np$
        $s = s + x(i)$
    end for
end for

Now, each instance of the external loop can use its own temporary variable:

for $j = 1$ **to** np
    $sp(j) = 0$
    for $i = (j - 1) \times n/np + 1$ **to** $j \times n/np$
        $sp(j) = sp(j) + x(i)$
    end for
end for
$s = 0$
for $j = 1$ **to** np
    $s = s + sp(j)$
end for

The different partial summations can now be performed in parallel since each instance of the external loop of the j index now works on distinct data.

This represents a first elementary example of an algorithm that permits parallelization.

It is important to note that the use of associativity leads to a modification in the order of which the operations will be executed. However, because of the limited accuracy in the representation of real numbers in a computer, the results are always imbued with errors due to truncation. Modifying the order of operation thus leads to a modification, *a priori* a slight one, of the result. To better illustrate this point, let us suppose that the numbers are represented with a mantissa of only three decimal digits. Thus, $1 + 1 + 1 + \cdots + 1$, with the addition repeated a thousand times, would give the result of exactly 1000, with $1000 + 1 = 1000$ for this particular computer. It is easy to understand that if we add values of different magnitudes, then the results will strongly depend on the order in which the operations are performed. However, without prior sorting, no order of execution can be chosen a *priori*. To put it simply, the results of parallel and sequential execution are both tainted by an error, though they are not the same one. Furthermore, execution in parallel mode will give a different result, depending upon how many processors are used.

2.3.5. *Nested loops*

Very often, the most important calculations conducted in a code reside in multi-level nested loops that handle multi-dimensional arrays. A typical example of this type of situation is the product of a matrix by a vector:

```
for  i = 1 to  n
    y(i) = 0
    for  j = 1 to  n
        y(i) = y(i) + a(i, j) × x(j)
    end for
end for
```

A priori, the highest performance will best be attained if the outermost loop is parallelizable, and has the greatest possible granularity, while the innermost loop, where each operation requires the least amount of memory access, has access to contiguous data that best favors spatial and temporal locality. Thus, the extra cost due to the parallel execution of the outer loop will be minimal and the speed of execution of the inner loop by each processor will be maximal.

It is not, however, always easy to analyze the dependence at the level of the outer loop, seeing as how the data of each of its iterations are the data used by all the instances of all the nested loops. Moreover, certain levels of intermediary loops may display better attributes for parallelization, or spatial and temporal locality for memory access, than the outermost loop, or the initial innermost one.

Therefore, it is necessary to consider the permutation of the loops. This is not always possible, since permutation of the loops implies changes to the order of execution. The existence of data or output dependence between different instances of the loops at different levels suggests a problem, *a priori*. However, in contrast to parallelization, loop permutation requires a transformation that preserves the temporal sequence of execution. Dependence does not necessarily prohibit permutations. It is necessary to do a specific analysis. Let us consider the following loop:

> **for** $i = i_1$ **to** i_2
>   **for** $j = j_1$ **to** j_2
> $v(i, j) = v(i, j) + v(i - 1, j) + v(i, j + 1)$
> $+ v(i + 1, j + 1) + v(i + 1, j - 1)$
>   **end for**
> **end for**

All the instances of the two levels of loops can be represented by a Cartesian diagram, see Figures 2.4 and 2.5. Data dependence is shown in the diagrams to the left by arrows that link the instance that generates data to that which uses it.

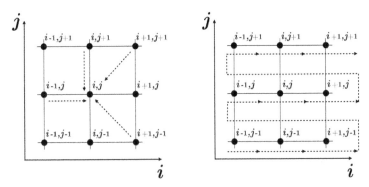

Figure 2.4. *Order of execution (j, i) and dependencies*

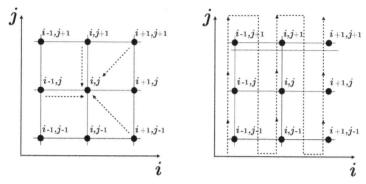

Figure 2.5. *Order of execution* (i, j) *and dependencies*

The diagrams to the right show the path of the temporal sequence of execution of the different instructions, depending on how the loops are nested.

In the case of Figure 2.4:

$$
\begin{aligned}
&\textbf{for } j = j_1 \textbf{ to } j_2 \\
&\quad \textbf{for } i = i_1 \textbf{ to } i_2 \\
&\qquad v(i, j) = v(i, j) + \ldots \\
&\quad \textbf{end for} \\
&\textbf{end for}
\end{aligned}
$$

In the case of Figure 2.5:

$$
\begin{aligned}
&\textbf{for } i = i_1 \textbf{ to } i_2 \\
&\quad \textbf{for } j = j_1 \textbf{ to } j_2 \\
&\qquad v(i, j) = v(i, j) + \ldots \\
&\quad \textbf{end for} \\
&\textbf{end for}
\end{aligned}
$$

For example, let us look at the instances $(i - 1, j)$ and (i, j). There is a data dependence between the two associated instructions: $v(i - 1, j)$ is modified with the instance $(i - 1, j)$ and is used with the instance (i, j). The permutation of the nested loops conserves the temporal sequence of execution in the two instances: $(i - 1, j)$ before (i, j). Therefore, it is allowed. It is obviously the same for the dependence between the instances $(i, j + 1)$ and (i, j): $(i, j + 1)$ is always executed after (i, j). An identical analysis can also be carried out for the dependence between the instances (i, j) and $(i + 1, j + 1)$. In a similar way, it is clear that the dependence between the instances $(i + k_i, j)$, $(i - k_i, j)$, $(i, j + k_j)$, $(i, j - k_j)$, $(i + k_i, j + k_j)$ or $(i - k_i, j - k_j)$ and the instance (i, j) do not prevent loop permutation if k_i and k_j are both positive integers.

Things are completely different for the dependence between the instances $(i + 1, j - 1)$ and (i, j). The permutation of nested loops does not conserve the temporal sequence of execution of both instances: $(i + 1, j - 1)$ is executed before (i, j) if the loop of index i is interior to the loop of index j, and afterward, in the opposite case. Thus, the permutation is not allowed since it causes a change in the result. It would be the same, by symmetry, with a dependence between the instances $(i - 1, j + 1)$ and (i, j).

In conclusion, we can postulate the following theorem:

THEOREM 2.2.– The two nested loops of indices i and j can be permuted if and only if there is no input and output dependence between the instances $(i + k_i, j - k_j)$ or $(i - k_i, j + k_j)$ and the instances (i, j), k_i and k_j being two strictly positive integers.

In the case of multiple levels, analysis is done in successive levels pairs. Among all the levels of nested loop permutation, we will seek to place loop parallelization at the outermost level, and the loop that displays the best configuration for memory access at the innermost level.

2.3.6. *OpenMP*

Some compilers analyze dependencies and automatically parallelize loops, regardless of whether they are nested or not. But, in certain cases, there is ambiguity. Let us consider, for example, the following loop:

```
for  i = 1 to  n
    v(index(i)) = v(index(i)) + α × x(i))
end  for
```

The question of dependence arises in the following formula:

$$\exists? i \neq j / index(i) = index(j)$$

Namely, if the array $index$ is injective, there is no dependence and the loop can be parallelized. Of course, the compiler cannot know in advance if the array is injective, and to verify this during execution by comparing values would evidently be much too expensive. However, the programmer generally knows whether the array is injective, because it serves to simply exclude certain terms from the array v, or if not, the loop represents operations of the partial reduction type. There are compilation directives that appear in the program as commentaries, which are only taken into account by certain compilers, which permit the programmer to force parallelization.

In order to standardize the syntax of these directives and, more generally, to define a parallel environment for shared memory machines, which use the traditional programming languages employed in scientific computing, in particular Fortran and C, the majority of machine manufacturers along with compiler software editors have defined a standard: OpenMP. The programming model of OpenMP is that of a unique code, executed by a single processor, in which parallel zones are defined, in particular, loops, which are performed by multiple processors. This mode of operation is called "multi-threading". There is, therefore, a "master thread" that activates "worker threads", which run in parallel for the duration of the execution of the task. Afterward, when the parallel code is completed, only the master task continues execution.

OpenMP directives have a syntax that uses commentary for the language employed, Fortran or C, so that the code remains compatible with all compilers. The definition of a parallel zone will take the following form, in Fortran and C, respectively:

```
!$OMP  PARALLEL                    #pragma  omp  parallel
   ...                                  {  ...  }
!$OMP  END  PARALLEL
```

In choosing a neutral syntax (neither Fortran nor C), and by using indentation to mark the limits of a directive field, the declaration of a parallel loop takes the following form:

```
omp  parallel  private(i,s)  shared(n,alpha,x)
    omp  for
        for  i = 1  to  n
            v(i) = v(i) + α × x(i))
        end  for
```

The "private" and "shared" directives are used to define the status of the different variables. A private variable possesses a different instance in each thread, whereas the shared variables only have one instance. Obviously, by default, the index of a parallel loop is a private variable, because each task will work with different values of the index.

An operation, such as a parallel scalar product, can *a priori* be written as:

omp parallel private (i , s_priv) shared (n , x , y , s)

$\quad s_{priv} = 0$

$\quad s = 0$

omp **for**

$\qquad$ **for** $i = 1$ **to** n

$\qquad\qquad s_{priv} = s_{priv} + x(i) \times y(i)$

$\qquad$ **end for**

$\quad s = s + s_{priv}$

The instructions that are in the parallel zone are executed by all the tasks. The same is true for the parallel loop, except that each of the tasks should not be executed for all the indexed values, but only for a subgroup of the values.

Two problems appear. The first is that the initial instruction for setting the shared variable s to 0 does not need to be executed by all the processes; one time suffices. Updating of s, at the end of calculations, must be executed by all the tasks – though only through "mutual exclusion". This signifies that a number of tasks cannot simultaneously execute this instruction, or the results will be false.

Let us suppose that all the tasks arrive simultaneously at that instruction, and then they will recuperate the initial value s in memory, namely 0, only to add it to their private variable, s_{priv}. The result is that the final value of s would be equal to the value of that of the private variable, s_{priv}, which will be written last. This kind of instruction is called a "critical section" at the interior of a parallel zone of code.

These problems of synchronization are managed with the help of directives:

omp parallel private (i , s_{ priv }) shared (n , x , y , s)

$\quad s_{priv} = 0$

omp single

$\qquad s = 0$

omp **for**

$\qquad$ **for** $i = 1$ **to** n

$\qquad\qquad s_{priv} = s_{priv} + x(i) \times y(i)$

$\qquad$ **end for**

omp atomic
$$s = s + s_{priv}$$

There are alternate forms of syntax, in particular for operations of reduction, as well as for other directives that permit us to manage synchronization. For example, the scalar product can be written by explicitly declaring the reduction variable s as follows:

omp parallel private(i) shared(n,x,y)
omp parallel reduction (+:s)
   omp **for**
      for $i = 1$ **to** n
         $s = s + x(i) \times y(i)$
      end for

Also, the OpenMP environment permits us, with the help of directives, to not only manage loop parallelism, but also multi-task parallelism, within a single program, by "section" definitions that can be simultaneously executed. In the framework of this book, multi-task parallelism will only be discussed in the context of message-passing programming, more adapted to distributed memory computers.

2.4. Vectorization: a case study

2.4.1. *Vector computers and vectorization*

Pipeline architecture, introduced in section 1.1.2, is especially conceived to accelerate identical arithmetic operations on a series of data; in other words, the execution of loops. To regularly supply data to pipelined units, the data must first be temporally stored in the memory space of the processor itself. These memory units are known as registers. For vector machines that use pipeline architecture, the registers have several blocks, so as to not only store single data items, but also to store a series of data, called vectors. It follows that these registers are referred to as vector registers.

To optimize the execution of a program on a computer conceived to perform the series of operations on vectors, the internal language of the computer uses vector instructions. A vector instruction is an instruction that handles a series of data, of the type: "Add the q data contained in register number 1, to the q data contained in register number 2 and store the result in register number 3".

Or, "Recuperate the q data stored in memory, from the address ia_0 onwards, and transfer it to register number 4". The parameter q is limited by the physical size of the registers, which can be either fixed or reconfigurable.

The execution of a vector instruction of the length of q by a pipelined functional unit will take $q + q_0$ cycles, taking into account preparation time. In this way, the control unit of the computer can successively launch different vector instructions, for which the execution times will overlap. This is to regularly supply the processor with data, on the one hand, and to launch the series of arithmetic operations, on the other hand.

Computers with pipelined architectures that feature vector instructions are called vector computers. These computers possess extremely fast processors that require high-speed memory, thus the use of interleaved multi-bank memory.

In the same way that adapting code for execution in parallel by its parallelization, formatting for vectorization permits efficient execution on a vector computer.

2.4.2. Dependence

Even if pipelined architecture, from a logical point of view, uses concepts of temporal, rather than spatial parallelism, the execution of tasks is carried out as if the arithmetic operation of a vector instruction is performed simultaneously, as with an SIMD architecture, and not successively. Thus, not all loops can be vectorized and it is necessary to analyze the dependencies. However, the problem is not exactly the same as in the case of parallelization. In fact, executing in vector mode does not produce random permutations of the execution order of different instances of the loop, but simply a quasi-simultaneous execution of packets. Specifically there is overlap of execution times of the different instances of the same chunk, without there being permutations in the order. To sum up: in vector mode, execution does not cause permutations in the order of execution, but begins executing a new instance before the prior ones are finished, so that the results of the previous instances are not available.

Thus, not all dependencies prevent vectorization. The problematic dependencies are those that involve the use of the result of a previous instance in a subsequent one. Forward dependence is not a problem, which is not the case for backward dependence – those calculations that are truly recurrent:

for $i = i_1$ **to** i_2
$\quad x(i) = x(i - k) + \alpha \times y(i)$
end for

with $k > 0$.

Moreover, the unavailability only lasts for the time it takes to execute a chunk of operations. In the above loop, if k is greater than the length of a vector register, it signifies that $x(i)$ and $x(i - k)$ are parts of two distinct chunks. The calculation of $x(i - k)$ will, therefore, be completed before beginning the corresponding series of operations on the chunk containing $x(i)$, so that vectorization is still possible. In this context, we refer to distance of dependence, which is the number of iterations that separate two instances that show dependence.

THEOREM 2.3.– A program loop can be vectorized if and only if the data of an instance have no dependence on a previous instance situated at a distance lower than the length of the vector registers.

As we saw, output dependence does not present any problems for vectorization, due to the fact that there are never any permutations in the execution orders. When two instances of a loop modify the same variable, it is that which has the superior value of the iteration index which will be executed last. The output value of the loop variable is thus the result of this, as it is in sequential operations.

2.4.3. *Reduction operations*

Reduction operations display a complete backward dependence and are thus not, *a priori*, vectorizable. However, like for the parallelization presented in section 2.3.4, the utilization of associativity permits the production of vectorizable operations.

The method is based on the use of the technique of cyclic reduction. It is possible to add terms together, two by two, instead of adding them recursively, which allows us to make them independent. To simplify, let us suppose that an even number of terms to add are equal to $2 \times n$. To recover the results of the addition, two-by-two, we will need a temporary table, of length n, noted by s. The first step of reduction is written in the following manner:

```
for  i = 1  to  n
    s(i) = x(2 × i − 1) + x(2 × i)
end  for
```

The above operation is clearly vectorizable. It permits the construction of an array half as long as the initial array, and for which it is sufficient to sum the terms. In order to vectorize the operation, we will use the same technique. Assuming that n is divisible by 2, the second step of cyclic reduction becomes:

```
for  i = 1  to  n/2
    s(i) = s(2 × i − 1) + s(2 × i)
end  for
```

It is unnecessary to use a new array to save the results. The above loop only has forward dependence, and is therefore totally vectorizable.

Recursively, in applying the same technique, we end up with p steps that are vectorizable, so that it is necessary only to total $n/2^p$ terms. When $n/2^p$ is sufficiently small, it suffices to carry out the classic non-vector summation of these terms.

Another way of doing this is to use the commutativity of the operation. The principle is quite similar, except that the two-by-two summations are carried out on successive data chunks equal in size to length of the registers. Let us assume that these are of length q. The initialization of the reduction is written as:

```
for  i = 1  to  q
    s(i) = x(i) + x(i + q)
end  for
```

Then, the successive chunks, termed x, will be added to the vector s, and supposing that n is a multiple of q can be written as:

```
for  p = 2  to  n/q − 1
    for  i = 1  to  q
        s(i) = s(i) + x(i + p × q)
    end  for
end  for
```

When all the x terms have been treated, the only remaining thing to do is a summation between them and the q coefficients of the s vector.

This method is all the more effective because there is absolutely no need to create array s in memory; it can simply reside in the vector registers. This reduces traffic toward the memory and enhances pipeline operations. This notion is detailed in the following section.

2.4.4. *Pipeline operations*

As is describes in the previous section in the case of reduction operations, data modified several times in a row can reside in the vector registers, which play a somewhat similar role as cache memory. If we need to execute numerous successive operations with the same data, the intermediate results do not need to be sent back to the memory, but can simply be stored in the registers between two successive uses. This is known as a pipeline operation, because we create a large composite pipeline to carry out successive operations.

A typical example is that of a linear combination of vectors:

$$\textbf{for}\ \ i = 1\ \ \textbf{to}\ \ n$$
$$y(i) = y(i) + a \times x(i)$$
$$\textbf{end}\ \ \textbf{for}$$

In the above loop, it is necessary to carry out two successive operations; one multiplication and one addition. The result of the multiplication $a \times x(i)$ needs to be used and added to $y(i)$. The intermediate result, $a \times x(i)$, can be temporarily stored in a register. This principle of functioning is shown in Figure 2.6, in which the notation $v(i_0 + 1 : i_0 + q)$ represents the vector of components $v(i_0 + 1), v(i_0 + 2), \cdots, v(i_0 + q)$.

The vector data are stored in the vector registers. Data a, which are used numerous times in a row, are stored in a unitary or scalar register. Using the intermediate vector register, register 2, is not always mandatory; some machines allow the output of an arithmetic unit to be sent directly to the input of the other. Figure 2.6 shows the state of registers; when the first chunk of the q elements of arrays x and y has been treated, the second chunk is at the input of the sum and the third chunk is at the input of the multiplication. The same mechanism is then repeated for all the subsequent packets.

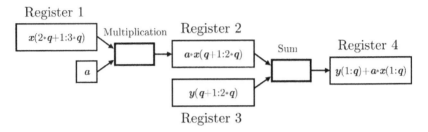

Figure 2.6. *Pipelining of the linear combination of vectors*

The mechanism creates a long pipelining of multiplication and addition. Once the pipeline starts, if we regularly feed data to registers 1 and 3, the computer can carry out a pair of operations $(+, \times)$ per clock cycle. Naturally, at any given instant, the multiplication and the sum are not carried out for the same instances of the loop, but on different chunks, in the same way that the different stages of a simple pipeline unit operate on successive instances. The fact remains that both can work simultaneously and that overall, the calculator can thus effectuate two operations per clock cycle, whereas each unitary operation requires several cycles.

Another example of pipelining is the scalar products of two vectors:

$$s = 0$$
$$\textbf{for } i = 1 \textbf{ to } n$$
$$\quad s = s + x(i) \times y(i)$$
$$\textbf{end for}$$

By using the reduction technique by chunks, described in the previous section, it is also possible to pipeline the multiplication of the coefficients $x(i)$ and $y(i)$ with the summations.

Obviously, the more complex the pipeline, the longer it takes to "issue" it, so they are only efficient for long loops. In the case of a scalar product of vectors, we have to add to this issue time the time for the sum of the final chunks in scalar mode.

Using these techniques, the vector architectures allow us to very rapidly accomplish multiple arithmetic operations, which are carried out on data that are divided up regularly in memory. The programmer, of course, does not need to deal with chunk management for operational pipelines; the compiler looks after that. However, the program must be suitable for vector optimization. This requires careful organization of the data structures and the calculations to bring up the long series of pipeline operations to be carried out on the data sets, which are preferably stored contiguously, so as to not impede and slow access to the memory banks.

2.5. Message-passing

2.5.1. *Message-passing programming*

Programming models such as OpenMP take into consideration a single code that manages the entire data set on the one hand, and launches the parallel execution of certain sections of the program on the other hand. This model is suitable for multiprocessor machines with shared memory.

For systems that use distributed memory, another model is needed, which must take into account the distinct processes that only have their own data stored on the various computing nodes. These processes must, therefore, be able to mutually communicate data. Data transfers among processes use message systems, accessible at the program level, which are associated with the different processes, by means of message-passing library functions, which can be used with both Fortran and C, as well as with other languages.

In the message-passing programming environment, the standard most widely used today is the MPI. In the following sections, only the basic functionalities of this type of environment will be discussed.

Programming by message-passing is relatively easy: the functions are intuitive, the parameters are few and their descriptions are easy to understand. The major difficulties lie in the conception of the algorithms; and we will consider the examples of those in the following chapters.

2.5.2. *Parallel environment management*

A priori, each process can be associated with its own code. Nonetheless, as is most often the case, the different processes have the same source code, since they all contribute to the same application. Only the data change from one process to another. In any event, each of the processes needs information from the parallel environment. At a minimum, this signifies that each of the processes must know the number of processes with which it shares the parallel application, and also be assigned a specific number.

The MPI functions that enable this are, respectively, called *MPI_Comm_size* and *MPI_Comm_rank*. The first determines the number of processes associated with a "communicator", and the second determines the rank attributed to the calling processes in the communicator, between 0 and the [number of processes – 1]. A communicator, in fact, designates a messaging service shared by a group of processes. In the same group of processes, different communicators can coexist, which are used to differentiate groups of processes, or different contexts.

For example, if only certain processes participate in a phase of calculations, that group can be attached to a specific communicator, so as to allow collective messages only within a group. Conversely, two communicators can be associated with the same group of processes to assure a perfect barrier between message-passing conducted in two different contexts.

All the processes of the same application, by default, belong to a global communicator. Each communicator is recognized by its unique identifier. By default, that of the global communicator is *MPI_COMM_WORLD*, an MPI environment parameter. Calls to the following routines: *MPI_Comm_size (MPI_COMM_WORLD,size)* and *MPI_Comm_rank (MPI_COMM_WORLD, rank)* respectively, permit us to recuperate, in the *size* and *rank* variable integers, the total number of attached processes to the parallel application and the unique ID numbers of the processes calling them.

2.5.3. *Point-to-point communications*

The main objective of a message-passing library is to permit "point-to-point" exchanges, that is to say, from one process to another. So that such a transfer can take place, the source (sending) processes send data through the network, which is then recuperated by the destination (receiving) processes.

The exchanges involve data, thus the content of a message is simply defined by an array, which is identified by its memory address, its length and the type of data it contains. To send a message, it is necessary to specify the communicator by which it will transit, and the rank of the destination process. Moreover, the message can optionally be identified by a tag.

In the program of the emitting processes, the sending of a message will be written as:

– *MPI_Send(array_sent,length_of_array,type_of_data,destination,tag,comm)*.

The type of data *type_of_data* is indicated by a parameter of the environment, *MPI_INTEGER* that designates, for example, the integer type. The parameter *length_of_array* designates the size of the data *array_sent* to be sent to the process of rank *destination*.

The reception is written in the following manner, in the program of the receiving processes:

– *MPI_Recv(array_received,size_of_array,type_of_data,source,tag,comm)*.

The parameter *size_of_array* designates the maximal length of the received message, because it is the size of the array in which it will be stored. The optional parameter *source* is the rank of the sending process, while *tag* serves to optionally sort the received messages, as an option.

A priori, the exchanges are asynchronous, but blocking. This means that the sending and receiving processes do not need to act simultaneously during the transfers. The message-passing library is the one in charge of temporally storing the message. However, the source process executes the instructions next to the *MPI_Send* once the message is sent and the array *array_sent* can be modified without altering the message. Conversely, the destination process can execute the instruction next to the *MPI_Recv* once the message has arrived and the data have been stored in the array *array_received*.

2.5.4. *Collective communications*

Collective communications are exchanges in which either one or all of the processes are both senders (source processes) and receivers (destination processes). When using a collective communications routine, all the processes belonging to the communicator which are used must imperatively call the function. This is why, it is necessary to specify a communicator for each subgroup for which we want to use this kind of exchange.

The simplest and most frequent example is the sending of one toward all; a process sends a message to all the other processes. Of course, this type of transfer could be achieved using successive point-to-point exchanges. But aside from this programming being simpler and clearer, calling the collective communications routine will allow putting into place strategies for the optimization of transfers. In effect, the sending operation using point-to-point exchanges toward the n members of a group, including itself, requires $n - 1$ successive sends.

As Figure 2.7 shows, in the case of 8 processes, the sending of 1 toward n can be carried out in only $Log_2(n)$ steps: at the end of the first transfer, two processes have the data, and can send toward two others during the second phase, and so forth. At the conclusion of the p-th phase, 2^p processes have received the information and will be able to send toward 2^p others in the following step. With this procedure, the total transfer time will be of the order of $Log_2(n)$ instead of $n - 1$, multiplied by the time for one transfer.

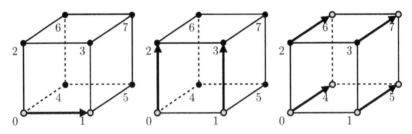

Figure 2.7. *One-to-all communication*

The MPI function that implements the transfer of one toward all is *MPI_Bcast*:

– *MPI_Bcast(array,length,type_of_data,source,comm)*.

The parameter *root* designates the rank of the process that sends the data *array* to all the other processes of the communicator *comm*. The parameters *array*, *length* and *type_of_data* describe the data sent from the source process to the destination processes, and the data received by these destination processes.

The exchange of all-to-one can be achieved by using the inverse exchange procedure of one-to-all. To carry out an all-to-all exchange, it will be possible to execute an exchange of all-to-one, followed by an exchange of one-to-all. Nevertheless, a procedure of simultaneous diffusion, starting from all the nodes, will permit performing the transfer in only $Log_2(n)$ steps, once again, as shown in Figure 2.8.

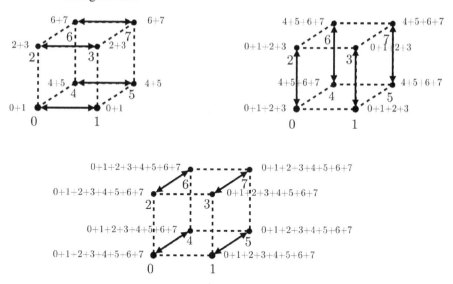

Figure 2.8. *All-to-all communication*

A particular case that is extremely frequent in the collective exchanges of the type all-to-one or all-to-all is of reduction operations. They serve to perform, term-by-term, associative operations, of the addition or multiplication kind, on the elements of arrays that are present in all the processes. In this case, instead of transferring all the data and only performing the calculations at the end, the operations are executed along the way. For example, in the case of a sum concerning an array of the length 1, as Figure 2.8 shows, instead of 2^{p-1} data, a single datum equal to the sum of the two data sent and received during the preceding phase is transmitted in the p step.

The syntax of the reduction operations is the following:

– *MPI_Reduce (initial_array,final_array,length,type_of_data, type_of_operation,root,comm);*

– *MPI_Allreduce(initial_array,final_array,length,type_of_data, type_of_operation,comm).*

The parameter *type_of_operation* designates the operation to be carried out: sum by using the MPI parameter *MPI_SUM*; maximum by using *MPI_MAX* and; minimum by using *MPI_MIN*. The reduction operation is carried out on the array *initial_array* of the different processes (the send buffer), and the result is placed on the array *final_array* (the receive buffer). In the case of the *MPI_Reduce* function, only the root process receives the result; whereas, in the case of the *MPI_Allreduce* function, the parameter *root* is omitted, because all the processes recuperate the result.

In iterative solvers, reduction operations are represented by scalar products. They are blocking operations and are thus synchronization points during the execution. Therefore, they strongly limit the scalability of the solvers. Recently, non-blocking reduction functions were implemented in the third version of MPI, namely MPI3. They have enabled the implementation of pipelined versions of classical solvers such as the pipelined conjugate gradient, where the communication of the reduction operations overlaps some computations such as matrix-vector product and preconditioning.

All the reduction functions work on the arrays in such a way that permit us to carry out simultaneously several reduction operations, each one dealing with an element of the arrays. This is to reduce the data transfer time. In a general manner, to transfer n data will take the time:

$$T(n) = T(0) + \frac{n}{C}$$

where $T(0)$ is the initialization time of the transfer and C is the speed of the network during the transfer phases.

The initialization time is qualified as the "latency" of the network. It is the time necessary to access data across the network. This notion of latency is more generally applied to all data access time to systems of storage, whether that be on the different levels of machine memory, or external storage systems; electronic, magnetic or optical.

For standard networks, latency time is extremely high in comparison to the flow rate, and more so in comparison to the clock rates of the processors awaiting the data. Technologically, it is much simpler to increase the flow rate, simply by increasing the bandwidth, than it is to reduce latency. Grouping reduction operations that simultaneously work with the arrays permits us to only lose time once, due to latency, for the different transfers of data. The same remark applies for all the transfers: it is always necessary, whenever possible, to regroup all the data to transfer, so that there is only one message exchange.

2.6. Performance analysis

The performance of a scientific code is hardly predictable. It depends on the particular scientific case under study, on the supercomputer on which the code is executed, the load of the system, etc. In addition, small details and variability can have an important impact on the overall computing time, e.g. a small load imbalance and a slower processor (for example, due to different heating. The study of the behavior of a code is, therefore, important in order to optimize it or to adjust the data of the simulation, and thus to increase its efficiency.

There exist performance analysis tools which enable us to study the behavior of a code along its execution. These tools provide relevant information, usually in a graphical way, on the "trace" generated by the code. The trace of a code is a binary file containing some information generated during its execution. The contents of the trace can be adjusted according to what is required, for example:

– MPI communications: point-to-point, collective;

– cache misses;

– number of instructions, etc.

A first diagnosis on the trace enables us to identify rapidly the load imbalances, sequences of collectives and cache misses. This valuable information gives indications to the programmer for a first optimization of the code: collectives can be merged into a single one in order to decrease the latency; cache misses can be reduced by numbering properly the nodes of the mesh, etc.

Some of these performance analysis tools present the results in a graphical way (for example, Paraver and Scalasca, see A3.4). Let us take the example of Paraver, a performance analysis tool developed at BSC-CNS. The horizontal axis represents the time and the vertical axis represents the core number (MPI task or thread). The GUI plots the state or the task carried out by a particular core at a given time by using different colors. We can then easily observe the synchronization of the different cores and detect load imbalances. Figure 2.9 shows the example of a computational fluid dynamics (CFD) code executed on 70 CPUs of a distributed memory supercomputer. The figure represents the first iteration of this code. According to the color, we can identify the tasks computed by the different CPUs:

1) the local matrix graph;

2) the local assembly of the matrix representing the Navier–Stokes equation;

3) the solution of the momentum equation using the GMRES method;

4) the solution of the continuity equation using the deflated conjugate gradient (DCG).

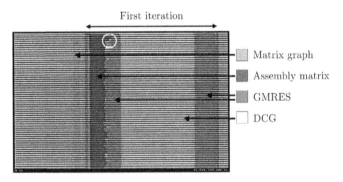

Figure 2.9. *Visualization of the trace of a CFD code. For a color version of the figure, see www.iste.co.uk/magoules/computing.zip*

In the assembly part, we encircled the processes which greater workload during this step. We thus clearly identified a small load imbalance: the mesh partitioner METIS assigned more elements to some processes.

Let us consider another example, the trace generated by MPI functions. The first part of Figure 2.10 shows the geometry of the network of vessels of a brain and a zoom on the mesh.

Figure 2.11 shows the different MPI functions called during the execution of an iterative method, namely the DCG used to solve the continuity equation. Some subdomains are encircled in order to show an imbalanced communication phase between some of them carried out after a local matrix-vector product. These communication phases use the MPI function *MPI_Sendrecv*, as will be explained in Chapter 14. The following operation is a reduction which uses the function *MPI_Allreduce*. This last operation will start only once the previous operation is finalized. We see that in this case, the lag of the encircled subdomains is almost one-third of the total time needed to carry out the *MPI_Allreduce*. We have thus identified a problem.

Now, let us go back to the geometry. In the bottom part of Figure 2.10, we can observe the connectivity of the subdomains, obtained using the library METIS to partition the mesh. The subdomains are colored according to the number of neighbors. We can observe that, in general, the vessels are sliced and have thus two neighbors. However, there exists a zone of converging vessels consisting of a sphere, where the number of neighbors goes up to nine for some subdomains. These subdomains are the ones that we previously identified by visualizing the trace and which exhibit more communication during the *MPI_Sendrecv* phase.

We have given two examples of common problems encountered in scientific simulation codes. After this first diagnosis, we can then enter into more detail. By selecting graphically a particular zone, we can have statistics on the different point-to-point and collective communication phases, compute-derived indices such as number of instructions per cycle, etc. These tools are of great help to the programmer and are widely used in supercomputing centers.

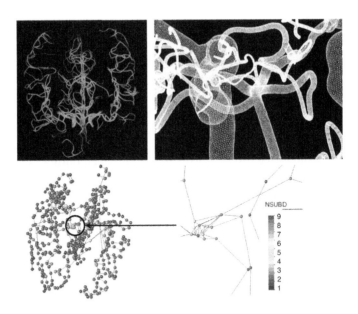

Figure 2.10. *Brain hemodynamics; (top) geometry and zoom on the mesh (from Raul Cebral, George Mason University, USA); (bottom). Subdomain connectivity and number of neighbors. For a color version of the figure, see www.iste.co.uk/magoules/computing.zip*

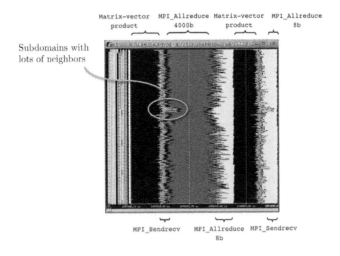

Figure 2.11. *Trace of a CFD code. MPI calls inside an iterative solver. For a color version of the figure, see www.iste.co.uk/magoules/computing.zip*

3

Parallel Algorithm Concepts

This chapter presents and examines two concrete examples of parallel algorithms. Our first example concerns reduction methods for linear recurrences, and allows us to illustrate how a change of algorithm can permit us to calculate, in parallel, a solution to a problem whose natural formulation is not parallelizable. Issues of algorithmic overhead and numerical stability are also discussed. The second example is the study of the product of matrices. It is fundamental in that it shows the importance of temporal and spatial locality of data. It allows us to explain how locality analysis, essential for obtaining good performance on hierarchical memory systems, leads to the development of a block approach, which can then easily be incorporated into a message-passing programming environment.

Whether we are working in an OpenMP programming environment with a global vision of the memory, or in a message-passing programming environment, MPI, with a distributed memory, the different parallel tasks that generate a method, or a parallel algorithm, are intended to be performed by separate processes – may they be light processes of the thread type, or standard processes. Thus, we will speak about parallel processes, it being understood that the parallelism provides an acceleration only if the different processes can be run simultaneously by different processors, or by different cores.

3.1. Parallel algorithms for recurrences

3.1.1. *The principles of reduction methods*

This analysis of dependence shows that it is impossible to parallelize, nor even to vectorize linear recurrences, such as in the below of order 1:

```
for  i = 2 to  n
    x ( i )  =  y ( i )  +  a ( i )  \star  x ( i − 1)
end  for
```

However, it is possible to consider other algorithms for solving the recurrence by using independent operations. The general idea is to reduce the calculations to a series of independent recurrence relations that will lead to smaller problems to be solved in a sequential mode. The same principle has already been applied to reduction operations.

Let us suppose that $n = p \times q + 1$; the recurrence relation, which links all the $x(i)$ among themselves, implies that the $p+1$ coefficients $\{x(1), x(q+1), \ldots, x(k \times q+1), \ldots, x(p \times q+1)\}$ all satisfy, among themselves, recurrence relations of the type:

$$x(k \times q + 1) = z(k) + b(k) \times x((k - 1) \times q + 1)$$

To find the coefficients $z(k)$ and $b(k)$, it is enough to solve the initial recurrence for the iteration indices between $(k - 1) \times q + 2$ and $k \times q$. In fact, if $x(i - 1) = z + b \times x(i_0)$, then in applying recurrence relations, we get:

$$x(i) = y(i) + a(i) \times x(i - 1) = (y(i) + a(i) \times z) + (a(i) \times b) \times x(i_0)$$

This leads to the following algorithm to determine $z(k)$ and $b(k)$:

$$z(k) = y((k - 1) \times q + 1)$$
$$b(k) = a((k - 1) \times q + 1)$$
$$\textbf{for} \ i = (k - 1) \times q + 2 \ \textbf{to} \ k \times q$$
$$z(k) = y(i) + a(i) \times z(k)$$
$$b(k) = a(i) \times b(k)$$
$$\textbf{end} \ \textbf{for}$$

The calculations of the p pairs of coefficients $z(k)$ and $b(k)$ are independent of each other and therefore can be performed in parallel by p processes.

Once the calculations of the coefficients $z(k)$ and $b(k)$ are finished, we need to solve the recurrence that connects, among themselves, the $p + 1$ coefficients $\{x(1), x(q+1), \ldots, x(k \times q + 1), \ldots, x(p \times q + 1)\}$. This small calculation can be executed by one process, using the algorithm:

> **for** $k = 1$ **to** p
> $\quad x(k \times q + 1) = y(k) + b(k) \times x((k-1) \times q + 1)$
> **end for**

Then, we have to calculate all the other coefficients of x, based on known values, in resolving each of the p recurrences:

> **for** $i = (k-1) \times q + 2$ **to** $k \times q$
> $\quad x(i) = y(i) + a(i) \times x(i-1)$
> **end for**

These calculations, conducted for the different values of k, from 1 to p inclusive, are independent of each other, and therefore can be performed in parallel by p processes.

3.1.2. *Overhead and stability of reduction methods*

The reduction method has two drawbacks. The first is the cost of the entire calculation. In fact, the number of necessary operations for the execution of the initial sequential algorithm:

> **for** $i = 2$ **to** n
> $\quad x(i) = y(i) + a(i) \times x(i-1)$
> **end for**

is equal to $n - 1$ pairs of operations $(+, \times)$.

With the reduction algorithm, the initial reduction phase requires $2q - 2$ products and $q - 1$ additions for each of the $p = (n-1)/q$ chunks:

$$z(k) = y((k-1) \times q + 1)$$
$$\quad b(k) = a((k-1) \times q + 1)$$
$$\quad \textbf{for} \ \ i = (k-1) \times q + 2 \ \textbf{to} \ \ k \times q$$
$$\quad\quad z(k) = y(i) + a(i) \times z(k)$$
$$\quad\quad b(k) = a(i) \times b(k)$$
$$\quad \textbf{end for}$$

This gives a total on the order of $2n$ products and n additions.

The resolution of the reduced recurrence:

$$\textbf{for} \ \ k = 1 \ \textbf{to} \ \ p$$
$$\quad x(k \times q + 1) = y(k) + b(k) \times x((k-1) \times q + 1)$$
$$\textbf{end for}$$

needs in return p pairs of $(+, \times)$ operations.

In the end, the final resolution of each of the p recurrences:

$$\textbf{for} \ \ i = (k-1) \times q + 2 \ \textbf{to} \ \ k \times q$$
$$\quad x(i) = y(i) + a(i) \times x(i-1)$$
$$\textbf{end for}$$

comes to $q - 1$ pairs of $(+, \times)$ operations, which result in a total of $n - p$ pairs of $(+, \times)$ operations for this phase.

We can see that the two reduction phases of recurrence resolutions and then the final resolution of independent p recurrences require, overall, the same number of arithmetic operations as with the standard sequential algorithm. The initial reduction phase thus accounts for computational overhead of about 1.5 times the initial cost. So, globally, the reduction method requires 2.5 times more arithmetic operations.

Moreover, the reduction method can create problems of numerical stability. The coefficient $b(k)$, calculated during the reduction operation, is the successive product of the coefficients $a(i)$, for $i = (k-1) \times q + 2$ to $i = k \times q$. If these coefficients are more than 1, their products can be so large as to make the machine unable to represent them and the algorithm diverges. Conversely, if these coefficients are less than 1, their products can become too small to be represented. In this latter case, we could imagine that setting the weakest coefficients to zero would settle the problem. However, this solution does not avoid the fact that the algorithm gives a sullied result with a very important error. In fact, if the coefficients $b(k)$ are null, or even simply too small before the coefficients $y(k)$, the reduced relationship:

> **for** $k = 1$ **to** p
> $x(k \times q + 1) = y(k) + b(k) \times x((k-1) \times q + 1)$
> **end for**

numerically degenerates to become the equivalent of:

> **for** $k = 1$ **to** p
> $x(k \times q + 1) = y(k)$
> **end for**

This signifies that by using a reduction method, the different values $x(k)$ are independent of each other, which is obviously false. The erroneous calculation of these coefficients obviously impacts the final results, obtained after the resolution of p recurrences:

> **for** $i = (k-1) \times q + 2$ **to** $k \times q$
> $x(i) = y(i) + a(i) \times x(i-1)$
> **end for**

are themselves also marred by the same level of error.

The numerical effects caused by the limitations of the precision in the representation of numbers, combined with the modification of the order in which the arithmetic operations are carried out, can prove catastrophic in the case of the direct application of the recurrence reduction algorithm presented here.

3.1.3. Cyclic reduction

In the context of vectorization, we look for the highest possible degree of parallelism and the disappearance of all recurrent operations. This implies taking the smallest possible q, that is to say $q = 2$ and thus $p = (n-1)/2$. So, the first reduction step will be written, for each k index between 1 and $(n-1)/2$:

$$z(k) = y(2 \times k - 1)$$
$$b(k) = a(2 \times k - 1)$$
$$z(k) = y(2 \times k) + a(2 \times k) \times z(k)$$
$$b(k) = a(2 \times k) \times b(k)$$

The computation of all the coefficients of the reduced system of the length $p + 1 = (n + 1)/2$ will, therefore, be performed by a vectorizable loop:

for $k = 1$ **to** $(n + 1)/2$
  $z(k) = y(2 \times k) + a(2 \times k) \times y(2 \times k - 1)$
  $b(k) = a(2 \times k) \times a(2 \times k - 1)$
end for

In the same way, once the reduced system is solved, where the unknowns are the coefficients of the odd-pairs of indices of the vector x, the calculation of the even-pairs terms will be performed by a vectorizable loop:

for $k = 1$ **to** $(n - 1)/2$
  $x(2 \times k) = y(2 \times k) + a(2 \times k) \times x(2 \times k - 1)$
end for

To resolve the reduced system itself, we will then again apply the same method, recursively, until the residual system is sufficiently small to be resolved, at negligible cost, in a non-vectorial manner.

This method is that of cyclic reduction. It still presents the same problems of overhead in cost and stability, than does the application of the former method using chunks.

3.2. Data locality and distribution: product of matrices

3.2.1. *Row and column algorithms*

We will look at three matrices A, B and C of dimension n. The usual formula for the product of matrices establishes that the coefficient $A(i, j)$ of the matrix $A = B \times C$ is equal to the scalar product of the row i of the matrix B, by the column j of the matrix C. The calculation of the product can, therefore, be written as:

```
for  i = 1  to  n
   for  j = 1  to  n
      for  k = 1  to  n
         A(i, j) = A(i, j) + B(i, k) × C(k, j)
      end  for
   end  for
end  for
```

This algorithm, in fact, calculates $A = A + B \times C$. To calculate $A = B \times C$, it is enough to initially cancel the coefficients of A. In this algorithm, the analysis of the dependence concerns only the matrix A, because it alone is modified. An analysis of the three nested loops shows that only the internal loop of the k index exhibits both input and output data dependencies in all its iterations. Indeed, this is a reduction operation. Besides, as there is no reference to the terms $A(i \pm k_i, \cdot)$ or $A(\cdot, j \pm k_j)$, there are no cross-dependencies and the loops can all be permuted two-by-two.

Thus, for example, the algorithm can be written as:

```
for  j = 1  to  n
   for  k = 1  to  n
      for  i = 1  to  n
         A(i, j) = A(i, j) + B(i, k) × C(k, j)
      end  for
   end  for
end  for
```

Here, we find that column j of the matrix A is obtained from the product of the matrix B by the column j of matrix C, which is a product equal to the linear combination of the columns of matrix B with the coefficients given by column j of matrix C. This is the definition of the product of matrices, as a representation of a combination of linear applications.

Which of the two algorithms will deliver the best performance? In both cases, the most external loop can be parallelized because there is no dependence. For the internal loops, we perform n pairs of $(+, \times)$ operations. The only difference resides in the access to memory.

With the loop of the k index at the interior, it is necessary, for each iteration, to recuperate two new coefficients $B(i,k)$ and $C(k,j)$ from memory. The initial value of $A(i,j)$ will be read first, and with the final value only being written at the end of the iterations, which leaves the intermediate results reside in the registers of the processor during the calculations. This means that it is necessary to access memory $2n + 1$ times in reading, and once in writing, for a total of $2n + 2$.

With the interior loop of index i, it is necessary in each iteration to read two new coefficients $A(i,j)$ and $B(i,k)$ in memory and then to rewrite the result $A(i,j)$. The coefficient, $C(k,j)$, will be read initially, and its value saved in the processor's registers during the iterations. The outcome is that it is necessary to access memory $2n + 1$ times in read mode, and n times in write mode, for a total of $3n + 1$.

The second solution thus appears to be worse than the first. However, if we consider the spatial locality of data, we see that in the case of the first algorithm, the access to the coefficients $B(i,\cdot)$ and $C(\cdot,j)$ take place, respectively, by row and column; whereas in the second algorithm, all the access to the coefficients $A(\cdot,j)$ and $B(\cdot,k)$ are done column-wise. If the coefficients of a matrix are arranged by columns in memory, the terms $A(\cdot,j)$ and $B(\cdot,k)$ are "contiguous" in memory, whereas the addresses of the term $B(i,\cdot)$ are separated by an increment equal to n. The spatial locality is, therefore, not as good as in the first case, and memory access will prove to be slower. We can see that neither of these two solutions is satisfactory.

NOTE 3.1.– If the matrices are not stored by columns, but by rows, then upon a permutation of the loops of the indices i and j, we find the same properties. In the following sections, we will assume that the matrices are always stored by column, but this comment still remains valid.

3.2.2. *Block algorithms*

If we consider the matrix–matrix product in its totality, we see that there are in fact $3n^2$ input data – the matrices A, B, C – and n^2 output data, the matrix A, whereas the calculation requires a total of n^3 pairs of $(+, \times)$ operations. This means that there should only be very little memory access compared to the number of operations, which none of the proceeding algorithms allows. The reason for this is that the temporal location is incorrectly exploited. Because of the three loop levels, each of the coefficients $A(i, j)$, $B(i, k)$ and $C(k, j)$ is used or modified a total of n times. However, each time, only the $A(i, j)$ coefficients, or the $C(k, j)$ coefficients, are stored in the registers; the others must be read, or rewritten in memory.

In practice though, this is not entirely true. If we implement the preceding algorithms, by rows or columns, on a computer with a cache memory, and measure the computational speed as a function of n, we will see that the speed begins to increase. Then, past a certain point, the maximum is reached, because the speed decreases when n increases and then stabilizes at an asymptotic variable that is significantly lower, as shown in Figure 3.1, for a calculation carried out by a core of a standard desktop computer.

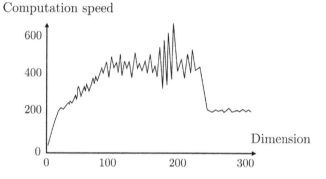

Figure 3.1. *The effect of cache memory on the speed of calculation*

As long as the dimensions stay sufficiently small so that the three matrices can simultaneously reside in the cache, the speed of calculation grows. Whichever of the algorithms is chosen, once all the pages containing the coefficients of the matrices have been used at least once, they will remain in the cache, and it is the high output of this that determines the performance. Temporal locality is at a maximum. Conversely, as the dimension becomes very large, temporal locality is no longer possible, except for the coefficients that are immediately reused, and then, it is the output of the main memory that limits the speed of calculation. The oscillations we see are due to the effects of how the data are aligned on the rows of the cache.

To reach peak performances, it is necessary to only operate on sufficiently small matrices, in comparison to the cache, so as to carry out calculations by block. We cut the $P \times P$ blocks of the dimension n/p, as in the A matrix, shown below in equation [3.1], in such a way so that the cache can hold three matrices of the dimension n/P, and to simplify our presentation, we will suppose that n is divisible by P.

$$
\begin{pmatrix}
A_{11} & A_{12} & \vdots & \vdots & A_{1J} & \vdots & A_{1P} \\
A_{21} & A_{22} & \vdots & \vdots & A_{2J} & \vdots & A_{2P} \\
\cdots & \cdots & \ddots & \vdots & \vdots & \vdots & \vdots \\
A_{I1} & A_{I2} & \cdots & \ddots & A_{IJ} & \vdots & A_{IP} \\
\cdots & \cdots & \cdots\cdots & & \ddots & \vdots & \vdots \\
\cdots & \cdots & \cdots\cdots & \cdots & & \ddots & \vdots \\
A_{P1} & A_{P2} & \cdots\cdots\cdots & A_{PJ} & \cdots & A_{PP}
\end{pmatrix}
\qquad [3.1]
$$

The algorithm of the block product of matrices is written as:

```
for  I = 1  to  P
   for  J = 1  to  P
      for  K = 1  to  P
         A_IJ = A_IJ + B_IK × C_KJ
      end  for
   end  for
end  for
```

The calculation of the products of $A_{IJ} = A_{IJ} + B_{IK} \times C_{KJ}$ now pertains to small enough blocks to obtain optimal spatial and temporal locality of data. There are no dependencies between the indices of the loops I and J. Therefore, the calculations of the different blocks of A_{IJ} can be performed in parallel on a multiprocessor machine with memory hierarchy. This type of algorithm enables us to obtain the best performance from the system, since the data can reside in the local caches, and that all the processors can work simultaneously.

We still need to establish precisely what the operation $A_{IJ} = A_{IJ} + B_{IK} \times C_{KJ}$ signifies; in other words, exactly how the blocks are defined in terms of their data structures.

The first possibility is to access the blocks of the matrix, but without changing its structure. The correspondence between the references to the coefficients in a block, and in the overall matrix, is written as:

$$A_{IJ}(i,j) \equiv A((I-1) \times n/P + i, (J-1) \times n/P + j)$$

Thus, the product of $A_{IJ} = A_{IJ} + B_{IK} \times C_{KJ}$ is written as:

```
for  i = 1  to  n/P
   for  j = 1  to  n/P
      for  k = 1  to  n/P
         A((I − 1) × n/P + i, (J − 1) × n/P + j) =
            A((I − 1) × n/P + i, (J − 1) × n/P + j)+
            B((I − 1) × n/P + i, (K − 1) × n/P + k)×
            C((K − 1) × n/P + k, (J − 1) × n/P + j)
      end for
   end for
end for
```

When the product of the loop $A_{IJ} = A_{IJ} + B_{IK} \times C_{KJ}$ is replaced by the three nested loops in the above block algorithm, we see that it was obtained by dividing each level of the loops of the initial algorithm into two, both by rows and columns, and then conducting the permutations.

In this first approach, the spatial locality of data is not complete: when coming to the end of a column in a block, the terms that follow in memory are not those of the following column of the same block, but those of the column in the following block – in other words, the following partition of the column in the overall matrix. Locality of data by blocks consists of effectively storing the matrices in the form of block matrices. A very simple way of doing this is to declare them as a four-dimensional array $(n/P, n/P, P, P)$. The correspondence among the coefficient references in a block, and in the overall matrix, is now written as:

$$A_{IJ}(i,j) \equiv A(i, j, I, J)$$

The product $A_{IJ} = A_{IJ} + B_{IK} \times C_{KJ}$ becomes:

```
for  i = 1  to  n/P
     for  j = 1  to  n/P
        for  k = 1  to  n/P
            A(i, j, I, J) = A(i, j, I, J) + B(i, k, I, K) × C(k, j, K, J)
        end for
     end for
  end for
```

Dividing things up this way shows interest, because of better data locality, which permits easier management of the different cache levels and limits the conflicts of access to the rows of cache. In the same way, it can also allow us to work with "out-of-core" memory, if the global matrices were to prove too large for the main memory.

3.2.3. *Distributed algorithms*

After our work in the previous example of locality, the development of a distributed algorithm does not present any new difficulties. Naturally, the data matrices will be distributed by blocks. For each number of the block (I, J), a process is associated among $P \times P$. From then on, each process will be identified by its block number.

The distributed calculation code only describes the operations carried out by each of the processes; that is for the (I, J) process:

```
for  K = 1  to  P
     A_IJ = A_IJ + B_IK × C_KJ
end for
```

The problem is that the process only has the blocks A_{IJ}, B_{IJ}. In iteration K of the algorithm, it needs the blocks B_{IK} and C_{KJ}, which are, respectively, held in the possession of the processes (I, K) and (K, J).

So that each of the processes receives the blocks it needs, they must obviously be sent by the owner processor. In iteration K, we notice that all the (I, J) processes need the block B_{IK}. It is, therefore, necessary that the (I, K) process sends its block of the matrix B to all the processes on row I.

Similarly, all the (I, J) processes need the block C_{KJ}, and so the (K, J) processes must send its block of the matrix C to all the processes on column J. Figures 3.2 and 3.3 illustrate these transfers of iteration 1, for a division into 16 blocks. The communications to be executed are thus one-to-all broadcast exchanges in each group of processes on either the same row, or the same column.

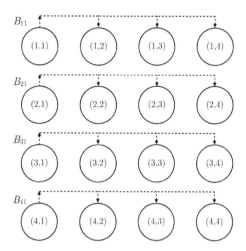

Figure 3.2. *Row-wise communication*

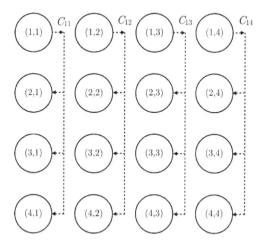

Figure 3.3. *Column-wise communication*

3.2.4. *Implementation*

In the context of message-passing programming, the source code of each process is the same. It is necessary to generate $P \times P$ processes. Each process has its own A, B and C matrices of dimensions n/P, which are, for the (I, J) processes, the blocks A_{IJ}, B_{IJ} and C_{IJ}. In the MPI environment, it is necessary to associate the pair (I, J) with the process with number $rank$ among the 64 processes (size = 64). Any bijective transformation will be appropriate. In particular, if we follow the logic of arranging the matrices by columns, the index (I, J) can be determined by the following equation:

$$rank = (J - 1) \times P + (I - 1), \text{ with } P = \sqrt{size}$$

To easily achieve these transfers of blocks of one-to-all in each group of processes on the same row, or on same column, we need to create the corresponding communicators. The MPI environment allows us to easily form such groups with the help of the function:

– *MPI_Comm_split(initial_communicator,color,criteria,final_communicator)*.

which permits partitioning the *initial_communicator* communicator into several *final_communicator* communicators, according to partitioning criterion set forth by the *color* parameter. All the processes of the *initial_communicator* communicator must call this function. Each process ends up in a *final_communicator* communicator that reunites all the processes that have the same *color* parameter value. To create communicators by row, it is enough to just call up this function with the variable I as the *color* parameter.

A priori, the processes are assigned an arbitrary number in the new communicator. In the case we are considering here, this means that the processes on the same row will not necessarily be numbered in their communicator by row, as a function of their column number, which is very annoying. It is the *criteria* parameter that serves the purpose of deciding the number assigned to the processes, according to the increasing *criteria* value. The variable J, or $rank$, provides the *criteria* parameter, which allows the processes (I, J) to receive the number $J - 1$ in the communicator of the row I. This finally gives the following two instructions to create the communicators, by row and column, for a division into 16 blocks, as represented in Figures 3.4 and 3.5:

– *MPI_Comm_split(MPI_COMM_WORLD,I,J,row_communicator);*

– *MPI_Comm_split(MPI_COMM_WORLD,J,I,column_communicator).*

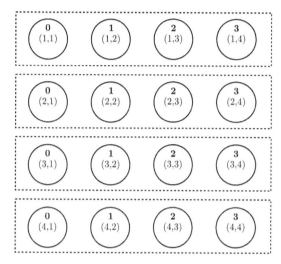

Figure 3.4. *Row-wise communicators*

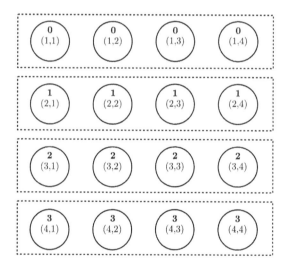

Figure 3.5. *Column-wise communicators*

Now, it is very easy to write the algorithm executed by each process. In each iteration, it is the process $K - 1$ that needs to send its block B to all the other processes in its row. Similarly, it is the process $K-1$ that must send its block C to all the other processes in its column. It is thus necessary to provide temporary blocks, B_{temp} and C_{temp}, to store the blocks which are received in each iteration. This finally results in the following:

$$
\begin{aligned}
&\textbf{for}\ \ K=1\ \textbf{to}\ \ P\\
&\quad \textbf{if}\ \ J=K\ \ \textbf{then}\\
&\quad\quad B_{temp}=B\\
&\quad \textbf{end\ if}\\
&\quad MPI\_Bcast(B_{temp}, length, type, K-1, row\_communicator)\\
&\quad \textbf{if}\ \ I=K\ \ \textbf{then}\\
&\quad\quad C_{temp}=C\\
&\quad \textbf{end\ if}\\
&\quad MPI\_Bcast(C_{temp}, length, type, K-1, column\_communicator)\\
&\quad A=A+B_{temp}\times C_{temp}\\
&\textbf{end\ for}
\end{aligned}
$$

where $length = (n/P)^2$ is the amount of transferred data and $type$ is the MPI type of matrices under consideration (integers, real, complex, double precision, etc.).

This example very clearly shows that the most difficult work lies in the locality of temporal and spatial access to data. Once this is achieved, distributed parallelism is generally easy to implement. Simply put, it is sufficient to begin to associate each block of data with the computational code carried out for these blocks. Then, it is necessary to analyze and program the necessary transfers to recuperate the data that are not local.

The programming in itself does not present any special difficulties. The parallel code for a distributed memory computer by using message-passing is often simpler than the sequential code from which it was derived, in the sense that the management of blocks is no longer an issue. This is the case here for the loops of the blocks (I, J). They are replaced by launching the $P \times P$ process, which with same source code, treats only one block.

NOTE 3.2.– The parallel algorithms presented here for the classic numerical linear algebra operations are for didactic purposes only. In practice, there are libraries of optimized programs, tailored to different types of processors and parallel systems, which obviously should be used first. The most classic libraries are basic linear algebra subroutines (BLAS), which contains the basic dense matrix and vector operations and is optimized for multi-core processors; linear algebra package (LaPack), which uses BLAS for algorithms for more advanced block matrix operations; and scalable linear algebra package (ScaLaPack), which performs an optimized implementation of LaPack on distributed-memory systems using MPI.

4

Basics of Numerical Matrix Analysis

In order to make this book as autonomous as possible, this chapter recalls the principle classical results and the notations that will be used in the following. This chapter is not intended to be a course in linear algebra, and only a few proofs are detailed. Similarly, it does not at all try to be exhaustive and only presents the concepts that will be used later in this book, and in particular, those discussed in the chapters concerning Krylov subspaces.

4.1. Review of basic notions of linear algebra

4.1.1. *Vector spaces, scalar products and orthogonal projection*

Let V be a vector space of the finite dimension n over the field $\mathbb{K}$, with $\mathbb{K} = \mathbb{R}$ (the set of real numbers), or $\mathbb{K} = \mathbb{C}$ (the set of complex numbers), and a basis of V, i.e. a set $\{e_1, e_2, \ldots, e_n\}$ of n linearly independent vectors of V, denoted by $(e_j)_{j=1}^n$. Each vector $v \in V$ allows a unique decomposition:

$$v = \sum_{j=1}^{n} v_j e_j$$

where the scalars v_i are called components of the vector v in the basis $(e_j)_{j=1}^n$. Subsequently, we will use matrix notations to represent vectors, namely:

DEFINITION 4.1 (Column vector).– *We define a column vector as an array with input $(v_i)_{1 \leq i \leq n}$ of elements (v_i) in $\mathbb{K}$ ($\mathbb{K} = \mathbb{R}$ or $\mathbb{C}$), where i is the row* *index, and we note:*

$$v = \begin{pmatrix} v_1 \\ \vdots \\ v_n \end{pmatrix}$$

We will denote by v^t the transposed (row) vector and by v^* the conjugated (row) vector: $v^t = (v_1, v_2, \ldots, v_n)$ and $v^* = (\overline{v}_1, \overline{v}_2, \ldots, \overline{v}_n)$, where $\overline{v}_i$ designates the complex conjugate of v_i.

DEFINITION 4.2 (Scalar product).– We call the canonical scalar product on $\mathbb{K}$, and more specifically, the Euclidean scalar product if $\mathbb{K} = \mathbb{R}$, and the Hermitian scalar product if $\mathbb{K} = \mathbb{C}$, the application defined by:

$$(\cdot, \cdot) : \mathcal{V} \times \mathcal{V} \to \mathbb{K}$$

$$(u, v) = v^t u = \sum_{i=1}^{n} u_i v_i \quad \text{if} \quad \mathbb{K} = \mathbb{R}$$

$$(u, v) = v^* u = \sum_{i=1}^{n} u_i \overline{v}_i \quad \text{if} \quad \mathbb{K} = \mathbb{C}$$

At times, we note $(u, v) = (u, v)^{(n)}$ as a reminder of the dimension of the vector space. Two vectors u and v of $\mathcal{V}$ are called orthogonal if $(u, v) = 0$.

DEFINITION 4.3 (Orthogonal space).– Let $\mathcal{W}$ be a vector subspace of $\mathcal{V}$. We call orthogonal complement to $\mathcal{W}$, noted as $\mathcal{W}^{\perp}$, the set of vectors of $\mathcal{V}$ which are orthogonal to all the vectors of $\mathcal{W}$.

THEOREM 4.1 (Complement space).– $\mathcal{W}$ and $\mathcal{W}^{\perp}$ are the complementary subspaces, or equivalently, $\mathcal{W}^{\perp}$ is a complement of $\mathcal{W}$. In other words, their intersection is reduced to the null vector and any vector v of $\mathcal{V}$ decomposes uniquely in the form: $v = w + u$, with $w \in \mathcal{W}$ and $u \in \mathcal{W}^{\perp}$.

We note that: $\mathcal{V} = \mathcal{W} \oplus \mathcal{W}^{\perp}$. The sum of the dimensions of two complementary subspaces is equal to the dimension of the complete space.

DEFINITION 4.4 (Affine space).– *Let W be a subspace of V and v_0 be an arbitrary vector of V. We call the affine space generated by v_0 and W, the set of vectors that are written as $v_0 + w$, for all w in W.*

The affine space generated by v_0 and W is denoted as: $v_0 + W$.

We see immediately that if w is any element of W, $v_0 + w$ and W gives rise to the same affine space as v_0 and W.

Let v be a vector of V. According to theorem 4.1, $v - v_0$ is uniquely written as: $v - v_0 = w + u$, with $w \in W$ and $u \in W^\perp$.

DEFINITION 4.5 (Orthogonal projection).– *We call orthogonal projection on $v_0 + W$, the application which, for every vector v of V, generates the unique element $v_0 + w$ of $v_0 + W$ such as $v = v_0 + w + u$, with $u \in W^\perp$.*

THEOREM 4.2.– If $P(v)$ is the image of v by the orthogonal projection on $v_0 + W$, then $P(v)$ is uniquely determined as the unique element of $v_0 + W$ that satisfies the following two equivalent properties:

1) $(v - P(v), v - P(v)) \leq (v - (v_0 + w'), v - (v_0 + w'))$ $\forall w' \in W$;

2) $(v - P(v), w') = 0$ $\forall w' \in W$.

PROOF 4.1.– If $v = v_0 + w + u$, with $w \in W^\perp$ and $u \in W^\perp$, then $P(v) = v_0 + w$. For all w' in W, $v - (v_0 + w') = v - P(v) + w' - w$. The vector $v - P(v)$ belongs to $W^\perp$, the vector $w' - w$ belongs to W, thus these two vectors are orthogonal and:

$$(v - (v_0 + w'), v - (v_0 + w')) = (v - P(v), v - P(v))$$
$$+ (w' - w, w' - w)$$

$(w' - w, w' - w)$ is strictly positive if $w' \neq w$. The minimum value of the left term is thus achieved for $w' = w$, which proves the first property.

If the first property is verified, then for every w' in W and all α in $\mathbb{K}$:

$$(v - P(v) + \alpha w'), v - P(v) + \alpha w') =$$
$$(v - P(v), v - P(v)) + 2Re(\alpha(v - P(v), w')) + |\alpha|^2(w', w') \geq$$
$$(v - P(v), v - P(v))$$

which implies that for all w' in $\mathcal{W}$:

$$2Re(\alpha(v - P(v), w')) + |\alpha|^2(w', w') \geq 0 \quad \alpha \in \mathbb{K}$$

This allows us to easily prove the second property by making α tend toward 0, with α being either pure real or pure imaginary, if $\mathbb{K} = \mathbb{C}$.

Finally, if an element of $v_0 + \mathcal{W}$, $v_0 + w'$ satisfies the second property, then $u' = v - (v_0 + w')$ belongs to $\mathcal{W}^\perp$. By the uniqueness of the decomposition $v - v_0 = w + u$, with $w \in \mathcal{W}$ and $u \in \mathcal{W}^\perp$, we necessarily have $w' = w$, and therefore, $v_0 + w' = P(v)$. $\square$

The first property tells us that $P(v)$ is the closest element of $v_0 + \mathcal{W}$ to v in the sense of the associated norm with the canonical scalar product. The general notion of norms is recalled in section 4.2.2.

The second property indicates that $P(v)$ is the unique element of $v_0 + \mathcal{W}$ for which the vector $P(v) - v$ is in $\mathcal{W}^\perp$, the orthogonal of $\mathcal{W}$.

4.1.2. *Linear applications and matrices*

Let $\mathcal{W}$ be a finite dimensional vector space of dimension m, with a basis $\{f_1, f_2, \ldots, f_m\}$.

DEFINITION 4.6 (Linear application).– *An application $\mathcal{A}$ of $\mathcal{V}$ in $\mathcal{W}$ is a linear application if and only if the following two conditions are met:*

1) $\forall x \in \mathcal{V}, \forall y \in \mathcal{V}, \mathcal{A}(x + y) = \mathcal{A}(x) + \mathcal{A}(y);$

2) $\forall \lambda \in \mathbb{K}, \forall x \in \mathcal{V}, \mathcal{A}(\lambda x) = \lambda \mathcal{A}(x).$

Let us consider $\mathcal{A}$ a linear application of $\mathcal{V}$ in $\mathcal{W}$, x a vector of $\mathcal{V}$ and y a vector of $\mathcal{W}$ equal to $y = \mathcal{A}(x)$. In writing the decomposition of the x in the basis $(e_j)_{j=1}^n$:

$$x = \sum_{j=1}^n x_j e_j$$

and in applying the definition of the linear application $\mathcal{A}$, the result is:

$$\mathcal{A}(x) = \sum_{j=1}^{n} x_j \mathcal{A}(e_j)$$

Because $\forall j, 1 \leq j \leq n, \mathcal{A}(e_j) \in \mathcal{W}, \mathcal{A}(e_j)$ decomposes in the basis $(f_i)_{i=1}^{m}$:

$$\mathcal{A}(e_j) = \sum_{i=1}^{m} a_{ij} f_i$$

or in vector form:

$$\mathcal{A}(e_j) = \begin{pmatrix} a_{1j} \\ \vdots \\ a_{mj} \end{pmatrix}$$

In the same way, the vector $y \in \mathcal{W}$ is written in the basis $(f_i)_{i=1}^{m}$ in the form:

$$y = \sum_{i=1}^{m} y_i f_i$$

and the equality $y = \mathcal{A}(x)$ reads, after substitution:

$$y = \mathcal{A}(x) = \sum_{j=1}^{n} x_j \mathcal{A}(e_j) = \sum_{i=1}^{m} y_i f_i$$

$$\begin{pmatrix} y_1 \\ \vdots \\ y_m \end{pmatrix} = \sum_{j=1}^{n} \begin{pmatrix} a_{1j} \\ \vdots \\ a_{mj} \end{pmatrix} x_j$$

or else:

$$y_i = \sum_{j=1}^{n} a_{ij} x_j, \quad 1 \le i \le m$$

We can thus write the linear application $\mathcal{A}$ of $\mathcal{V}$ in $\mathcal{W}$ in matrix form.

DEFINITION 4.7 (Matrix).– *We call a matrix a rectangular array* $(a_{ij})_{1 \le i \le m, 1 \le j \le n}$ *of elements* (a_{ij}) *in* $\mathbb{K}$ *(*$\mathbb{K} = \mathbb{R}$ *or* $\mathbb{C}$*); i is the index of the row and j is the index of the column, and we note:*

$$A = \begin{pmatrix} a_{11} & \cdots & a_{1n} \\ \vdots & & \vdots \\ a_{m1} & \cdots & a_{mn} \end{pmatrix}$$

where the elements a_{ij} of the matrix A are defined uniquely by the relations:

$$\mathcal{A}(e_j) = \sum_{i=1}^{m} a_{ij} f_i, \quad 1 \le j \le n$$

That is the j-th column vector of matrix A

$$\begin{pmatrix} a_{1j} \\ \vdots \\ a_{mj} \end{pmatrix}$$

represents the vector $\mathcal{A}(e_j)$ in the basis $(f_i)_{i=1}^{m}$:

$$\begin{pmatrix} y_1 \\ \vdots \\ y_m \end{pmatrix} = \begin{pmatrix} a_{11} & \cdots & a_{1n} \\ \vdots & & \vdots \\ a_{m1} & \cdots & a_{mn} \end{pmatrix} \begin{pmatrix} x_1 \\ \vdots \\ x_n \end{pmatrix}$$

A matrix A with m rows and n columns is called a matrix of type (m, n). A matrix A with elements a_{ij} is noted as $A = (a_{ij})$, and is said to be real or complex, depending on whether its elements are in $\mathbb{R}$ or $\mathbb{C}$.

In the following, the null matrix and the null vectors are identified by the same character, "0".

DEFINITION 4.8 (Transposed and adjoint matrices).– *The transposed matrix of a matrix A, with m rows and n columns, is the matrix A^t, with n rows and m columns, defined uniquely by:*

$$(Av, w)^{(m)} = (v, A^t w)^{(n)}, \quad \forall v \in V, w \in W \quad \text{if} \quad \mathbb{K} = \mathbb{R}$$

The coefficients of A^t and A satisfy the following relationship:

$$a_{ij}^t = a_{ji}$$

The adjoint matrix of a matrix A, with m rows and n columns, is the matrix A^*, with n rows and m columns, defined uniquely by:

$$(Av, w)^{(m)} = (v, A^* w)^{(n)}, \quad \forall v \in V, w \in W \quad \text{if} \quad \mathbb{K} = \mathbb{C}$$

The coefficients of A^* and A satisfy the following relationship:

$$a_{ij}^* = \bar{a}_{ji}$$

From the algebraic point of view, the multiplication of matrices corresponds to the composition of linear applications. If $\mathcal{U}$ is a vector space of dimension l, let $\mathcal{C}$ and $\mathcal{B}$ be two linear applications defined by the following:

$$\mathcal{C} : V \rightarrow \quad \mathcal{U} \qquad \mathcal{B} : \mathcal{U} \rightarrow \quad W$$
$$x \mapsto z = \mathcal{C}(x) \qquad z \mapsto y = \mathcal{B}(z)$$

and $\mathcal{A} = \mathcal{B} \circ \mathcal{C}$ the composed application defined by:

$$\mathcal{A} : \mathcal{V} \to \mathcal{W}$$

$$x \mapsto y = \mathcal{A}(x) = \mathcal{B}(\mathcal{C}(x))$$

Writing $y = \mathcal{A}(x)$ as the succession of two operations $\mathcal{C}(x) = z$ and $\mathcal{B}(z) = y$, and then writing in the matrix form, we obtain $A = BC$ with:

$$A e_j = \begin{pmatrix} a_{1j} \\ \vdots \\ a_{mj} \end{pmatrix} = B(Ce_j) = B \begin{pmatrix} c_{1j} \\ \vdots \\ c_{lj} \end{pmatrix}$$

that signifies that the j-th column of matrix A corresponds to the product of matrix B by the j-th column of matrix C. Hence, we can introduce the following definition:

DEFINITION 4.9 (Matrix multiplication).– *Let $B = (b_{ik})$ be a matrix of type (m, l) and $C = (b_{kj})$ be a matrix of type (l, n), then the matrix multiplication $A = BC$ is defined by:*

$$(A)_{ij} = (BC)_{ij} = \sum_{k=1}^{l} b_{ik} c_{kj}$$

Among the important properties of matrix multiplication, we have that $(BC)^t = C^t B^t$, and that $(BC)^* = C^* B^*$.

DEFINITION 4.10 (Square matrix).– *Matrix $A = (a_{ij})$ of the type (n, n) is said to be a square matrix if $m = n$, and rectangular if $m \neq n$. If A is a square matrix, the elements a_{ii} are called diagonal elements, and the elements a_{ij}, $i \neq j$ extra-diagonal elements. The matrix unit for the matrix multiplication is the matrix $I = \delta_{ij}$ where δ_{ij} is the symbol of Kronecker: $\delta_{ij} = 1$ if $i = j$, $\delta_{ij} = 0$ if $i \neq j$.*

DEFINITION 4.11 (Invertible matrix).– *A matrix A is invertible if there is a matrix, called the inverse of matrix, denoted by A^{-1}, such that $AA^{-1} = A^{-1}A = I$.*

Among the important properties of the inverse of a matrix, we are reminded that $(AB)^{-1} = B^{-1}A^{-1}, (A^t)^{-1} = (A^{-1})^t, (A^*)^{-1} = (A^{-1})^*$.

4.2. Properties of matrices

4.2.1. *Matrices, eigenvalues and eigenvectors*

DEFINITION 4.12 (Matrix properties).– *A matrix A is symmetric if A is real and $A = A^t$, Hermitian if $A = A^*$, orthogonal if A is real and $AA^t = A^tA = I$, normal if $AA^* = A^*A$ and unitary if $AA^* = A^*A = I$.*

Relations	Type of matrix	Properties of the elements
$A^t = A$	Symmetric	$a_{ji} = a_{ij}$
$A^t = -A$	Antisymmetric	$a_{ji} = -a_{ij}, a_{ii} = 0$
$(A^t)^{-1} = A$	Orthogonal	$\sum_k a_{ki}a_{kj} = \sum_k a_{ik}a_{jk} = \delta_{ij}$
$\overline{A} = A$	Real	
$\overline{A} = -A$	Pure imaginary	
$A^* = A$	Hermitian	$\overline{a}_{ij} = a_{ji}$
$A^* = -A$	Anti-Hermitian	$\overline{a}_{ij} = -a_{ji}$
$AA^* = A^*A$	Normal	
$(A^*)^{-1} = A$	Unitary	$\sum_k \overline{a}_{ki}a_{kj} = \sum_k a_{ik}\overline{a}_{jk} = \delta_{ij}$

Let us take the case of a square matrix A of type (n, n), a vector column v that has n rows and a scalar λ. Consider the following equation: $Ax = \lambda x$. For non-zero x, the values of λ that satisfy this equation are called "eigenvalues" of the matrix A. The corresponding vectors are called "eigenvectors" . The equation $Ax = \lambda x$ can also be written as: $(A - \lambda I)x = 0$. This system of equations has a non-trivial solution, if and only if, the matrix $(A - \lambda I)$ cannot be inverted. If λ is an eigenvalue, the set of vectors $\mathcal{V}$ such that $(A - \lambda I)v = 0$ is a vector subspace. By definition, it contains the zero vector, and all the eigenvectors A associated with λ. We call this associated subspace eigenvector subspace λ. We should also note that an eigenvector can be associated with only one eigenvalue.

DEFINITION 4.13 (Spectral radius).– *The spectral radius of a matrix A is the number defined by:*

$$\rho(A) = max\{|\lambda_i(A)|; 1 \leq i \leq n\}$$

where $\lambda_i(A)$ is the i-th eigenvalue of the matrix A.

DEFINITION 4.14 (Kernel and image of a matrix).– *Let $\mathcal{A}$ be a linear application of $\mathcal{V}$ in $\mathcal{W}$. We define the kernel of $\mathcal{A}$, and the image of $\mathcal{A}$, the two subspaces:*

$$Ker\mathcal{A} = \{x \in \mathcal{V}; \mathcal{A}(x) = 0_{\mathcal{W}}\}$$
$$Im\mathcal{A} = \{y \in \mathcal{W}; \exists x \in \mathcal{V} \text{ such that } y = \mathcal{A}(x)\}$$

THEOREM 4.3.– Let $\mathcal{V}$ and $\mathcal{W}$ be two vector spaces of finite dimension on $\mathbb{K}$ and let $\mathcal{A}$ be a linear application of $\mathcal{V}$ in $\mathcal{W}$. We have:

$$\dim Ker\mathcal{A} + \dim Im\mathcal{A} = \dim\mathcal{V}$$

With the above notations, the eigenspace associated with λ is none other than the subspace $Ker(A - \lambda I)$.

4.2.2. *Norms of a matrix*

There are several ways to define the norm for a vector. Certainly, the most commonly used of all is the Euclidean norm, defined for a vector v by:

$$\|v\| = \sqrt{\sum_{i=1}^{n} v_i^2}$$

The definition of a norm is, however, more general.

DEFINITION 4.15.– An application $\| \cdot \| : \mathcal{V} \longrightarrow \mathbb{R}$ (here, $\mathcal{V}$ is a real vector space) is called a vector norm if it satisfies the following properties:

1) $\|v\| \geq 0, \forall v \in \mathcal{V}$ and $\|v\| = 0 \Leftrightarrow v = 0.$

2) $\|av\| = |a|\|v\|, \forall a \in \mathbb{R}, v \in \mathcal{V}$.

3) $\|v + u\| \leq \|v\| + \|u\|, \forall v, u \in \mathcal{V}$.

There are several norms for the a vector space, like the p-norms defined by:

$$\|v\|_p = \left(\sum_{i=1}^{n} |v_i^p| \right)^{1/p}$$

When $p = 2$, we find the definition of the Euclidean norm. There is also the norm known as infinite, which is defined as follows:

$$\|x\|_\infty = \max_{1 \leq i \leq n} |x_i|$$

This last norm is one of the most widely used, along with 1 and 2-norms.

Like the vectors of $\mathbb{R}^n$, matrices have a norm, and here is the definition.

DEFINITION 4.16.– Let $A, B \in M_{n \times n}$, $M_{n \times n}$ being the set of real matrices of size (n, n). Then, the application $\| \cdot \| : M_{n \times n} \longrightarrow \mathbb{R}$ is a matrix norm if it satisfies the following properties:

1) $\|A\| \geq 0, \forall A \in M_{n \times n}$ and $\|A\| = 0 \Leftrightarrow A = 0$.

2) $\|\beta A\| = |\beta|\|A\|$, for all scalars β and every A in $M_{n \times n}$.

3) $\|A + B\| \leq \|A\| + \|B\|$, for every A and B in $M_{n \times n}$.

4) $\|AB\| \leq \|A\|\|B\|$, for every A and B in $M_{n \times n}$.

Let us now look at some matrix norms. Those most commonly used, which are called induced norms, are derived from the vector norms described above. Thus, for each p vector norm, we associated a matrix p-norm in the following way:

$$\|A\|_p = \max_{\|v\|_p \neq 0} \frac{\|Av\|_p}{\|v\|_p} = \max_{\|v\|_p = 1} \|Av\|_p$$

This relationship means that the induced norm of a matrix corresponds to the maximum norm of the vector, resulting from the multiplication of matrix A, by all the vectors with norms equal to 1.

In particular, for a matrix of dimension (n, n), we can show that:

$$\|A\|_2 = \sqrt{\rho(A^*A)} \tag{4.1}$$

$$\|A\|_1 = \max_{1 \leq j \leq n} \sum_{i=1}^{n} |a_{ij}| \tag{4.2}$$

$$\|A\|_\infty = \max_{1 \leq i \leq n} \sum_{j=1}^{n} |a_{ij}| \tag{4.3}$$

The 1-norm consists of the maximum column sum of absolute values, while the infinite-norm is the maximum row sum of absolute values.

In the following, unless otherwise indicated, the vector norm will be the norm $\| \cdot \|_2$ and the matrix norm, the induced norm.

THEOREM 4.4.– Any symmetric matrix accepts an orthonormal basis of eigenvectors.

DEFINITION 4.17.– Let A be a real symmetric matrix of type (n, n). It is called positive definite if it satisfies one of the three following equivalent properties:

– For all non-zero column vectors x with n rows, we have:

$$(Ax, x) = x^t Ax > 0$$

– All eigenvalues of A are strictly positive, which means:

$$\lambda_i(A) > 0$$

– The symmetric bilinear form defined by the relation:

$$(x, y)_A = (Ax, y) = y^t Ax$$

is a scalar product on $\mathbb{R}^n$.

THEOREM 4.5.– Let A be a real symmetric positive definite matrix of type (n, n). Then, the associated bilinear form is coercive, that is to say:

$$\exists \alpha > 0, \forall x \in \mathcal{V}, \ (Ax, x) = x^t A x \geq \alpha \|x\|^2$$

4.2.3. Basis change

Let us look at the matrix A of the linear application $\mathcal{A}$ of $\mathcal{V}$ in $\mathcal{V}$, in the basis $(e_j)_{j=1}^n$. Let $(\widetilde{e}_j)_{j=1}^n$ be another basis of $\mathcal{V}$. Let us consider B the basis change matrix (also referred to as matrix of the identity application) from the space $\mathcal{V}$ provided with the basis $(e_j)_{j=1}^n$, to the same space provided with the base $(\widetilde{e}_j)_{j=1}^n$. Then the j-th column of B is the vector of the components of $\widetilde{e}_j$ in the basis $(e_j)_{j=1}^n$, so that its coefficients are $b_{ij} = e_i^t \cdot \widetilde{e}_j$ (see exercise A2.8). The matrix of the identity application of $\mathcal{V}$ provided with the basis $(e_j)_{j=1}^n$ in $\mathcal{V}$, provided with the basis $(\widetilde{e}_j)_{j=1}^n$, is clearly equal to B^{-1}, as illustrated in Figure 4.1.

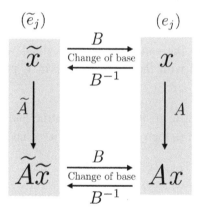

Figure 4.1. *Basis change and linear application*

If x and $\widetilde{x}$ are, respectively, the components of the same vector of $\mathcal{V}$ in the basis $(e_j)_{j=1}^n$ and $(\widetilde{e}_j)_{j=1}^n$, respectively, we have the relation:

$$x = B\widetilde{x}$$

where matrix B is given by:

$$B = \begin{pmatrix} (e_1^t \cdot \tilde{e}_1) & (e_1^t \cdot \tilde{e}_2) & \cdots & (e_1^t \cdot \tilde{e}_n) \\ (e_2^t \cdot \tilde{e}_2) & (e_2^t \cdot \tilde{e}_2) & \cdots & (e_2^t \cdot \tilde{e}_n) \\ \vdots & \vdots & \ddots & \vdots \\ (e_n^t \cdot \tilde{e}_2) & (e_n^t \cdot \tilde{e}_2) & \cdots & (e_n^t \cdot \tilde{e}_n) \end{pmatrix} \qquad [4.4]$$

THEOREM 4.6.– The matrix of the linear application $\mathcal{A}$ of $\mathcal{V}$ in $\mathcal{V}$, in the basis $(\tilde{e}_j)_{j=1}^n$, is given by:

$$\tilde{A} = B^{-1}AB$$

PROOF 4.2.– The proof comes immediately, considering the fact that $\tilde{A}$ is the matrix of the application obtained by composing: the identity application of $\mathcal{V}$ provided with the basis $(\tilde{e}_j)_{j=1}^n$ in $\mathcal{V}$ to $\mathcal{V}$ provided with the basis $(e_j)_{j=1}^n$; application $\mathcal{A}$ of $\mathcal{V}$ to the same space $\mathcal{V}$ provided with the basis $(e_j)_{j=1}^n$; identity of $\mathcal{V}$ provided with the basis $(e_j)_{j=1}^n$ in $\mathcal{V}$ provided with the basis $(\tilde{e}_j)_{j=1}^n$. □

If A is a real symmetric positive definite matrix, and we consider the scalar product associated with it, then the change of basis has the following effect:

$$(Ax, y) = (AB\tilde{x}, B\tilde{y}) = (B^t AB\tilde{x}, \tilde{y})$$

hence, the following theorem:

THEOREM 4.7.– The scalar product associated with the matrix A in the basis $(e_j)_{j=1}^n$ is associated in the basis $(\tilde{e}_j)_{j=1}^n$ with the matrix:

$$\tilde{A} = B^t AB$$

If the matrix B is orthogonal, in other words, if the basis $(\tilde{e}_j)_{j=1}^n$ is orthonormal, the two matrices, obtained by a change of basis in the sense of the linear applications or in the sense of the scalar products, are identical.

More generally, if A is a symmetric positive definite matrix, the matrix $B^t AB$ is symmetric and positive. It is defined if and only if B is invertible since:

$$(B^t ABx, x) = (ABx, Bx) \geq \alpha \|Bx\|^2$$

4.2.4. *Conditioning of a matrix*

Modeling and discretization of a physical problem often leads to the resolution of large linear systems, which are represented by a matrix system like $Ax = b$. Sometimes, a small variation on the vector side b causes a great variation of the solution x. It is said that in this case the matrix, or the problem, is poorly conditioned. For example, we will consider the following linear system $Ax = b$:

$$\begin{pmatrix} 10 & 7 & 8 & 7 \\ 7 & 5 & 6 & 5 \\ 8 & 6 & 10 & 9 \\ 7 & 5 & 9 & 10 \end{pmatrix} \begin{pmatrix} x_1 \\ x_2 \\ x_3 \\ x_4 \end{pmatrix} = \begin{pmatrix} 32 \\ 23 \\ 33 \\ 31 \end{pmatrix}$$

whose solution is:

$$x = \begin{pmatrix} 1 \\ 1 \\ 1 \\ 1 \end{pmatrix}$$

We note that the matrix A is invertible. Now, we will consider the following problem in which the vector b is slightly modified:

$$\begin{pmatrix} 10 & 7 & 8 & 7 \\ 7 & 5 & 6 & 5 \\ 8 & 6 & 10 & 9 \\ 7 & 5 & 9 & 10 \end{pmatrix} \begin{pmatrix} x_1 \\ x_2 \\ x_3 \\ x_4 \end{pmatrix} = \begin{pmatrix} 32.1 \\ 22.9 \\ 33.1 \\ 30.9 \end{pmatrix}$$

The solution of the perturbed system is:

$$x = \begin{pmatrix} 9.2 \\ -12.6 \\ 4.5 \\ -11 \end{pmatrix}$$

In other words, very small variations of b have led to wide variations of x. Similarly, if we perturb the matrix elements:

$$\begin{pmatrix} 10 & 7 & 8.1 & 7.2 \\ 7.08 & 5.04 & 6 & 5 \\ 8 & 5.98 & 9.89 & 9 \\ 6.99 & 4.99 & 9 & 9.98 \end{pmatrix} \begin{pmatrix} x_1 \\ x_2 \\ x_3 \\ x_4 \end{pmatrix} = \begin{pmatrix} 32 \\ 23 \\ 33 \\ 31 \end{pmatrix}$$

the solution is:

$$x = \begin{pmatrix} -81 \\ 137 \\ -34 \\ 22 \end{pmatrix}$$

A small variation in the data causes a large variation of the solution. Specifically, we have the following definition:

DEFINITION 4.18.– We call conditioning of a matrix A associated with the norm p, the real number $\kappa_p(A)$ given by the relationship $\kappa_p(A) = \|A\|_p \|A^{-1}\|_p$.

In the previous example, we find $\kappa(A)_\infty = 2.9841 \times 10^3$, for the matrix infinite norm.

More generally, let A be a square matrix and $Ax = b$, a linear system. Let us look more closely at the linear system:

$$A(x + \delta x) = b + \delta b$$

where δb is a perturbation of b and δx, which is the error committed in the resolution of the linear system. From $\delta x = A^{-1}\delta b$ and $b = Ax$, we deduce:

$$\|\delta x\| \leq \|A^{-1}\|\|\delta b\|, \quad \|b\| \leq \|A\|\|x\|$$

and consequently:

$$\frac{\|\delta x\|}{\|x\|} \leq \|A\|\|A^{-1}\|\frac{\|\delta b\|}{\|b\|}$$

In summary, if the right-hand side, assumed to be non-zero, is marred by a δb error, the relative error $\frac{\|\delta x\|}{\|x\|}$ on the solution x is bounded by:

$$\frac{\|\delta x\|}{\|x\|} \leq \kappa(A)\frac{\|\delta b\|}{\|b\|}$$

Now, let us look at the linear system:

$$(A + \delta A)(x + \delta x) = b$$

From $\delta x = -A^{-1}\delta A(x + \delta x)$, we deduce:

$$\|\delta x\| \leq \|A^{-1}\|\|\delta A\|\|x + \delta x\|$$

and consequently:

$$\frac{\|\delta x\|}{\|x + \delta x\|} \leq \|A\|\|A^{-1}\|\frac{\|\delta A\|}{\|A\|}$$

In summary, if the matrix A is flawed by a δA error, the relative error in the solution is bounded by:

$$\frac{\|\delta x\|}{\|x + \delta x\|} \leq \kappa(A)\frac{\|\delta A\|}{\|A\|}$$

Let us define $\lambda_{max} = \max_i|\lambda_i|$ and $\lambda_{min} = \min_i|\lambda_i|$ as the greatest and lowest eigenvalues absolute values of matrix A, respectively.

COROLLARY 4.1.– For a square matrix A:

1) The conditioning $\kappa(A)$ satisfies the following property:

$$\kappa(A) \geq \frac{\lambda_{max}}{\lambda_{min}}$$

2) The conditioning of matrix A remains unchanged upon multiplication of the matrix:

$$\kappa(\alpha A) = \kappa(A), \quad \forall \alpha \in \mathbb{K}$$

PROOF 4.3.– Let us prove the first property. Let e_i be the eigenvector associated with the eigenvalue λ_i such that:

$$Ae_i = \lambda_i e_i \tag{4.5}$$

Then:

$$\|Ae_i\| = \|\lambda_i e_i\| = |\lambda_i|\|e_i\| \leq \|A\|\|e_i\| \quad \forall i$$

so that

$$\|A\| \geq \lambda_{max} \tag{4.6}$$

If A is invertible, we can multiply equation [4.5] by A^{-1}:

$$\frac{1}{\lambda_i}e_i = A^{-1}e_i$$

and establish the following result:

$$\|A^{-1}e_i\| = \|1/\lambda_i e_i\| = 1/|\lambda_i|\|e_i\| \leq \|A^{-1}\|\|e_i\| \quad \forall i$$

which gives:

$$\|A\| \geq \frac{1}{\lambda_{min}} \tag{4.7}$$

Considering this last equation and equation [4.6], we obtain the inequality.

$\square$

COROLLARY 4.2.– Let A be a square Hermitian matrix, the conditioning $\kappa_2(A)$ for the 2-norm satisfies the following equation:

$$\kappa_2(A) = \frac{\lambda_{max}}{\lambda_{min}}$$

PROOF 4.4.– As A is Hermitian, the basis $(e_i)_{i=1}^n$ formed by the eigenvectors is orthogonal (see the solution of exercise A2.10). Thus, we can decompose a vector in the basis as:

$$v = \sum_{i=1}^{n} x_i e_i$$

whose norm is:

$$\|v\|_2^2 = \sum_{i=1}^{n} x_i^2$$

We have also:

$$Av = \sum_{i=1}^{n} x_i \lambda_i e_i$$

which implies that:

$$\|Av\|_2^2 = \sum_{i=1}^{n} x_i^2 \lambda_i^2$$

From the latter equation, we have:

$$\left(\sum_{i=1}^{n} x_i^2\right) \lambda_{min}^2 \leq \|Av\|_2^2 \leq \left(\sum_{i=1}^{n} x_i^2\right) \lambda_{max}^2$$

and after dividing by $\|v\|_2^2$

$$\lambda_{min}^2 \leq \frac{\|Av\|_2^2}{\|v\|_2^2} \leq \lambda_{max}^2$$

which implies that:

$$\|A\|_2 \leq \lambda_{max}$$

By choosing $v = e_{max}$ as the eigenvector associated with λ_{max}, the upper bound of the matrix norm is reached:

$$\frac{\|Ae_{max}\|_2}{\|e_{max}\|_2} = \lambda_{max}$$

so that:

$$\|A\|_2 = \lambda_{max} \tag{4.8}$$

Let us now see the norm $\|A^{-1}\|_2$. If A is invertible, we have:

$$\frac{1}{\lambda_i} e_i = A^{-1} e_i$$

so that the eigenvalues of A^{-1} are λ_i^{-1}. We have, therefore:

$$\frac{1}{\lambda_{max}^2} \leq \frac{\|A^{-1}v\|^2}{\|v\|^2} \leq \frac{1}{\lambda_{min}^2}$$

which yields:

$$\|A^{-1}\|_2 \leq \frac{1}{\lambda_{min}}$$

As before, by choosing for v the eigenvector associated with λ_{min}, we reach the lower bound and therefore:

$$\|A^{-1}\|_2 = \frac{1}{\lambda_{min}} \tag{4.9}$$

Multiplying equations [4.8] and [4.9], we finally obtain:

$$\|A\| \, \|A^{-1}\| = \frac{\lambda_{max}}{\lambda_{min}}$$

□

We saw above that the number $\kappa(A)$, called conditioning of the matrix A, measures the sensitivity of the solution x of the linear system $Ax = b$ in relation to the variations of the data A and b. The value of this number also has a great influence on the solution methods, either for direct methods, where it is directly related to the round-off errors during the calculations, or for iterative methods where it is directly linked to the number of iterations necessary to reach convergence.

In taking eigenvectors associated with λ_{max} or λ_{min} as second members of the problem $Ax = b$, or as a variation of the second member δb, we easily show that the estimates of sensitivity, depending on the conditioning, are clear; the extreme values are reached.

5

Sparse Matrices

In this chapter, we are particularly interested in matrices arising from the discretization of partial differential equations of physics using the finite difference (FD), finite volume (FV) or finite element (FE) methods. By construction, these matrices have a sparse structure. It encourages reduced storage of the coefficients of the matrix, which facilitates the temporal and spatial localities of data. An obvious application is the formation of the matrix in parallel. These are issues that we address in the following sections.

5.1. Origins of sparse matrices

Most codes of numerical simulation in fluid mechanics, structures or electromagnetics use discretizations of partial differential equations of physics, using the finite difference (FD), finite volume (FV) or finite element (FE) methods. These methods are based on the approximation of the solution using piecewise polynomial functions, defined on a mesh representing the calculation domain. They transform the problem of a continuous partial differential to an algebraic problem of finite dimension. Its unknowns are the coefficients of the approximate solution in a base of functions whose supports are limited to a single cell, or a small number of cells with a point, edge or a given common face. In the case where each basic function is associated with a node of the mesh, taking the value of 1 in it, and 0 in all others, the support of a basic function is restricted to elements containing this point, as shown in Figure 5.1.

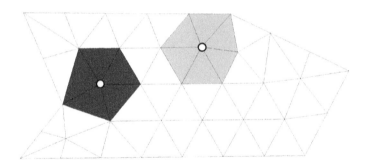

Figure 5.1. *Supports of the basis functions associated with two vertices*

The coefficients of the matrices of discretized problems represent the interactions between the basis functions, and the result of a spatial integration. Due to the nature of bounded supports of the basis functions, most coefficients are null, since the spatial integration is done only in the mesh belonging to the intersection of the supports. Thus, these matrices are sparse. These sparse matrices have special properties. In particular, they have a symmetrical structure: the existence of a non-empty intersection between the supports of basis functions, which determines the appearance of a non-zero coefficient, where coefficient (i, j) is non-zero. And it is the same for the coefficient (j, i). Similarly, the diagonal coefficients are generally non-zero.

DEFINITION 5.1 (Graph).– *A graph is a set of vertices S and edges A, where A is a subset of $S \times S$. The graph is said to be undirected if the edges (s, t) and (t, s) cannot be distinguished.*

The structure of a sparse matrix can be described in terms of its graph. The vertices of the graph are the row numbers, that is the equation numbers of the system, and the edges of the graph represent the non-zero coefficients of the matrix. We note that the edges (i, j) and (j, i) always coexist. The connectivity graph of the matrix is, therefore, undirected. It can be deduced directly from the mesh. In the case of basis functions associated with vertices of triangular meshes in two-dimensional (2D), or tetrahedrical meshes in three-dimensional (3D), the graph of the matrix is directly associated with the edges of the mesh, as shown in Figures 5.2 and 5.3. For meshes composed of other elements (like quadrilaterals in 2D), some non-zero coefficients are not connected by an edge (this is the case of the nodes connected by the diagonal of the quadrilaterals).

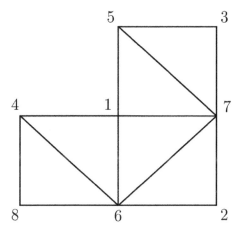

Figure 5.2. *Mesh*

11			14		16		18
	22				26	27	
		33		35		37	
41			44	45	46	47	
		53	54	55		57	
61	62		64		66	67	68
	72	73	74	75	76	77	
81					86		88

Figure 5.3. *Sparse matrix*

In a more general case, the solution can be a vector field with several components, so that we have several basis functions associated with the same point. Thus, the matrix has the same structure of blocks with their dimensions equal to the number of components.

The graph of the sparse matrix defines, for each row, the list of column numbers of non-zero coefficients. Only these coefficients are stored. If we, respectively, arrange in arrays $list\_column\_i$ and $coef\_i$, the n_i column numbers of non-zero coefficients and the coefficients themselves, for the row i, the algorithm of the product of a sparse matrix by a vector (SMVP) can be written as:

```
for  i = 1 to  n
    y(i) = 0
    for  k = 1 to  n_i
        y(i) = y(i) + coef_i(k) × x(list_column_i(k))
    end for
end for
```

In practice, the arrays $list\_column\_i$ are stored one after another in a single one-dimensional array. It suffices to go directly to the row i in this concatenated array, to have the pointer that gives the sum of the lengths of the preceding rows:

$$pointer\_row(i) = \sum_{k=1}^{i-1} n_k$$

The matrix coefficients are also ranged in an array $coef$ having a dimension equal to the total number of non-zero coefficients in the matrix, with the same structure, which can be accessed by the same pointer. The storage of the sparse matrices in two one-dimensional arrays optimizes memory access, due to the temporal localization of data, regardless of the programming language used.

With this storage method, described as compressed sparse row (CSR), the matrix-vector product is:

```
for  i = 1 to  n
    y(i) = 0
    for  k = pointer_row(i) + 1 to  pointer_row(i + 1)
        y(i) = y(i) + coef(k) × x(list_column(k))
    end for
end for
```

To calculate the product by the transposed matrix, we need only to consider that a row of the original matrix now describes a column of the transposed matrix, and then carry out a matrix-vector product by column such that the product of the transposed matrix can be written:

```
for  i = 1  to  n
  y(i) = 0
end for
for  i = 1  to  n
  for  k = pointer_row(i) + 1  to  pointer_row(i + 1)
    y(list_column(k)) = y(list_column(k)) + coef(k) × x(i)
  end for
end for
```

Moreover, if the matrix is symmetric, it is enough to store only its upper triangular part with the diagonal included. To perform the matrix-vector product, we thus calculate the product by the upper triangular part, and then the product by its transposition, without the diagonal. If the coefficients of the different rows are sorted by increasing column numbers, the diagonal coefficient is the first. This in such a way that the product by a symmetric sparse matrix, stored as compressed by the top row, can be written as:

```
for  i = 1  to  n
  y(i) = 0
  for  k = pointer_row(i) + 1  to  pointer_row(i + 1)
    y(i) = y(i) + coef(k) × x(list_column(k))
  end for
end for
for  i = 1  to  n
  for  k = pointer_row(i) + 2  to  pointer_row(i + 1)
    y(list_column(k)) = y(list_column(k)) + coef(k) × x(i)
  end for
end for
```

Another mode of compressed storage is to describe each non-zero coefficient by three parameters; the row number, column number and value. This storage is known as coordinate (COO). The matrix is then described by three arrays equal in size to the number of non-zero terms of the matrix; $list\_row$, $list\_column$ and $coef$, so the matrix-vector product is written as:

```
for  i = 1  to  n
  y(i) = 0
end for
for  k = 1  to  number_coef
  y(list_row(k)) = y(list_row(k)) + coef(k) × x(list_column(k))
end for
```

This last storage method is *a priori* more flexible since it requires no sorting of the coefficients. However, it has several disadvantages: it requires two indirect addressing in order to achieve the product; *a priori* it does not localize access to data; and it cannot quickly find a term of the matrix from its row and column numbers.

5.2. Parallel formation of sparse matrices: shared memory

For some methods, such as the FD method, the coefficients of the sparse matrix are calculated independently at each point, or each edge of the mesh. In this case, the parallelization of the matrix formation is obviously trivial.

However, for many methods, such as FE and FV methods, the calculation of the matrix is carried out on the cells (elements) of the mesh. In the case of the FE method, each elementary matrix calculated on an element contributes to the interactions of the nodes of the element. The formation of the matrix thus implies going through a procedure called "assembly", in which the coefficients of each elementary matrix are added to the corresponding coefficients of the complete matrix.

So, there is an output dependence between the assembly operations of two elementary matrices associated with neighboring cells, or to put this another way, those cells with common vertices. To remove this dependence, the solution is to work on subsets of cells that are not connected. Therefore, we establish lists of unconnected cells, which amounts to coloring the mesh, as shown in Figure 5.4, if we associate a different color to each list. The assembly of elementary matrices associated with the cells of a given color shows no dependence and can be performed in parallel, and hence, *a fortiori*, be vectorized.

This approach allows for parallel assembly of the matrix, and consequently increases the efficiency of the code. From the start, parallelization is already involved in the construction of the problem, and not just in its resolution. The coloring technique enables us to avoid the so-called critical sections of OpenMP, which can drastically penalize the speedup.

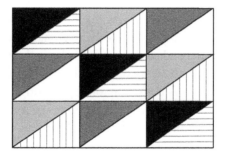

Figure 5.4. *Coloring the elements of a mesh*

5.3. Parallel formation by block of sparse matrices: distributed memory

The formation of matrices in distributed memory computers depends on the nature of the discretization method. In the case of the FD method, where the coefficients of the matrix are obtained by looping over the vertices of the mesh, the parallelization by sets of vertices appears natural. On the contrary, parallelization by sets of elements is ideal for the FE method. We will now describe both types of parallelization and compare them through a simple one-dimensional example.

5.3.1. *Parallelization by sets of vertices*

In a message-passing programming environment on a distributed machine, parallelization will consist of simultaneously producing block matrices. Assigning a block matrix to a process amounts to assigning it a portion of the graph of the matrix. Generally speaking, a sub-block of a matrix consists of coefficients associated with a set of rows and a set of columns. For the graph of the matrix, a set of rows, or columns, corresponds to a set of vertices. The objective of an efficient allocation of blocks of the matrix is, on the one hand, that load balancing will be achieved if the blocks are the same size and, on the other hand, minimizing data transfers and thus interdependencies between blocks. We must, therefore, limit the number of edges of the graph that connect two subsets of vertices assigned to separate processes.

The diagonal coefficients of the matrix are naturally assigned to the processes that treat the corresponding rows. Therefore, all the columns of a process necessarily contain all rows assigned to the same process, such that the corresponding block matrix contains the diagonal block determined by all the rows. To limit the dependencies, we must limit the number of columns, which do not belong to all the rows of each block. We must, therefore, assign to each process, a set of rows consisting of neighboring vertices of the graph, so that the connecting edges are found in the diagonal block assigned to the process, and then try to limit, as much as possible, the number of edges that connect these vertices to other sets.

Decomposing the matrix effectively, amounts to achieving a balanced partition of the set of vertices, such that the different subsets have a minimal number of interconnected edges. Which means achieving a spatial slicing of the graph into subgraphs, with the same number of vertices, using the smallest possible set of separating edges. And since the graph of the matrix originates from a mesh, we must apply the same partitioning principle.

With a partitioning by vertices, like that shown in Figure 5.5, for a division into two, two types of areas appear for the edges and elements. The area inside each subgraph contains the edges corresponding to the coefficients of the diagonal block of the matrix, defined by the subset of the vertices, and determines a subset of elements that only contribute to the diagonal block. The interface area is formed by the edges that connect the vertices located in two distinct subsets of the partition, which also correspond to the coefficients of the off-diagonal blocks of the matrix. The elements that contain these edges contribute to several diagonal and off-diagonal blocks.

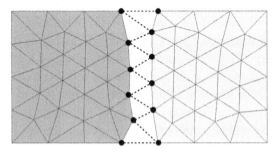

Figure 5.5. *Mesh partitioning by sets of vertices*

5.3.2. *Parallelization by sets of elements*

When the calculation of the matrix consists of the sum of elementary matrices, the distribution of these elementary calculations can naturally be based on a partitioning by sets of elements. Each process thus computes the submatrix coming from the contributions of the elements it has been assigned. In this situation, illustrated in Figure 5.6, there exist two areas for the edges and vertices of the graph: the internal area, which corresponds to a matrix subblock and is completely specific to the process, and the interface area, formed by the edges and vertices known in the distinct blocks of elements. These contributions will have to be taken into account, through communication of the missing coefficients between neighboring processes or through communications after the matrix-vector products of the iterative solvers.

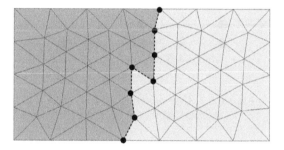

Figure 5.6. *Mesh partitioning by sets of elements*

As in the case of parallelization by sets of vertices, the dependence between the computations carried out on the different blocks of elements depends on the size of the interface coming from the subdomain decomposition. In any case, in a distributed environment, it is out of the question to assemble the global matrix in a single process. In the chapters on resolution methods for sparse matrices, we will see how to use matrices calculated in parallel by the two approaches presented here.

5.3.3. *Comparison: sets of vertices and elements*

In Figure 5.7, we present the two types of parallelization applied to a simple one-dimensional example, on a mesh with five nodes and two subdomains.

We compare the FD method, the FE method, and the FV method. Let us note that in this last case, the degrees of freedom are located at the center of the cells (cell-centered) and there only exist four of these instead of the previous methods.

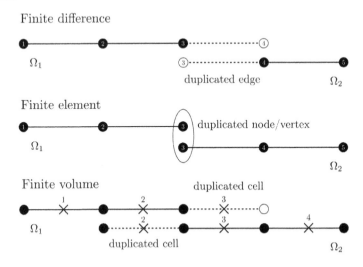

Figure 5.7. *One-dimensional case. Typical decomposition of FD, FE and FV*

In Figure 5.8, we can identify the coefficients computed by each of the subdomains: in each cell of the matrix, we indicate the subdomain number which calculates it. The global degrees of freedom are indicated in the previous figure and correspond to the rows and columns of Figure 5.8. We have identified with a black border the owner of the coefficients (subdomain 1 or 2). We have also colored in gray the coefficients that could be computed by both subdomains, as the edges are duplicated. We observe in Figure 5.7 that for a typical assembly using the FD method, the edges connecting both subdomains are duplicated. On this edge, subdomain 1 will only assemble coefficient $(3, 4)$, while subdomain 2 will assemble coefficient $(4, 3)$. That is the two subdomains will assemble disjoint subblocks of the global matrix: subdomain 1 will be in charge of the complete row 1 through 3 and subdomain 2 will be in charge of rows 4 and 5. The case of the FE method is different, because the partitioning is done element-wise. The two elements connected to the interface, one in subdomain 1 and the other in subdomain 2, have contributions to the coefficient $(3,3)$. Finally, in the case of the FV method, two layers of edges are necessary. Subdomain 1 will be in charge of the first and second degrees of freedom, while subdomain 2 will be in charge of rows 3 and 4. We will see in section 14.3 that in this case, in order to carry out a parallel matrix-vector, subdomain 1 will require the value of the third degree of freedom, while subdomain 2 will require the value of the second degree of freedom. In the aforementioned section, we will compare the matrix-vector product for the three discretization methods.

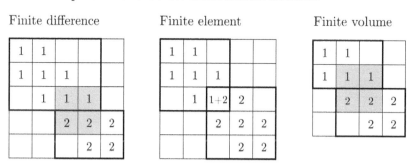

Finite difference   Finite element   Finite volume

Figure 5.8. *One-dimensional case. Submatrices coming from the FD (left), FE (center) and FV (right) methods*

6

Solving Linear Systems

Within the scientific codes, the solution of large linear systems is often the most expensive, both in terms of memory and computation time. This part of the book presents different methods for solving large linear systems and concentrates on their parallelization. Resolution methods fall into two categories: direct methods and iterative methods.

6.1. Direct methods

Direct methods are based on the initial factorization of the matrix and easy-to-solve products of matrices by a direct algorithm, in other words, an algorithm that requires no transformation of the matrix and which gives the result in a number of exactly predictable operations. The solution is obtained by successively solving the problems associated with each factor of the product of matrices. The types of matrices that can be solved by direct algorithms are diagonal matrices, lower or upper triangular matrices and orthogonal, or unitary, matrices.

For the direct methods, in this book, we will focus on LU-type factorizations, or LDU, where L and U are, respectively, lower and upper triangular matrices, and D is diagonal. Once the factorization is achieved, the system is resolved by solving the triangular factors by successive substitutions. The concepts of filling and tree elimination for sparse matrices will be addressed, both to reduce the cost of factorization and to analyze its parallelization.

The disadvantage of direct methods lies in the high costs in terms of the number of arithmetic operations, and also, in terms of the memory footprint of the matrices that were initially sparse, from the initial phase of factorization. However, the resolution itself has a low cost, which can be particularly useful when it is necessary to solve the same system with multiple right-hand sides.

6.2. Iterative methods

An iterative method is a method that solves a problem by finding a succession of approximations from an initial value. The principle of the simplest iterative method is: to solve a system $Ax = b$, we assume to know an invertible approximation M of A^{-1}. Starting from an approximate solution x_p, obtained after p iterations, we calculate the residual vector $Ax_p - b$. The correction necessary to apply to x_p, to find x, would be $-A^{-1}(Ax_p - b)$. We use M to approximate this correction, so that:

$$x_{p+1} = x_p - M(Ax_p - b)$$

It is clear that whatever M is, if the method converges, it converges toward the solution of the problem. However, the method might not converge, and its speed of convergence depends on M.

Specifically, we have:

$$x_{p+1} - x = x_p - x - M(Ax_p - b) = (I - MA)(x_p - x)$$

And therefore:

$$\|x_{p+1} - x\| \leq \|I - MA\|\|x_p - x\|$$

The method converges for all initial approximate solutions, if there is a matrix norm for which $\|I - MA\| < 1$, that is if M is a sufficiently good approximation of A^{-1}.

The simplest approximation of A^{-1} is D^{-1}, where D is the diagonal of the matrix A; this is called the Jacobi method. If $A = D - E - F$, where D

is the diagonal; E is the strict lower triangular part and F is the strict upper triangular part of A, we know how to solve a linear system associated with the lower triangular matrix, $D - E$, or the upper triangular matrix, $D - F$, by successive substitutions. If we choose $M = (D - E)^{-1}$ or $M = (D - F)^{-1}$, this is called the Gauss–Seidel method.

All these methods can be accelerated by the addition of ρ, an *ad hoc* parameter:

$$x_{p+1} = x_p + \rho M(Ax_p - b)$$

The method defined in this way, called the Richardson method, converges faster if $\|I + \rho MA\| < \|I - MA\|$. Richardson's method can converge even when the method of simple iteration, with $\rho = -1$, does not converge.

The coefficient $\rho = -1$ can be calculated according to certain criteria of optimization at each iteration:

$$x_{p+1} = x_p + \rho_p M(Ax_p - b)$$

Further on, we will see a method for calculating an optimal coefficient for symmetric positive-definite matrices, as part of the preconditioned gradient method. This method always converges if M is also symmetric definite positive, even if it is a very poor approximation of A^{-1}, and in particular for $M = I$.

The disadvantage of all the methods presented here is that they do not keep track of changes, and thus, in a manner of speaking, "forget" the history of the iterations. If the application of $p + 1$ iterations, starting from x_0, gives an approximation of x_{p+1}, a single iteration starting from x_p as the initial value gives exactly the same approximate solution.

For the remainder of this book, we will only concern ourselves with Krylov methods, which allow defining an optimal approximation of the solution – not by using only the vector $M(Ax_p - b)$, but all the subspaces generated by the successive vectors $M(Ax_j - b)$. As a result, these methods obviously converge more rapidly than the previous methods that we have studied.

The advantage of iterative methods is that they basically involve matrix-vector operations, and they require nothing more than non-zero coefficients of the matrix, which is particularly interesting for sparse matrices. In addition, they avoid the costly factorization phase. However, in practice, their convergence is difficult to predict, and may even be excessively slow for matrices with poor conditioning. It is, therefore, necessary to invest heavily in the determination of the approximate inverse M, called the preconditioner. Toward the end of this book, we will discuss methods for preconditioning using direct methods at the subblock level of the matrices. The technique employed consists of decomposing the original domain into subdomains, and calculating the exact solution of a local problem in each subdomain to determine the approximate inverses of the system. Each iteration on the global level, therefore, requires solving, in parallel, the local problems defined in each subdomain. This is the case of the Schur and Schwarz methods, which will be discussed in Chapter 15, where examples of hybrid direct-iterative methods are presented.

7

LU Methods for Solving Linear Systems

In this chapter, we present the principle of LU factorization to solve a linear system. We then detail Gauss factorization and, subsequently, Gauss–Jordan factorization for matrices of any kind. The notion of the pivoting of rows is also discussed in detail. Finally, the special case of symmetric matrices is considered and illustrated by Crout factorization, and later, by Cholesky factorization.

7.1. Principle of LU decomposition

DEFINITION 7.1 (LU factorization).– *To calculate the LU factorization of an invertible matrix A is to determine L, a lower triangular matrix and U, an upper triangular matrix, such that $A = LU$.*

Since matrix A is invertible, it follows that matrices L and U are as well.

Once the LU factorization is performed, the system $Ax = b$ is solved into two steps: the first, solving the system $Ly = b$, and second, solving the system $Ux = y$.

Since L is an invertible lower triangular matrix, its diagonal coefficients are non-zero, so the system $Ly = b$ can be solved by successive substitutions, from the first row to the last row. This phase is called "forward substitution", and the algorithm for this can be written as follows:

```
for  i = 1  to  n
    for  j = 1  to  i − 1
```
$$b(i) = b(i) - l(i, j) \times y(j)$$
```
    end  for
```
$$y(i) = b(i)/l(i, i)$$
```
end  for
```

Similarly, since U is an invertible upper triangular matrix, its diagonal coefficients are non-zero, so the system $Ux = y$ can be solved by "backward substitution", that is to say, by successive substitutions from the last row to the first row, and the algorithm for this can be written as follows:

```
for  i = n  to  1
    for  j = i + 1  to  n
```
$$y(i) = y(i) - u(i, j) \times x(j)$$
```
    end  for
```
$$x(i) = y(i)/u(i, i)$$
```
end  for
```

The main cost of a direct method resides in the factorization phase, to which we will devote this chapter.

NOTE 7.1.– In the following, for the algorithm descriptions, to more clearly dissociate the blocks from the coefficients, we will continue to denote the matrices by using uppercase italic letters, while references to coefficients will be denoted in lowercase italic characters.

Let us consider an invertible matrix A decomposed into 2×2 blocks:

$$A = \begin{pmatrix} A_{11} & A_{12} \\ A_{21} & A_{22} \end{pmatrix}$$

The blocks A_{11} and A_{22} are square matrices, respectively, of dimensions n_1 and n_2. The blocks A_{12} and A_{21} are square matrices, respectively, of dimensions (n_1, n_2) and (n_2, n_1).

DEFINITION 7.2 (Partial LU factorization of a matrix).– *We call partial LU factorization of the matrix A, block factorization of a matrix:*

$$\begin{pmatrix} A_{11} & A_{12} \\ A_{21} & A_{22} \end{pmatrix} = \begin{pmatrix} L_{11} & 0 \\ L_{21} & I \end{pmatrix} \begin{pmatrix} U_{11} & U_{12} \\ 0 & S_{22} \end{pmatrix} \qquad [7.1]$$

in which the blocks L_{11} and U_{11} are, respectively, lower and upper-triangular.

Partial factorization is the basic operation of all the algorithms that will be studied in this chapter.

LEMMA 7.1.– So that matrix A allows the partial factorization of equation [7.1], it is necessary, and sufficient, that the block A_{11} is factorizable in $A_{11} = L_{11}U_{11}$.

PROOF 7.1.– Matrix A allows the partial factorization of equation [7.1] if and only if:

$$\begin{pmatrix} A_{11} & A_{12} \\ A_{21} & A_{22} \end{pmatrix} = \begin{pmatrix} L_{11} & 0 \\ L_{21} & I \end{pmatrix} \begin{pmatrix} U_{11} & U_{12} \\ 0 & S_{22} \end{pmatrix}$$

$$= \begin{pmatrix} L_{11}U_{11} & L_{11}U_{12} \\ L_{21}U_{11} & L_{21}U_{12} + S_{22} \end{pmatrix}$$

By identification:

$$\begin{aligned} A_{11} &= L_{11}U_{11} \\ A_{21} &= L_{21}U_{11} \\ A_{12} &= L_{11}U_{12} \\ A_{22} &= L_{21}U_{12} + S_{22} \end{aligned}$$

The first relation represents the factorization $A_{11} = L_{11}U_{11}$ of the main diagonal block. The following two relationships determine the two extra-diagonal blocks.

$$\begin{aligned} L_{21} &= A_{21}U_{11}^{-1} \\ U_{12} &= L_{11}^{-1}A_{12} \end{aligned} \qquad [7.2]$$

Finally, the last relationship determines the block S_{22}:

$$S_{22} = A_{22} - L_{21}U_{12} \tag{7.3}$$

Block S_{22} is called the Schur complement.   □

LEMMA 7.2.– The Schur complement does not depend on the factorization of block A_{11}, and is:

$$S_{22} = A_{22} - A_{21}A_{11}^{-1}A_{12}$$

PROOF 7.2.– The immediate consequence of the previous lemma, and more precisely equations [7.2] and [7.3], is:

$$S_{22} = A_{22} - L_{21}U_{12} = A_{22} - A_{21}U_{11}^{-1}L_{11}^{-1}A_{12}$$

□

Finally, we obtain the fundamental theorem for the LU factorization methods.

THEOREM 7.1.– Matrix A allows LU factorization, if and only if, the block A_{11} and the Schur complement $S_{22} = A_{22} - A_{21}A_{11}^{-1}A_{12}$ can be themselves factorized.

The LU factorization of the matrix is determined by the factorization of the blocks $A_{11} = L_{11}U_{11}$ and $S_{22} = L_{22}U_{22}$, using the formula:

$$\begin{pmatrix} A_{11} & A_{12} \\ A_{21} & A_{22} \end{pmatrix} = \begin{pmatrix} L_{11} & 0 \\ L_{21} & L_{22} \end{pmatrix} \begin{pmatrix} U_{11} & U_{12} \\ 0 & U_{22} \end{pmatrix}$$

in which the blocks L_{21} and U_{12} are those of the partial factorization of the matrix:

$$\begin{pmatrix} A_{11} & A_{12} \\ A_{21} & A_{22} \end{pmatrix} = \begin{pmatrix} L_{11} & 0 \\ L_{21} & I \end{pmatrix} \begin{pmatrix} U_{11} & U_{12} \\ 0 & S_{22} \end{pmatrix}$$

PROOF 7.3.– LU factorization of the matrix is written as:

$$\begin{pmatrix} A_{11} & A_{12} \\ A_{21} & A_{22} \end{pmatrix} = \begin{pmatrix} L_{11} & 0 \\ L_{21} & L_{22} \end{pmatrix} \begin{pmatrix} U_{11} & U_{12} \\ 0 & U_{22} \end{pmatrix}$$

$$= \begin{pmatrix} L_{11}U_{11} & L_{11}U_{12} \\ L_{21}U_{11} & L_{21}U_{12} + L_{22}U_{22} \end{pmatrix}$$

By identification, we again find that the blocks L_{11}, U_{11}, L_{21} and U_{12} are the same as those of the partial factorization of lemma 7.1 and finally:

$$A_{22} = L_{21}U_{12} + L_{22}U_{22} = L_{21}U_{12} + S_{22} \text{ if and only if } S_{22} = L_{22}U_{22}. \ \square$$

This theorem provides a convenient way to construct algorithms for LU factorization. Indeed, if we know how to factorize small-sized matrices, we first factorize the small main diagonal block A_{11}, then calculate the blocks L_{21} and U_{12} and finally the Schur complement, S_{22}. To complete the factorization, it suffices to calculate that of S_{22}, using the same method recurrently.

7.2. Gauss factorization

The Gauss factorization algorithm is based on the recurrent application of the method of partial factorization, taking for block A_{11}, the block of dimension 1 $(a(1,1))$. Its factorization is trivial, $L_{11} = (l(1,1))$, $U_{11} = (u(1,1))$, with $a(1,1) = l(1,1) \times u(1,1)$. The Gauss factorization chooses to take $l(1,1) = 1$ and $u(1,1) = a(1,1)$.

The blocks A_{21} and L_{21} are composed, respectively, of a single column, and the blocks A_{12} and U_{12} are composed, respectively, of a single row. Thus, the partial factorization is easily calculated, using the following algorithm, in which the matrix S_{22}, which is of dimension $n - 1$, is described, to simplify the notations, as a matrix whose indices, of both rows and columns, vary between 2 and n:

```
l(1, 1) = 1
u(1, 1) = a(1, 1)
  for i = 2 to n
    l(i, 1) = a(i, 1)/u(1, 1)
  end for
```

```
for  j = 2  to  n
    u(1, j) = a(1, j)
end  for
for  j = 2  to  n
    for  i = 2  to  n
        s(i, j) = a(i, j) − l(i, 1) × u(1, j)
    end  for
end  for
```

To finish the factorization, it now suffices to apply the same algorithm recursively to S_{22} and then to the different Schur complements of decreasing dimensions, thereby produced.

We can see that each of the coefficients, of the initial matrix A, is used only once to calculate the corresponding coefficient, L_{21}, U_{12} or S_{22}. Afterward, only the matrix S_{22} is used. It is, therefore, unnecessary to work with three matrices: we can substitute the coefficients of L_{21}, U_{12} and S_{22} to those of matrix A. Similarly, $u(1, 1)$ can be substituted for $a(1, 1)$, whereas for $l(1, 1)$, there is no need to keep it; by construction, we know that it is equal to 1.

Finally, the complete Gauss factorization algorithm, with substitution of the terms of L and U, respectively, to those of the strict lower triangular part of A, and its upper triangular part, diagonal included, is written:

```
for  k = 1  to  n − 1
    for  i = k + 1  to  n
        a(i, k) = a(i, k)/a(k, k)
    end  for
    for  j = k + 1  to  n
        for  i = k + 1  to  n
            a(i, j) = a(i, j) − a(i, k) × a(k, j)
        end  for
    end  for
end  for
```

The algorithm constructs, if it exists, the Gauss factorization of the matrix $A = LU$, where L is a lower triangular matrix, whose diagonal coefficients are all equal to 1, and U is an upper triangular matrix.

By construction, step number n_1 of the Gauss factorization algorithm calculates the column number n_1 of L, the row number n_1 of U, as well as, a lower diagonal block of dimension n_2 with $n_1 + n_2 = n = dim(A)$. Applying the Gauss factorization algorithm to this block gives the last n_2 rows and columns of the completed matrix. Therefore, according to lemma 7.1, this block is none other than the Schur complement.

Hence, the following theorem:

THEOREM 7.2.– After the first n_1 iterations of the Gauss algorithm, the blocks A_{11}, A_{21}, A_{12} and A_{22}, respectively, contain the Gauss factorization $L_{11}U_{11}$ of block A_{11}, the blocks L_{21}, U_{12} of the partial factorization of the matrix A and the Schur complement $S_{22} = A_{22} - A_{21}U_{11}^{-1}L_{11}^{-1}A_{12}$.

COROLLARY 7.1.– So that the complete Gauss factorization exists, it is necessary and sufficient that for any value of n_1, the first diagonal coefficient of the Schur complement $S_{22} = A_{22} - A_{21}U_{11}^{-1}L_{11}^{-1}A_{12}$ is different from 0.

PROOF 7.4.– Step n_1 of the above factorization algorithm can only be achieved if the coefficient $a(n_1, n_1)$, resulting from the first $n_1 - 1$ iterations, is different from 0.

Conversely, if the Gauss factorization exists, theorem 7.1 shows that the Schur complement is factorizable, implying that the first diagonal coefficient, equal to the product of the first two coefficients of the invertible matrices L_{22} and U_{22}, is different from 0.   □

NOTE 7.2.– An alternative factorization of the first diagonal term at each step does not change this condition, since, as we have seen in theorem 7.1, the lower diagonal block of any partial factorization is always the Schur complement. This also means that both methods of LU factorization only differ in the choice of the factorization of the diagonal term, at each iteration.

7.3. Gauss–Jordan factorization

As we saw in the previous section, two methods of LU factorization can only differ by the choice of the factorization of the first diagonal term at each iteration. To clarify this, we will begin by proving a lemma on solving triangular systems.

LEMMA 7.3.– We consider the linear system $Lx = y$. If the first n_1 coefficients of y are null, the same is true for those of x. In addition, the vector x_2 of the $n_2 = n - n_1$ last coefficients of x is the solution of the subsystem $L_{22}x_2 = y_2$, where L_{22} is the lower diagonal block of L.

PROOF 7.5.– The system, decomposed by blocks, is written as:

$$\begin{pmatrix} L_{11} & 0 \\ L_{21} & L_{22} \end{pmatrix} \begin{pmatrix} x_1 \\ x_2 \end{pmatrix} = \begin{pmatrix} y_1 \\ y_2 \end{pmatrix}$$

thus, $L_{11}x_1 = y_1 = 0$, which obviously implies that $x_1 = 0$.

In addition, $L_{21}x_1 + L_{22}x_2 = y_2$ and so $L_{22}x_2 = y_2$, since $x_1 = 0$.   □

It is now easy to prove the following theorem:

THEOREM 7.3.– If LU and L_1U_1 are two LU factorizations of the same matrix, then *a fortiori*, a diagonal matrix D exists, such that: $L_1 = LD^{-1}$ and $U_1 = DU$.

PROOF 7.6.– If $L_1U_1 = LU$, then $L^{-1}L_1 = U_1U^{-1} = B$. The matrix B satisfies $LB = L_1$. Therefore, the j column vector of B, which we will denote as x, is the solution of the $Lx = y$ system, where y is the j column vector of L_1. As L_1 is a lower triangular matrix, the $j - 1$ first coefficients of y are null, and the same is true for the $j - 1$ first coefficients of x, in accordance with lemma 7.3.

Thus, we deduce that if L and L_1 are two lower triangular matrices, the same is true for $L^{-1}L_1$.

Similarly, if U_1 and U are two upper triangular matrices, the same is true for U_1U^{-1}. In fact, the transposed matrix of U_1U^{-1} is equal to $U^{-t}U_1$, with U^{-t} designating either the transposed matrix of the inverse of U, or the inverse of its transpose, which are both identical. Therefore, we have just proved that a lower triangular matrix signifies that U_1U^{-1} is an upper triangular.

Matrix B is simultaneously lower triangular and upper triangular. It is, therefore, diagonal.   □

COROLLARY 7.2.– The Gauss factorization, if it exists, is unique.

PROOF 7.7.– In fact, if LU and L_1U_1 are two Gaussian factorizations of the same matrix, then $L_1 = LD^{-1}$. L and L_1, both being lower triangular matrices with diagonal coefficients equal to 1, D can only be the identity matrix.   □

Another choice for the factorization of the diagonal coefficient in each iteration consists of putting forward: $l(1,1) = 1$, $d(1,1) = a(1,1)$ and $u(1,1) = 1$. It now produces three matrices: L, lower triangular; U, upper triangular – both with diagonal coefficients equal to 1 – and a diagonal matrix D such that $A = LDU$.

DEFINITION 7.3 (Gauss–Jordan factorization).– *The factorization of a matrix of the form $A = LDU$, where L is a lower triangular, U is an upper triangular, both with diagonal coefficients equal to 1, and D is a diagonal matrix, is called Gauss–Jordan factorization.*

The previous corollary on the uniqueness of the Gauss factorization leads to the following corollary:

COROLLARY 7.3.– The Gauss–Jordan factorization, if it exists, is unique.

PROOF 7.8.– If $A = LDU$ is a Gauss–Jordan factorization, then L and DU are the factors of the Gauss factorization.   □

This proof also shows that the Gauss–Jordan factorization is obtained simply by starting with the Gauss factorization and then by factorizing the diagonal term into each row of U. Factorizing the diagonal term of row k of U can be performed as soon as it ceases to be used, that is to say, at the end of step k of the Gauss factorization. This gives us the following algorithm for the Gauss–Jordan factorization:

```
for  k = 1 to n − 1
    for  i = k + 1 to  n
        a(i, k) = a(i, k)/a(k, k)
    end for
    for  j = k + 1 to  n
        for  i = k + 1 to  n
            a(i, j) = a(i, j) − a(i, k) × a(k, j)
        end for
    end for
    for  j = k + 1 to  n
```

$$a(k, j) = a(k, j)/a(k, k)$$
      end for
   end for

Obviously, after these calculations, the coefficients of the strictly lower and upper triangular parts of A are, respectively, those of L and U, the diagonal coefficients being those of D.

7.3.1. *Row pivoting*

If the first diagonal coefficient of the Schur complement is zero, the matrix is not, *a priori*, factorizable. However, there is necessarily always at least one non-zero coefficient in the first column of the Schur complement. Otherwise, it would not be invertible and, because of the formula for the partial factorization [7.1], neither would the matrix A. We would, therefore, like to permute the first row of the Schur complement with one containing a non-zero term in the first column. To do this, we will apply a transformation called "elementary permutation".

DEFINITION 7.4 (Permutation matrix).– *The elementary permutation matrix P^{i_1,i_2} is the matrix obtained by permuting the rows i_1 and i_2 of the identity matrix.*

All the rows and columns, except those of i_1 and i_2 of matrix P^{i_1,i_2}, are the same as those of the identity matrix. In row i_1, all the coefficients are zero except for the coefficient (i_1, i_2), which is 1. Similarly, in row i_2, all the coefficients are zero, except the coefficient (i_2, i_1), which is 1. The matrix is symmetric.

LEMMA 7.4.– The result of the product of matrix P^{i_1,i_2} by matrix A is obtained by permuting the rows i_1 and i_2 of A.

PROOF 7.9.– By definition of the product of two matrices, the coefficient (i, j) of the matrix $P^{i_1,i_2}A$ is equal to the scalar product of row i of P^{i_1,i_2} by column j of A. Since $IA = A$, the scalar product of row i of the identity matrix by column j of A is equal to the coefficient (i, j) of A.

With P^{i_1,i_2} being formed by the permutation of rows i_1 and i_2 of the identity matrix, we see that the product $P^{i_1,i_2}A$ is obtained from the product IA by permutation of the rows i_1 and i_2.   □

Suppose that the coefficient $(i_1, 1)$ of the matrix S_{22} is non-zero. We would like to multiply the matrix S_{22} to the left by the permutation matrix of dimension n_2: $P_{n_2}^{1,i_1}$. To do this, we will multiply the complete matrix, to the left, by the matrix:

$$\begin{pmatrix} I & 0 \\ 0 & P_{n_2}^{1,i_1} \end{pmatrix} = P^{n_1+1,n_1+i_1}$$

Let us now continue the partial factorization of equation [7.1] and multiply it to the left by the permutation matrix P^{n_1+1,n_1+i_1}:

$$\begin{aligned}
P^{n_1+1,n_1+i_1} A &= \begin{pmatrix} I & 0 \\ 0 & P_{n_2}^{1,i_1} \end{pmatrix} \begin{pmatrix} L_{11} & 0 \\ L_{21} & I \end{pmatrix} \begin{pmatrix} U_{11} & U_{12} \\ 0 & S_{22} \end{pmatrix} \\
&= \begin{pmatrix} L_{11} & 0 \\ P_{n_2}^{1,i_1} L_{21} & P_{n_2}^{1,i_1} \end{pmatrix} \begin{pmatrix} U_{11} & U_{12} \\ 0 & S_{22} \end{pmatrix}
\end{aligned}$$

from where:

$$P^{n_1+1,n_1+i_1} A = \begin{pmatrix} L_{11} & 0 \\ P_{n_2}^{1,i_1} L_{21} & I \end{pmatrix} \begin{pmatrix} U_{11} & U_{12} \\ 0 & P_{n_2}^{1,i_1} S_{22} \end{pmatrix} \qquad [7.4]$$

Equation [7.4] shows that to calculate the partial factorization of the matrix obtained by the permutation of rows $n_1 + 1$ and $n_1 + i_1$ of A, it is sufficient to apply a permutation of the rows 1 and i_1, to the blocks L_{21} and S_{22} of the partial factorization of A.

In practice, since these blocks are actually stored in the corresponding locations of matrix A, which signifies that they simply apply the permutation of rows $n_1 + 1$ and $n_1 + i_1$ to matrix A resulting from the n_1 first stages of the factorization.

At each iteration of the Gauss algorithm, there, therefore, exists, at least one elementary permutation that allows us to obtain a first non-zero diagonal coefficient in the Schur complement. This gives us the following theorem:

THEOREM 7.4.– If A is an invertible matrix, then there exists a sequence of elementary permutations such as matrix $\prod_{k=n-2}^{0} P^{k+1,k+i_k} A$ that allows a Gauss factorization.

The sequence of permutations is obviously not unique. The permutation of the rows is called "pivoting". To solve the system $Ax = b$, it is replaced by the system:

$$\prod_{k=n-2}^{0} P^{k+1,k+i_k} Ax = LUx = \prod_{k=n-2}^{0} P^{k+1,k+i_k} b$$

Thus, it suffices to successively apply to b the permutations of rows $k + 1$ and $k+i_k$ for k going from 0 to $n-1$, before solving the system using forward–backward substitution.

Pivoting can be applied even if the first diagonal coefficient is not null, which permits improving the stability of the Gauss factorization algorithm. To illustrate this fact, let us consider the first step of the factorization. The calculation of the Schur complement is written as:

$$s(i, j) = a(i, j) - l(i, 1) \times u(1, j) = a(i, j) - a(i, 1) \times a(1, j)/a(1, 1)$$

If the coefficient $a(1, 1)$ is very small, the term $a(i, 1) \times a(1, j)/a(1, 1)$ will dominate the term $a(i, j)$. Given that the accuracy of calculations on a computer is limited by its representation of numbers, a certain number of significant digits of $a(i, j)$ will disappear. This disappearance, or at least the modification of the terms $a(i, j)$, amounts to changing the initial matrix in such a way that it can no longer be invertible. At the very worst, the result is the same as if $a(i, j)$ were zero. The algorithm will become numerically unstable.

In the opposite case, if the coefficient $a(1, 1)$ is very large, the term $a(i, 1) \times a(1, j)/a(1, 1)$ will be dominated by the term $a(i, j)$ to such a point that it will eventually disappear before it. This returns to considering that the terms $a(i, 1)$ and $a(1, j)$ are negligible compared with $a(1, 1)$, which is certainly a source of inaccuracy, but does not throw into question the invertibility of the matrix. Doing this is what we call "numerical pivoting".

DEFINITION 7.5 (Numerical pivoting).– *In the Gauss factorization, the method which consists of permuting the rows of the matrix at each iteration, in such a way as to move the largest terms onto the diagonal, is called numerical pivoting.*

7.4. Crout and Cholesky factorizations for symmetric matrices

If matrix A is symmetric, then its diagonal blocks A_{11} and A_{22} are as well, and its extra-diagonal blocks are transposed from one to another: $A_{12} = A_{21}^t$. Because of this, the Schur complement, $S_{22} = A_{22} - A_{21}A_{11}^{-1}A_{12}$, is obviously also symmetric. During the Gauss factorization, it is therefore sufficient to calculate the lower triangular part, or the upper triangular part, of the Schur complement only. However, the Gauss factorization does not preserve the symmetry: $U \neq L^t$.

The Gauss–Jordan factorization retains the symmetry since, if A is a factorizable symmetric matrix, then $A = LDU = A^t = U^tL^t$. From the uniqueness of the Gauss–Jordan factorization, it follows that $U = L^t$. Consequently, blocks L and U of the Gauss factorization of the matrix satisfy the equation: $U = DL^t$.

Hence, we just proved the following theorem:

THEOREM 7.5.– If A is a factorizable symmetric matrix, then A allows a Crout factorization: $A = LDL^t$.

For example, Crout's algorithm can be written by using only the lower triangular part of the matrix, and by only calculating L and D.

```
for  k = 1  to  n − 1
  for  i = k + 1  to  n
    v(i) = a(i, k)
    a(i, k) = a(i, k)/a(k, k)
  end for
  for  j = k + 1  to  n
    for  i = j  to  n
      a(i, j) = a(i, j) − a(i, k) × v(j)
    end for
  end for
end for
```

The utility vector v is used to conserve the values of the coefficients of row k of U, which, by symmetry, are in fact equal to the coefficients of column k of L prior to their division by the diagonal coefficient.

NOTE 7.3.– The Crout's algorithm requires two times less data and operations than those of the Gauss–Jordan algorithm, since we are using only half of the matrix, and also because we carry out only half the arithmetic operations. To truly benefit from the reduced number of necessary data, obviously it is necessary to store the lower triangular part of the matrix in a different manner.

Let us write the partial Gauss factorization of a symmetric matrix:

$$\begin{pmatrix} A_{11} & A_{12} \\ A_{21} & A_{22} \end{pmatrix} = \begin{pmatrix} L_{11} & 0 \\ L_{21} & I \end{pmatrix} \begin{pmatrix} U_{11} & U_{12} \\ 0 & S_{22} \end{pmatrix}$$

Due to the relations of symmetry, we have:

$$\begin{pmatrix} A_{11} & A_{12} \\ A_{21} & A_{22} \end{pmatrix} = \begin{pmatrix} L_{11} & 0 \\ L_{21} & I \end{pmatrix} \begin{pmatrix} D_{11}L_{11}^t & D_{11}L_{12}^t \\ 0 & S_{22} \end{pmatrix}$$

Factoring in the diagonal blocks, we finally obtain:

$$\begin{pmatrix} A_{11} & A_{12} \\ A_{21} & A_{22} \end{pmatrix} = \begin{pmatrix} L_{11} & 0 \\ L_{21} & I \end{pmatrix} \begin{pmatrix} D_{11} & 0 \\ 0 & S_{22} \end{pmatrix} \begin{pmatrix} L_{11}^t & L_{12}^t \\ 0 & I \end{pmatrix} \qquad [7.5]$$

Equation [7.5] clearly appears as a formula of a change of basis to the sense of quadratic forms. We thus deduce the following theorem:

THEOREM 7.6.– If A is symmetric positive definite, the same is true for the Schur complement.

COROLLARY 7.4.– If A is symmetric positive definite, it is factorizable, and all the diagonal coefficients of the Crout factorization are strictly positive.

PROOF 7.10.– Since the Schur complement is symmetric positive definite, its diagonal coefficients are strictly positive. Thus, the first diagonal coefficient of the Schur complement is never null. The diagonal coefficients of the Crout factorization are equal to the first diagonal coefficients of the successive Schur complements.   □

Since the diagonal terms are strictly positive, there is another method of factorization that preserves the symmetry. In step one of the factorization algorithm, we take: $l(1,1) = u(1,1) = \sqrt{a(1,1)}$, and then the same at each iteration. By doing so, we will calculate the Cholesky factorization of the matrix $A = LL^t$. Of course, by the uniqueness of the Gauss–Jordan factorization, and therefore of Crout for a symmetric matrix, we immediately realize that if the Crout factorization of the positive definite matrix is written as $A = LDL^t$, then the Cholesky factorization applies:

$$A = \left(L\sqrt{D}\right)\left(L\sqrt{D}\right)^t$$

The Cholesky's algorithm can thus be written in the following manner:

```
for  k = 1  to  n − 1
    a(k, k) = √a(k, k)
    for  i = k + 1  to  n
        a(i, k) = a(i, k)/a(k, k)
    end for
    for  j = k + 1  to  n
        for  i = j  to  n
            a(i, j) = a(i, j) − a(i, k) × a(j, k)
        end for
    end for
end for
```

Cholesky factorization requires a square root extraction to calculate the diagonal coefficients of the matrix; a costly operation and a source of numerical imprecision. Crout's method can also be applied to non-positive matrices and does not cost more than that of Cholesky, and is thus the preferred method.

8

Parallelization of LU Methods for Dense Matrices

In this chapter, we focus on the parallelization of LU methods. As with the product of matrices, we will see that the concern about temporal and spatial localities of data leads to a block-wise approach. Block factorization easily lends itself to implementation in a message-passing programming environment. Then, block-wise forward-backward substitution is described, as well as its parallelization in a message-passing programming environment.

8.1. Block factorization

To study parallelization, it suffices to consider Gauss factorization; from that, the parallelization of other algorithms will immediately result. Let us begin by considering the Gauss algorithm:

```
for  k = 1  to  n − 1
    for  i = k + 1  to  n
        a(i, k) = a(i, k)/a(k, k)
    end for
    for  j = k + 1  to  n
        for  i = k + 1  to  n
            a(i, j) = a(i, j) − a(i, k) × a(k, j)
        end for
    end for
end for
```

There are no dependencies at the level of the two inner loops, since the indices i and j are always greater than k. However, the k loop shows obvious input and output dependencies. The permutability cannot be studied using the analytical tools we presented in Chapter 2, because the bounds of the inner loops depend on the value of the index of the outer loop. Clearly, this dependence prevents the permutation. The algorithm is highly recursive: in each iteration of the loop of index k, we change the whole lower diagonal block, and the data used to do this are the result of operations in the previous iterations. Hence, on the one hand, parallelization can only be done at the level of the loop:

> **for** $i = k + 1$ **to** n
> $\quad a(i, k) = a(i, k)/a(k, k)$
> **end for**

and, on the other hand, at the level of the two nested loops:

> **for** $j = k + 1$ **to** n
> $\quad$ **for** $i = k + 1$ **to** n
> $\quad\quad a(i, j) = a(i, j) - a(i, k) \times a(k, j)$
> $\quad$ **end for**
> **end for**

which clearly represents the largest of the operations.

Thus, we will focus our efforts on these. They do not exhibit any dependencies and, therefore, are parallelizable and permutable. In terms of memory access, whether we consider the index i or j for the inner loop, there are two reads and one write per iteration, for a pair of operations $(-, \times)$. However, with the loop index j, the accesses to the matrices are by row, and they are accessed by column with the loop index i. If the matrices are stored in memory by column, spatial locality is much better with the loop index i, so it is best to leave that at the internal level; while leaving loop index j, which is parallelizable, at the external level.

As with the product of matrices, this result is still far from satisfactory. In fact, the total number of pairs of operations $(-, \times)$ in the algorithm is:

$$\sum_{k=1}^{n-1}(n-k)^2 = \sum_{k=1}^{n-1}k^2 \simeq \frac{n^3}{3}$$

The input data of the algorithm are the coefficients of matrix A, the total of which is n^2 and the same applies for the output data. It should thus be possible to access memory only $2n^2$ times, for a total of $n^3/3$ pairs of $(-, \times)$ operations. Temporal locality access should be very good, which is not the case of the row algorithm, in the way we wrote it.

Once again, the solution lies in the implementation of a block-wise strategy. In reality, if the matrix is of a sufficiently small size to fit in cache memory, it will reside there throughout the calculations, and the total number of access operations to the main memory will be limited to n^2 reads and n^2 writes. However, unlike the case of the product of matrices, it is not enough to duplicate the three levels of loops of the indices k, j and i, and perform permutations: the recursive nature of the algorithm prevents any automatic permutation. The block algorithm is, therefore, not constructed by using simple manipulations of nested loops.

In fact, we have already laid the foundations of the block factorization algorithm, by writing the partial factorization 7.1. To achieve the partial factorization, four operations are needed:

1) Factorization of the diagonal block, $A_{11} = L_{11}U_{11}$.

2) Determination of the upper block, $U_{12} = L_{11}^{-1}A_{12}$.

3) Determination of the lower block, $L_{21} = A_{21}U_{11}^{-1}$.

4) Calculation of the Schur complement, $S_{22} = A_{22} - L_{21}U_{12}$.

If the dimension of A_{11}, n_1, is small enough, the first operation can be performed in the cache. The number of pairs of $(-, \times)$ operations required is of the order of $n_1^3/3$.

The second operation requires solving $n_2 = n - n_1$ linear systems associated with a lower triangular matrix, since block U_{12} is the solution of the equation $L_{11}U_{12} = A_{12}$. The cost of a forward substitution, being of the order of $n_1^2/2$ pairs of $(-, \times)$ operations, the calculation of U_{12} requires $n_2 \times n_1^2/2$ operations. For each substitution, if the block L_{11} already resides in the cache, it is sufficient to access memory n_1 times in read mode for the second member of the vector, and then n_1 times to write the resulting vector, so that memory is accessed $2n_1$ times for $n_1^2/2$ pairs of $(-, \times)$ operations.

The third operation is identical to the preceding operation. In fact, the transposition of the equation $L_{21}U_{11} = A_{21}$ gives $U_{11}^t L_{21}^t = A_{21}^t$, so therefore, once again, we must make n_2 forward substitutions for linear systems associated with the lower triangular matrix of dimension n_1, U_{11}^t.

Calculating the Schur complement, $S_{22} = A_{22} - L_{21}U_{12}$, is a product of block matrices which can be organized block-wise to ensure the temporal and spatial localities of data. It requires $n_2^2 \times n_1$ pairs of $(-, \times)$ operations, since each of the n_2^2 matrix coefficients of S_{22} is obtained by using the scalar product of n_1 terms of a row of L_{21} by those of a column of U_{12}.

To complete the factorization of the matrix, it will now be sufficient to carry out a fifth step, which consists of factorizing the Schur complement, $S_{22} = L_{22}U_{22}$, which would require of the order of $n_2^3/3$ pairs of $(-, \times)$ operations. To ensure the proper temporal and spatial localities of data, this factorization itself is done by recursively applying the same block-wise methodology.

We have just proved that the cost of calculating the block Gauss factorization was the same as the classical algorithm. In reality, the five steps described above require a total number of pairs of $(-, \times)$ operations of the order of:

$$\frac{n_1^3}{3} + n_2 \times \frac{n_1^2}{2} + n_2 \times \frac{n_1^2}{2} + n_2^2 \times n_1 + \frac{n_2^3}{3} = \frac{(n_1 + n_2)^3}{3}$$

Calculating the Schur complement requires that the largest part of arithmetic operations is performed at each step of the block algorithm. To obtain good temporal and spatial localities to access memory in this product of matrices, it is necessary to decompose them in such a way that three subblocks can be held simultaneously in the cache. To this end, it is the entire matrix A that is divided into $P \times P$ blocks of dimension n/P, so that the cache can contain three matrices of dimension n/P:

$$
\begin{pmatrix}
A_{11} & A_{12} & \vdots & \vdots & A_{1J} & \vdots & A_{1P} \\
A_{21} & A_{22} & \vdots & \vdots & A_{2J} & \vdots & A_{2P} \\
\cdots & \cdots & \ddots & \vdots & \vdots & \vdots & \vdots \\
A_{I1} & A_{I2} & \cdots & \ddots & A_{IJ} & \vdots & A_{IP} \\
\cdots & \cdots & \cdots\cdots & & \ddots & \vdots & \vdots \\
\cdots & \cdots & \cdots\cdots & \cdots & \ddots & \vdots \\
A_{P1} & A_{P2} & \cdots\cdots & \cdots & A_{PJ} & \cdots & A_{PP}
\end{pmatrix}
$$

The algorithm for Gauss block factorization is finally written as:

```
for  K = 1  to  P
    A_KK = L_KK U_KK
    for  J = K + 1  to  P
        A_KJ = L_KK^{-1} × A_KJ
    end for
    for  I = K + 1  to  P
        A_IK = A_IK × U_KK^{-1}
    end for
    for  J = K + 1  to  P
        for  I = K + 1  to  P
            A_IJ = A_IJ − A_IK × A_KJ
        end for
    end for
end for
```

During the factorization of the diagonal block, blocks L_{KK} and U_{KK} clearly substitute block A_{KK}. Calculations of blocks $L_{KK}^{-1} \times A_{KJ}$ and $A_{IK} \times U_{KK}^{-1}$ are obtained by forward substitutions of lower triangular systems, as described in step 1. The calculations loops of these blocks are parallelizable.

Similarly, calculations of different Schur complements of $A_{IJ} = A_{IJ} - A_{IK} \times A_{KJ}$ are independent and can be performed simultaneously.

8.2. Implementation of block factorization in a message-passing environment

As with the product of matrices, the implementation of a block-wise strategy has already provided the initial temporal and spatial localities of data for parallelization in a message-passing programming environment. With all operations being block-type products, they have high granularity. Finally, there only remains the actual effective distribution of the blocks to different processes, to obtain the greatest possible efficiency. This will depend on the effective degree of parallelism, load balancing and the organization of data transfers.

During the course of the algorithm, each processor will treat the blocks allocated to it. We will assume that all the processes have a *distribution* table of dimension (P, P), which for each block, gives the process number to which it is assigned. In terms of calculation, each process is only going to do the operations that modify its own block, so that the code could be written:

```
for  K = 1  to  P
    if  distribution(K, K) = rank  then
        A_{KK} = L_{KK}U_{KK}
    end  if
    for  J = K + 1  to  P
        if  distribution(K, J) = rank  then
            A_{KJ} = L_{KK}^{-1} × A_{KJ}
        end  if
    end  for
    for  I = K + 1  to  P
        if  distribution(I, K) = rank  then
            A_{IK} = A_{IK} × U_{KK}^{-1}
        end  if
    end  for
    for  J = K + 1  to  P
        for  I = K + 1  to  P
            if  distribution(I, J) = rank  then
                A_{IJ} = A_{IJ} − A_{IK} × A_{KJ}
            end  if
        end  for
    end  for
end  for
```

It remains for us to handle the data exchange. Consider an arbitrary distribution of the blocks, as shown in Figure 8.1, for 16 blocks distributed to four processes according to their shade.

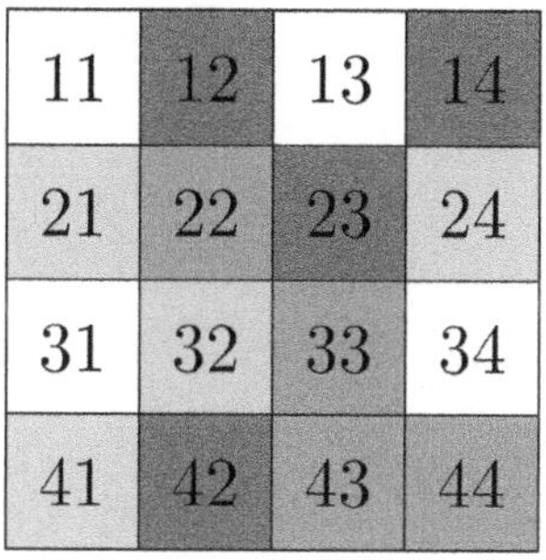

11	12	13	14
21	22	23	24
31	32	33	34
41	42	43	44

Figure 8.1. *Random distribution*

We see that after the factorization of the first diagonal block A_{11} by the white process, the factor L_{11} must be transmitted to all other processes responsible for block A_{1J}, on the first row, in this case, the dark gray process. Similarly, the factor U_{11} must be sent to all other processes responsible for block A_{I1} on the first column, i.e. the light gray process. It is only after receiving these factors that the processes will be able to carry out their part in the calculation of the new blocks:

```
for  J = 2 to  P
   if  distribution(1, J) = rank  then
       A₁J = L₁₁⁻¹ × A₁J
   end  if
end  for
for  I = 2 to  P
   if  distribution(I, 1) = rank  then
       A_I1 = A_I1 × U₁⁻¹
   end  if
end  for
```

$$\textbf{for } J = 2 \textbf{ to } P$$
$$\quad \textbf{if } distribution(1, J) = rank \textbf{ then}$$
$$\qquad A_{1J} = L_{11}^{-1} \times A_{1J}$$
$$\quad \textbf{end if}$$
$$\textbf{end for}$$
$$\textbf{for } I = 2 \textbf{ to } P$$
$$\quad \textbf{if } distribution(I, 1) = rank \textbf{ then}$$
$$\qquad A_{I1} = A_{I1} \times U_1^{-1}$$
$$\quad \textbf{end if}$$
$$\textbf{end for}$$

Similarly, the blocks A_{1J} and A_{I1} thus calculated must be, respectively, transmitted to all the processes calculating the Schur complement of the column J and row I. Figures 8.2 and 8.3 illustrate the different types of block transfers, row-wise or column-wise, required for the first iteration of the Gauss algorithm.

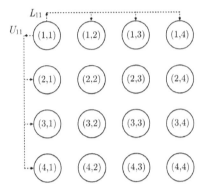

Figure 8.2. *Diagonal block transfers at iteration 1*

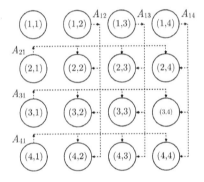

Figure 8.3. *Block transfers of the first row and the first column at iteration 1*

Finally, we see that we will have to develop block transfer functions, on a row and a column. The transfer of block L_{KK} on row K will be carried out using the process $distribution(K, K)$ toward all the processes with $distribution(K, J)$, $J > K$. Those of a block A_{IK} on row I will use processes $distribution(I, K)$ toward all the processes $distribution(I, J)$, $J > K$. Similarly, the transfer of a block U_{KK} on row K will use processes $distribution(K, K)$ toward all the $distribution(I, K)$, $I > K$ processes.

Those of a block A_{KJ} will use processes $distribution(K, J)$ toward all the processes $distribution(I, J), I > K$.

Let us define two procedures:

$$diffusion\_by\_row \quad \text{or} \quad diffusion\_by\_column$$

with arguments I or J for the row or column number and K which indicates that the destination processes are only:

$$distribution(I, K) \text{ for } I > K \quad \text{or} \quad distribution(K, J) \text{ for } J > K$$

By doing this, we want to mimic the arguments of function *MPI_Bcast*, since this is a transfer of one-to-all in a group. With management of data transfers included, the algorithm executed by each process is now written as:

```
for  K = 1  to  P
   if  distribution(K, K) = rank  then
      A_KK = L_KK U_KK
   end  if
   diffusion_by_row(K, K, L_KK, distribution(K, K))
   diffusion_by_column(K, K, U_KK, distribution(K, K))
   for  J = K + 1  to  P
      if  distribution(K, J) = rank  then
         A_KJ = L_KK^{-1} × A_KJ
      end  if
      diffusion_by_column(J, K, A_KJ, distribution(K, J))
   end  for
   for  I = K + 1  to  P
      if  distribution(I, K) = rank  then
         A_IK = A_IK × U_KK^{-1}
      end  if
      diffusion_by_row(I, K, A_IK, distribution(I, K))
   end  for
   for  J = K + 1  to  P
      for  I = K + 1  to  P
         if  distribution(I, J) = rank  then
```

$$A_{IJ} = A_{IJ} - A_{IK} \times A_{KJ}$$
$$\textbf{end if}$$
$$\textbf{end for}$$
$$\textbf{end for}$$
$$\textbf{end for}$$

Efficient distribution must ensure that the greatest number of processes are employed in each phase, while still balancing the work load. The random distribution of Figure 8.1 is certainly not very effective. For example, at the first iteration, the medium gray process has nothing to do and remains idle during the block updating phase of the first row and first column, but in contrast, it treats four of nine blocks in the calculation phase of the Schur complement.

One possibility to achieve high efficiency is to shade the blocks cyclically by row and column, as shown in Figure 8.4, with a total number of blocks on each row or column, a multiple of the number of processes. With this distribution, all the processes are working at all the iterations for each parallel updating phase of the rows and columns of the blocks, or on calculating the Schur complement. In addition, the procedures *diffusion_by_row* or *diffusion_by_column* can be simply replaced by the function *MPI_Bcast*, since the distribution cycle ensures that all processes have blocks on each row and each column.

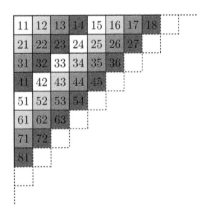

Figure 8.4. *Cyclic distribution*

However, this distribution has the disadvantage of separating into a large number of blocks, which can harm the granularity. In addition, in each block Gauss iteration, all the processes will need all the blocks on the row and on the column to calculate their contributions to the Schur complement. This requires a large amount of memory space.

There are other methods of distribution that require a breakdown into a number of smaller blocks. But, whatever the method of distribution, the problem of memory required to temporarily store the blocks used in the calculations does arise for large matrices.

NOTE 8.1.– The scientific library ScaLaPack performs block factorization and the resolution of dense matrices on distributed memory systems, using a block-wise distribution, which is a little bit more complex than cyclic distribution that we have discussed here, but it has the advantage of needing a smaller number of blocks.

8.3. Parallelization of forward and backward substitutions

Forward and backward substitutions are the transposed operation of each other. It is, therefore, sufficient to study the parallelization of a forward phase, that is solving a system $Lx = y$:

for $i = 1$ **to** n
  for $j = 1$ **to** $i - 1$
    $y(i) = y(i) - l(i, j) \times x(j)$
  end for
  $x(i) = y(i)/l(i, i)$
end for

A priori, the outer loop shows a dependence on the variable x. The inner loop is a reduction operation: it is the scalar product of the left side of row i of matrix L by the vector of the $i - 1$ first coefficients of x, already calculated, to be deducted from $y(i)$. This operation is parallelizable, but its granularity is low. The algorithm presented here comes down to accessing matrix L by row.

The correction operation $y(i) = y(i) - l(i, j) \times x(j)$ can actually be performed as soon as $x(j)$ is known. It is thus possible to permute the two loops, with a slight modification of the algorithm, a modification that is not automatic, given that the boundaries of the inner loop depend on the index of the outer loop:

```
for  j = 1  to  n
    x(j) = y(j)/l(j, j)
    for  i = j + 1  to  n
        y(i) = y(i) − l(i, j) × x(j)
    end for
end for
```

The outer loop has a dependence on the variable y. The inner loop shows no dependence; thus, it is parallelizable. It amounts to subtracting to the last $n - j$ terms of y, the lower part of column j of L, multiplied by the coefficient $x(j)$. This algorithm thus accesses matrix L by column. Once again, this operation has low granularity.

In the case of block factorization of the matrix, the operations are similar, except that rather than the operations being on coefficients of matrix L, they are on the blocks. So, there is one side of the matrix-vector product for the lower blocks, and forward substitutions for the diagonal blocks that are themselves lower triangular. The granularity is a bit better, since they are products of matrix blocks by vectors that can be performed simultaneously.

For example, the column algorithm, in the case of a division of blocks $P \times P$ of dimension n/P, is written:

```
for  J = 1  to  P
    Resolve  :  L_{JJ}X_J = Y_J
    for  I = J + 1  to  P
        Y_I = Y_I − L_{IJ} × X_J
    end for
end for
```

Gathering the operations in blocks improves the granularity at the cost of a decrease in the degree of parallelism. Nevertheless, whatever the approach used, the granularity stays limited, because of the fact that we cannot perform more than a single pair of $(+, \times)$ operations by coefficient of matrix L. The ratio of the number of arithmetic operations, compared to the number of times memory is accessed, is 2 maximum.

The forward-backward substitution is a phase in which the efficiency of parallelism is low. However, this is not a problem *a priori*, as the relative cost of forward-backward substitution is very low compared to that of the factorization of n^2 compared to Cn^3.

The situation is different if we have to solve the same system for a large number of right-hand sides. In this case, however, if the right-hand sides are all known *a priori*, it is sufficient to perform all the forward-backward substitutions simultaneously. Operations of the $L_{IJ} \times X_J$ type are products of rectangular matrices, with the number of columns X_J being equal to the number of right-hand sides. The granularity is greatly improved, and thereby, so is the effectiveness.

However, if the right-hand sides cannot be simultaneously processed, because they are all dependent on each other, for example, because they are derived from an external iterative procedure, this methodology is faulty.

9

LU Methods for Sparse Matrices

We begin this chapter with a discussion of the factorization of sparse matrices. After a brief presentation of filling that occurs during the factorization, we introduce symbolic factorization, and the renumbering of the equations of a matrix. The notion of elimination trees for achieving symbolic factorization at a lesser cost is then discussed. Elimination trees permit the analysis of dependencies, and thus parallelization of the factorization. The method of nested dissections thus appears as a technique naturally suited for renumbering, which enables efficient parallelization. In conclusion, forward-backward substitution is analyzed for parallelization.

9.1. Structure of factorized matrices

The first stage of Gauss factorization consists of calculating the first row of U, the first column of L and then the Schur complement of rows 2 to n.

$l(1,1) = 1$
$u(1,1) = a(1,1)$
for $i = 2$ **to** n
    $l(i,1) = a(i,1)/u(1,1)$
end for
for $j = 2$ **to** n
    $u(1,j) = a(1,j)$
end for
for $j = 2$ **to** n
    for $i = 2$ **to** n
        $s(i,j) = a(i,j) - l(i,1) \times u(1,j)$
    end for
end for

The first row of U and the first column of L thus have non-zero coefficients exactly at the same locations of non-zero coefficients of the first column and first row of the initial matrix. Due to the structural symmetry of the initial matrix, the full set of indices of column $j > 1$, for which $u(1, j)$ is non-zero, is identical to the set of indices of row $i > 1$ for which $l(i, 1)$ is non-zero. Let us denote this set as C1.

The calculation of the Schur complement has an impact only on the coefficients (i, j), for which $l(i, 1)$ and $u(1, j)$ are simultaneously non-zero; that is to say that the submatrix composed of terms (i, j) such that i and j both belong to C_1. For one of the coefficients of the submatrix, two situations can occur:

– the coefficient was already in the initial matrix and is modified by calculating the Schur complement.

– the coefficient was not in the initial matrix, and thus will be created.

The appearance of non-zero terms during the factorization, in places where the original sparse matrix of coefficients did not have any, implies that the structure of the factorized matrix will be less sparse than the initial matrix. This phenomenon is called "filling". Since the modified, or created coefficients form a submatrix, filling retains a symmetrical structure in the Schur complement.

In Figure 9.1, the non-zero coefficients in the first row of U and the first column of L appear as black squares. All the positions in the matrices involved in the first stage of factorization correspond to the rows and columns of non-zero terms in the first row of U, and the first column of L. They are illustrated as squares with solid borders. Those squares that already contain a non-zero coefficient are colored in gray, while the white squares do not have a coefficient.

In Figure 9.2, the matrix of coefficients, modified when calculating the Schur complement, are represented by squares with asterisk. Among these squares, those that correspond to the coefficients that already existed are colored in gray with an asterisk, and those which did not are white with an asterisk.

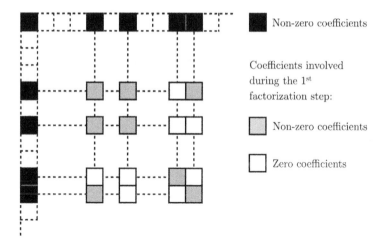

Figure 9.1. *Structure of the factorized matrix before filling*

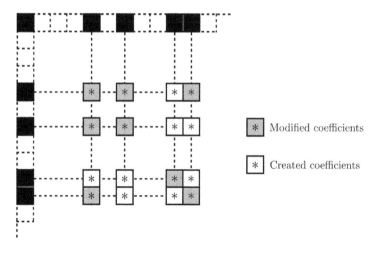

Figure 9.2. *Structure of the factorized matrix after filling*

In each iteration of the Gauss algorithm, the same phenomenon will occur in the factorization of the first row and first column of the Schur complement. Therefore, filling has a cumulative effect, with the rows and columns of successive Schur complements becoming less and less sparse due to filling provoked by previous iterations.

Regarding the graphs, the graph of the Schur complement at the end of the first stage of factorization is deduced from the graph of the initial matrix, in which we removed vertex number 1, but in which all the vertices of the set C_1 are connected two-by-two by the edges, as shown in Figure 9.3. The subgraph formed by the set of vertices fully connected two-by-two is referred to as a "clique". Each edge of the clique, which did not initially exist, corresponds to the pair of coefficients (i, j) and (j, i) that appear in the Schur complement.

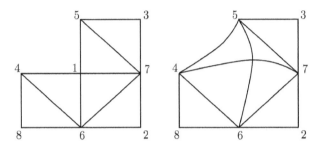

Figure 9.3. *The initial graph on the left, and the emergence of a clique, on the right*

The graph of the Schur complement, at step $k+1$ of the Gauss factorization, is deduced in the same manner as that of the Schur complement resulting from the first k iterations of the algorithm.

9.2. Symbolic factorization and renumbering

Due to the phenomenon of filling, the graph of the matrix is modified during factorization. In order to factorize the matrix, without having to modify the data structures in each step, the structure of the factorized matrix must be determined beforehand; but it is impossible to simply calculate filling *a priori*. It does not only depend on the size and number of non-zero coefficients of the matrix, but also on their position. A renumbering of the unknowns can thus be modified, as the following small example clearly shows:

$$
\begin{pmatrix}
* & * & * & * & * \\
* & * & 0 & 0 & 0 \\
* & 0 & * & 0 & 0 \\
* & 0 & 0 & * & 0 \\
* & 0 & 0 & 0 & *
\end{pmatrix}
,
\begin{pmatrix}
* & 0 & 0 & 0 & * \\
0 & * & 0 & 0 & * \\
0 & 0 & * & 0 & * \\
0 & 0 & 0 & * & * \\
* & * & * & * & *
\end{pmatrix}
$$

The factorization of the matrix on the left creates a dense structure. Renumbering the equations in reverse order, from the largest to the smallest, we obtain the structure on the right, for which there is no filling during factorization.

To calculate the actual filling, we need to proceed to a phase called "symbolic factorization" of the matrix, which consists of determining the number and position of the new coefficients created during factorization. This procedure allows us to construct a data structure capable of accommodating all the coefficients during the factorization of the Schur complements, and finally, the L and U coefficients. Then, within this structure, we will proceed to "numerical factorization", in other words, the actual calculation of the L and U coefficients.

A priori, symbolic factorization of the matrix requires doing all the Gauss algorithm iterations, and for each one of them, examining the list of coefficients on which the Schur complement calculations have an impact, and then adding those that are created, to the structure of the matrix. This amounts to carrying out all the iterations while replacing the calculations of the coefficients by a test of their pre-existence. Hence, the term, "symbolic factorization".

The numbering of the equations plays an essential role in filling, and therefore in the cost of factorization, both in terms of the volume of data and in the number of arithmetic operations. Prior to proceeding to the symbolic factorization of the matrix, we will try to find a renumbering of the equations that permits reducing the filling. There are no optimal renumbering algorithms for sparse matrices whose cost does not vary exponentially with their dimensions. The renumbering problem is called "NP-complete". We will, therefore, be satisfied with algorithms called "heuristics", which give a reasonable, if not optimal solution, at a reduced cost.

Among these algorithms, one of the oldest is referred to as "frontal numbering". Its premise is that in a column in the upper triangular part of the matrix, a non-zero term in the factorization cannot appear above the first non-zero coefficient of the initial matrix. Indeed, we have seen that if the coefficient located in a column j in the first row of the matrix is zero, then the first iteration of the Gauss algorithm does not change the column in question. By recurrence, we see that if the $i_0(j)$ first coefficients of the column are initially zero, they remain that way during the $i_0(j)$ first iterations of the factorization. By structural symmetry of the factorized matrix, the same is true for the first coefficients $i_0(j)$ of the row j. The zone that is situated in the upper triangular part of the matrix for each column, between the first non-zero coefficient of the column and the diagonal, is called the "profile" of it. Obviously, the profile of the lower triangular part, which is the zone composed of each row, between the first non-zero coefficient of the row and the diagonal, is the symmetric profile of the upper triangular part, as shown in Figure 9.4.

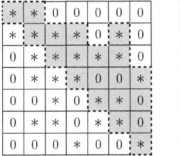

Figure 9.4. *Upper and lower profiles*

The smaller the surface of the profile, the lower the maximum possible filling. To reduce the profile, it is necessary that the equations connected together in the graph of the matrix have nearby numbers, which is the objective of frontal numbering. This consists of a method of numbering from any vertex, initially numbering those to which it is connected, then its neighbors, proceeding onto the neighbors that have not yet been numbered from vertex number 2 and so on. This is shown in Figure 9.5. This numbering shows the fronts, the first consisting of the initial vertex, with each edge being formed by the full set of vertices numbered from the vertex of the preceding front, as is shown in Figure 9.5. Frontal numbering gives special properties to the profile of the matrix.

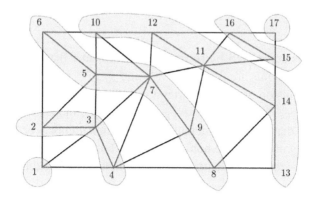

Figure 9.5. *Frontal numbering*

THEOREM 9.1.– Frontal numbering creates a monotonic profile that is completely filled during factorization.

PROOF 9.1.– Le us first prove that the profile is monotonic. That is to say that the function $i_{first}(j)$, which gives the row number of the first non-zero coefficient in column j, is increasing. In fact, $i_{first}(j)$ is the first neighboring vertex of j, numbered during frontal numbering. Thus, j was given a number during the numbering the neighbors of $i_{first}(j)$ that had not yet been numbered. So, if $j_1 < j_2$, j_2 has been numbered after j_1, then $i_{first}(j_1) \leq i_{first}(j_2)$.

For each row i, let us call $j_{last}(i)$ the number of the last non-zero coefficient on the row, after the first steps of the $i - 1$ factorization. We will prove that the function j_{last} is increasing, and that for all the terms of row i of U, of the column number between i and $j_{last}(i)$ inclusive, are non-zero.

Because of the monotonic nature of the profile, the first $j_{last}(1)$ coefficients of the first row are non-zero. The calculation of the Schur complement, in the first iteration of the Gauss factorization, will thus completely fill the diagonal block of 1 to $j_{last}(1)$. In particular, on row number 2, all the coefficients of column numbers between 2 and $j_{last}(1)$ inclusive will be non-zero in the factorized matrix, and therefore, $j_{last}(2) \geq j_{last}(1)$.

If $j_{last}(2) > j_{last}(1)$, all the coefficients of column numbers between $j_{last}(1)$ and $j_{last}(2)$ inclusive, in row 2, are non-zero, due to the monotonic nature of the profile. All the coefficients of 2 to $j_{last}(2)$ are thus non-zero in row 2, after the first stage of the Gauss factorization, so that the Schur complement calculation in the second iteration will completely fill the diagonal block of $j_{last}(2)$.

The proof is completed by recurrence. We assume that in row $k + 1$, all the column coefficients are between $k + 1$ and $j_{last}(k)$ inclusive, and are non-zero at the conclusion of the first k iterations of the Gauss factorization. Thus, $j_{last}(k + 1) \geq j_{last}(k)$. If $j_{last}(k + 1) > j_{last}(k)$, the monotonic nature of the profile requires that all the coefficients of the column numbers between $j_{last}(k)$ and $j_{last}(k + 1)$ inclusive are non-zero. The Schur complement calculation in iteration $k + 1$ of the Gauss factorization completely fills the diagonal block of $k + 1$ to $j_{last}(k + 1)$.

Figure 9.6 illustrates the complete filling mechanism of a monotonic profile. The gray squares, with dotted borders, indicate the areas filled by different stages of factorization. The asterisks show the position of non-zero coefficients to the right of the already filled areas in previous factorization stages.   □

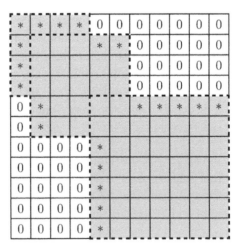

Figure 9.6. *Filling of monotonic profile*

When using frontal numbering, the symbolic factorization is extremely simple. It is enough to calculate the profile, which in practice means determining for each j equation, the smallest vertex number connected to j in the graph of the matrix, $i_{first}(j)$. The factorized matrix will be stored as a profile, that is to say as a set of columns of variable length in the upper triangular part and of rows in the lower triangular part; both of them having the same structure due to the symmetry of the profile.

9.3. Elimination trees

There are algorithms that provide less important filling than with frontal numbering. But, they lead to non-monotonic profiles that will not be completely filled during factorization. To really benefit from the improvements provided by these algorithms, we must accurately manage matrix filling and then store the factorized matrix in sparse form.

Symbolic factorization is much more complex in this case. If we carry out all the Gauss algorithm iterations; replace the calculations of the coefficients by a test of their pre-existence; and in each case modify the sparse structure of the matrix in consequence; symbolic factorization will be as costly, if not more so, than numerical factorization. There is, however, an essential difference between the two phases. Indeed, once a coefficient is created during symbolic factorization, there is no need to re-examine it in the following stages. Obviously, however, the successive modifications of the same coefficient during the numerical factorization must all be calculated.

The problem is how to avoid repeatedly testing the existence of the same coefficient. Yet, without doing a test, it is impossible to know whether a coefficient already exists. Though if we know that a coefficient will be re-examined later, we can postpone its eventual creation.

For example, in Figure 9.7, all the terms created or modified during the elimination of the first line are those that are found in the squares situated at the intersection of the dotted lines, beginning from the non-zero coefficients in the first row and the first column. In the row and column number 5, there are three types of squares: those colored in gray with a question mark are those that correspond to non-zero terms before the first stage of factorization; the white squares with an asterisk are those created during this step; finally, the gray squares with an asterisk correspond to the pre-existing coefficients modified during the first stage.

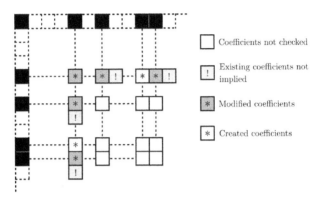

Figure 9.7. *Coefficients created or modified in step 1*

Figure 9.8 shows the positions of the terms, created or modified, during the fifth stage of factorization, represented by the squares situated at the intersection of the dotted lines starting from the non-zero coefficients of the fifth row and fifth column. The gray squares, located in the lower diagonal block, are all those involved in the first stage of factorization. For the symbolic factorization, it is thus sufficient to calculate the filling resulting from the lower diagonal block in the fifth step.

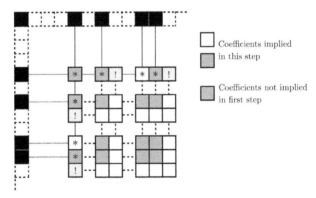

Figure 9.8. *Coefficients created or modified in step 5*

For any row i, we denote C_i as the set of indices $j > i$ for which $u(i, j)$, and thus $l(j, i)$, also is non-zero. This set is only known at the end of the $i - 1$ first stages of the symbolic factorization. The sets C_i determine the structure of the factorized matrix. The calculation of the Schur complement in step i of the Gauss factorization modifies or reveals all the coefficients (k, l), where k and l belong to C_i. To formalize the mechanism of successive modifications shown in Figure 9.8, we are going to start by proving a lemma.

LEMMA 9.1.– If i_1 is an element of C_i, then $\{j > i_1 \,/\, j \in C_i\} \subset C_{i_1}$.

PROOF 9.2.– If i_1 and j belong to C_i, then the coefficients $u(i, i_1)$ and $u(i, j)$, and in the same way $l(i_1, i)$ and $l(j, i)$, are non-zero. Therefore, if $i_1 < j$, the i stage of the Gauss factorization will reveal the coefficients (i_1, j) and (j, i_1) in the Schur complement, or will modify them if they already exist.   □

This implies that the coefficients of row j of the upper triangular part, and column j of the lower triangular part of the matrix created by step i of the factorization, will again be examined in step i_1. So, if we fail to consider the row and column j in step i, these coefficients will be created in step i_1. Hence, the idea of only examining, during the symbolic factorization, the filling in step i, resulting from the row and column i_1, with i_1, being the smallest element of C_i.

The question then is to know that whether in doing so, we might not be forgetting to create some terms. Indeed, in the situation where j belongs to C_i with $j > i_1 1$, the terms that should have appeared in the row and column j during step i of the symbolic factorization will actually be created in step i_1, but only if j is the smallest element of C_{i_1}. If the smallest element of C_{i_1} is $i_2 < j$, the row and column j will not be considered during step i_1.

In fact, these terms will actually be created, but later on. The proof will be based on the following lemma.

LEMMA 9.2.– If j is an element of C_i, then there is a sequence, $i_0 = i < i_1 < \ldots < i_p = j$, such that for all k between 0 and $p - 1$ inclusive, $j \in C_{i_k}$ and i_{k+1} is the smallest element of C_{i_k}.

PROOF 9.3.– From lemma 9.1, if i_1 is the smallest element of C_i, then $j \in C_{i_1}$. Similarly, if $j \in C_{i_k}$ and if we denote i_{k+1} as the smallest element of C_{i_k}, $j \in C_{i_{k+1}}$. By recurrence, there exists an increasing sequence that satisfies the two properties: that $j \in C_{i_k}$ and that i_{k+1} is the smallest element of C_{i_k}. This sequence is bounded by j and is finite. If i_{p-1} is the last term of the sequence, then i_p, the smallest element of $C_{i_{p-1}}$, is equal to j.   □

This leads us to define a method, with minimal costs, with which to perform the symbolic factorization in the following theorem:

THEOREM 9.2.– To calculate the total filling of the matrix during factorization, it is enough, in step i of the symbolic factorization, to determine the filling in the row and column i_1, with i_1 being the smallest element of C_i.

PROOF 9.4.– Let us consider the sequence defined in lemma 9.2. Lemma 9.1 implies that for all k between 0 and $p - 1$ inclusive, $\{j > i_k \, / \, j \in C_{i_{k-1}}\} \subset C_{i_k}$. We immediately deduce, by recurrence that $\{j > i_{p-1} \, / \, j \in C_i\} \subset C_{i_{p-1}}$. So, by calculating the resulting filling provoked in row and column j in step i_{p-1}, we necessarily create the coefficients that normally appear in step i of the factorization.   □

The set of pairs (i, i_1), where i_1 is the smallest element of C_i, allows us to define the previous symbolic factorization method, which has remarkable properties.

THEOREM 9.3.– The subundirected graph of the factorized matrix formed by the edges (i, i_1), where i_1 is the smallest element of C_i, is a spanning tree, that is to say a graph with $n - 1$ edges, without cycles, nor connections.

DEFINITION 9.1 (Elimination tree).– *The subundirected graph of the factorized matrix formed by the edges (i, i_1), where i_1 is the smallest element of C_i, is called an elimination tree.*

PROOF 9.5.– Let us start by proving that the elimination tree has $n - 1$ edges. By definition, there is at most, one edge (i, i_1), with $i < i_1$, starting from any i between 1 and $n - 1$ inclusive. Let us show that one actually exists. We assume that the graph of the initial matrix is connected. Otherwise, there are several independent systems to factor and we will apply the factorization method to each of them. As we saw in Figure 9.3, each step of the factorization modifies the graph of the matrix by removing a vertex and by creating a clique of its neighbors. If the initial graph is connected, of course, the new graph will be as well. By induction, the graphs of the Schur complements are all connected, which means that when we have completed $i - 1$ steps of the factorization, there is necessarily at least one non-zero extra-diagonal term in the row and column i. C_i is thus non-empty for all $i < n$.

The elimination tree is acyclic. In fact, if there were a cycle, $(i_0, i_1), (i_1, i_2),$ $\ldots,(i_{p-1}, i_p)$, with $i_p = i_0$, then for k, such that i_k is the minimum number of vertices of the cycle, the two edges (i_{k-1}, i_k) and (i_k, i_{k+1}) satisfy: $i_k \neq i_{k+1}$,

$(i_k < i_{k-1})$ and $(i_k < i_{k+1})$, which is obviously impossible, since it starts at most, from one edge of the tree i_k toward j with $j > i_k$.

The elimination tree thus has $n - 1$ edges and is acyclic. It is necessarily connected. Indeed, if it had p connected components with, respectively, n_1, n_2, ... and n_p vertices, one of these components would necessarily have a number of edges at least equal to the number of vertices. This contradicts the fact that the elimination tree is acyclic, because a connected graph, with a number of edges greater than or equal to the number of its vertices, necessarily has a cycle. In fact, let us carry out a frontal renumbering of such a graph. From point number 1, we connect its nv_1 neighbors by nv_1 edges. Similarly, nv_2 neighbors of point 2 that are not yet renumbered can be connected to point 2 by two edges nv_2, which allows us to connect $nv_1 + nv_2$ vertices to the first vertex, with $nv_1 + nv_2$ edges. By induction, we prove that we can connect $n - 1$ vertices in the graph to the first by using $n - 1$ edges. If there is an extra edge in the graph, it necessarily connects two already connected vertices by another route, which reveals a cycle.   □

COROLLARY 9.1.– The calculation of the Schur complement in step i of the Gauss factorization only changes the row and column number j, if there is a path from i to j, formed by edges (i_k, i_{k+1}), with $(i_k < i_{k+1})$, in the elimination tree.

PROOF 9.6.– This corollary is a simple reformulation of lemma 9.2. The calculation of the Schur complement in step i of the Gauss factorization only changes the row and column number j, if j is an element of C_i. The rest, $i_0 = i < i_1 < \ldots < i_p = j$, defines a path from i to j in the elimination tree, formed of edges (i_k, i_{k+1}), with $(i_k < i_{k+1})$, for k between 0 and $p - 1$ inclusive.   □

NOTE 9.1.– This condition is necessary, but it is not sufficient. To know which vertices, located lower than i in the tree, are actually involved in step i of the factorization, we must examine all the non-zero terms of row i of U, whereas the elimination tree only provides the first. The fact that a dense matrix and a tridiagonal matrix have the same elimination tree, formed by the edges $(i, i + 1)$, for all i between 1 and $n - 1$ inclusive, well illustrates this problem. For the first, the graph of the factorized matrix is the complete clique; for the second, it is identical to elimination tree. Therefore, in each iteration of the Gauss algorithm for a dense matrix, all the rows and columns of the lower diagonal block are changed, while for a tridiagonal matrix, only the subsequent rows and columns are affected.

9.4. Elimination trees and dependencies

Corollary 9.1 provides an initial tool for analyzing dependencies of the Gauss factorization of a sparse matrix. In fact, it means that if two vertices $i < j$ are not connected between each other by a path formed by the edges (i_k, i_{k+1}) of the elimination tree, with $(i_k < i_{k+1})$, then the coefficient values of row and column j do not depend on iteration i of the Gauss factorization. This allows us to consider achieving, at least in part, the calculations of the i and j iterations in parallel.

More precisely, if we isolate several subsets of vertices in the graph, forming branches of it, such that the two branches are not connected by a path formed by the edges (i_k, i_{k+1}) of the elimination tree, with $(i_k < i_{k+1})$, then the factorization of the subdiagonal blocks associated with these different branches can be performed in parallel, as shown in Figure 9.9.

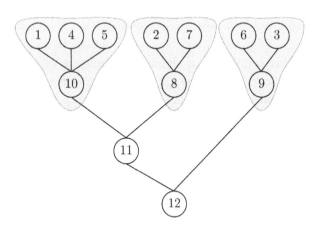

Figure 9.9. *Elimination tree and dependence*

However, the calculation of the Schur complements of the various subblocks will change some of the rows and columns located further down in the elimination tree. These multiple corrections must be cumulative.

Thus, it appears that the degree of parallelism and granularity will be, *a priori*, even greater as the elimination tree becomes broader and shallower. The numbering of the equations will, therefore, play a key role in the possibilities for parallelization. Moreover, this type of renumbering has the added advantage of leading, *a priori*, to reduced filling: the shallower the elimination tree, the less the risk of filling is high, since the elimination of a row and a column can only cause filling in the rows and columns located further down in the elimination tree.

Parallelization methods based on algorithms for renumbering, which allow revealing independent branches in the elimination tree, are called multifrontal methods. Indeed, one way to achieve this type of elimination tree is to renumber the equations simultaneously from different starting points far from one another in the graph of the factorized matrix, or grid, and progress in a frontal manner from each of them, until the fronts meet to form a separator. Similarly, during parallel factorization, the elimination of rows and columns when descending a branch in the graph goes back to it frontally.

The last section will focus on detailing this methodology, in the context of one of these renumbering algorithms, allowing for good parallel performance while ensuring reduced filling.

9.5. Nested dissections

In order to obtain degree 2 parallelism with maximum granularity in the elimination tree, we need two branches of the largest possible size, linked to the smallest possible trunk, as shown in Figure 9.10.

Consequently, with this kind of elimination tree, the factorized matrix and the initial matrix have the same block structures:

$$\begin{pmatrix} A_{11} & 0 & A_{13} \\ 0 & A_{22} & A_{23} \\ A_{31} & A_{32} & A_{33} \end{pmatrix} = \begin{pmatrix} L_{11} & 0 & 0 \\ 0 & L_{22} & 0 \\ L_{31} & L_{32} & L_{33} \end{pmatrix} \begin{pmatrix} U_{11} & 0 & U_{13} \\ 0 & U_{22} & U_{23} \\ 0 & 0 & U_{33} \end{pmatrix} \qquad [9.1]$$

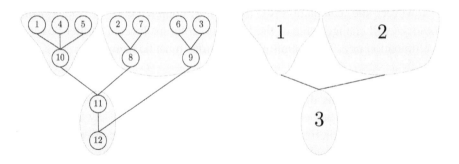

Figure 9.10. *Level 1 binary tree*

The Schur complement calculation of block 3 will require the accumulated contributions from blocks 1 and 2. We can uncouple the calculation phase from the corrections of the summing phase, by arbitrary decomposing the initial lower diagonal block, in the form of:

$$A_{33} = A_{33}^{(1)} + A_{33}^{(2)}$$

Applying the block Gauss factorization algorithm reveals two phases:

– a degree 2 parallel phase for the partial factorization of the first two diagonal blocks:

$$
\begin{array}{l|l}
A_{11} = L_{11}U_{11} & A_{22} = L_{22}U_{22} \\
L_{31} = A_{31}U_{11}^{-1} & L_{32} = A_{32}U_{22}^{-1} \\
U_{13} = L_{11}^{-1}A_{13} & U_{23} = L_{22}^{-1}A_{23} \\
S_{33}^{(1)} = A_{33}^{(1)} - L_{31}U_{13} & S_{33}^{(2)} = A_{33}^{(2)} - L_{32}U_{23}
\end{array}
\qquad [9.2]
$$

– a non-parallel phase of assembly and factorization of the Schur complement:

$$S_{33} = S_{33}^{(1)} + S_{33}^{(2)}$$
$$S_{33} = L_{33}U_{33}$$

Partitioning the factorized matrix of the graph into two disjoint subsets 1 and 2 connected to a separator 3, as shown in Figure 9.10, obviously has its counterpart in the mesh. It corresponds to a partitioning of the spatial domain, represented by the mesh in two subdomains, separated by an interface, as shown in Figure 9.11.

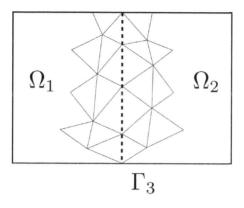

Figure 9.11. *Decomposition into two subdomains*

In fact, this procedure consists of partitioning the set of cells of the mesh into two subsets, which divide the vertices into three blocks: the internal vertices of the first subdomain, those of the second, and finally the vertices located at the interface between the subdomains that form the separator. In order to obtain load balancing, it is required to ensure that there are the same number of vertices in each subdomain, while making sure that the separator is minimal, so that the non-parallel phase of assembly and factorization of the Schur complement has the minimum possible cost.

The mesh-partitioning approach has the advantage of leading to a natural parallelization of the formation phase of the matrix. Let us suppose that we attribute the distinct submeshes associated with the two subdomains to two different processes, as shown in Figure 9.12. Given that the coefficients are obtained by spatial integration, and that the support of a base function associated with an internal vertex of a subdomain is included in this subdomain, then the matrices calculated by the two processes are equal to:

$$A_1 = \begin{pmatrix} A_{11} & 0 & A_{13} \\ 0 & 0 & 0 \\ A_{31} & 0 & A_{33}^{(1)} \end{pmatrix}, \quad A_2 = \begin{pmatrix} 0 & 0 & 0 \\ 0 & A_{22} & A_{23} \\ 0 & A_{32} & A_{33}^{(2)} \end{pmatrix} \quad [9.3]$$

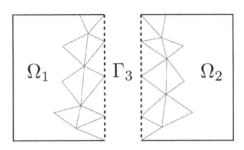

Figure 9.12. *Local meshes of the two subdomains*

Blocks $A_{33}^{(1)}$ and $A_{33}^{(2)}$, respectively, represent the coefficients of interaction between the base functions associated with the vertices of the interface calculated in each of the subdomains. These base functions are the only ones that have the support of the union of the two non-empty parts, respectively, included in each of the two subdomains. Local integration thus naturally leads to a mesh partitioning that satisfies:

$$A_{33} = A_{33}^{(1)} + A_{33}^{(2)}$$

We see that the parallel phase of factorization of the two diagonal blocks, equation [9.2] is simply the partial factorization of the two matrices A_1 and A_2, equation [9.3], in which we shifted the numbering of the equations in order to remove the empty rows and columns:

$$\begin{pmatrix} A_{11} & A_{13} \\ A_{31} & A_{33}^{(1)} \end{pmatrix} = \begin{pmatrix} L_{11} & 0 \\ L_{31} & I \end{pmatrix} \begin{pmatrix} U_{11} & U_{13} \\ 0 & S_{33}^{(1)} \end{pmatrix}$$

$$\begin{pmatrix} A_{22} & A_{23} \\ A_{32} & A_{33}^{(2)} \end{pmatrix} = \begin{pmatrix} L_{22} & 0 \\ L_{32} & I \end{pmatrix} \begin{pmatrix} U_{22} & U_{23} \\ 0 & S_{33}^{(2)} \end{pmatrix}$$

To obtain a 2^p degree order of parallelism, we can recursively apply the same strategy of mesh partitioning, as shown in Figure 9.13. This method is referred to as "nested dissections".

The matrix obtained by nested dissections of level p has a block structure similar to that of equation [9.1], in which each of the two diagonal blocks itself has a matrix structure obtained by nested dissections of level $p-1$. In the case of partitioning into eight subdomains, as in Figure 9.13, this results in the level 3 matrix shown in Figure 9.13.

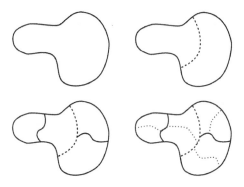

Figure 9.13. *Mesh-partitioning by nested dissections*

The partial factorization of the matrix obtained by eliminating the 2^p blocks of level p gives a Schur complement, which itself has a matrix structure obtained by the nested dissections of level $p-1$, see Figure 9.14. The upper level blocks, which correspond to the interior vertices of the 2^p subdomains, are sparse. After the first partial factorization, the blocks become dense, since the Schur complement of each subdomain is a dense matrix.

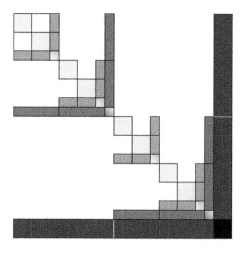

Figure 9.14. *The matrix structure obtained by nested dissections*

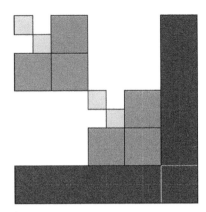

Figure 9.15. *Structure of the matrix after the first partial factorization*

If we choose a parallelization strategy based on the blocks, the degree of parallelism decreases from 2^p to 1 during the p steps of the partial factorization. What is particularly bothersome is that the blocks are dense and become increasingly large; a separator also becomes larger as the area it bisects increases. Therefore, to achieve a good level of efficiency, we need to parallelize the factorization of the blocks at the lower levels. In addition, these blocks vary greatly in size. As much as it is possible to ensure that the various subdomains have the same number of vertices, when the mesh is irregular, the separators of the same level can vary greatly in size. Thus, it is necessary to adapt the number of processors allocated to each block.

All this makes implementation in a message-passing programming environment very complex. At the highest level of partitioning, things are certainly very simple. Each of the 2^p processes will deal with one of the subdomains; this means forming the local matrix first, and then performing the partial factorization of the interior vertices to compute the Schur complement on the interfaces. This becomes much more complicated afterward, as is suggested by the partitioning diagram in Figure 9.13.

The Schur complement, calculated on a subdomain, only contributes to part of the matrices associated with the lower level separators. Moreover, it is necessary to redistribute these matrices to different processors, depending on their size, and to parallelize their factorization using the block methods explored in Chapter 8.

Because of these complexities, it is very difficult to achieve high scalability with parallel factorization methods for sparse matrices.

NOTE 9.2.– There are a number of sparse matrix parallel factorization libraries. Among the most employed is Pardiso available from the Intel mathematics library, MKL, which uses multi-threading-type parallelism for shared memory machines. The MUMPS library is a reference in the field. This library has the characteristic of targeting shared memory machines and using MPI.

9.6. Forward and backward substitutions

The analysis of the parallelization of forward and backward substitutions is based on the same methodology as that used for the factorization; successive substitutions can be performed simultaneously on two independent branches of the elimination tree. Updating the second members for equations located lower in the tree are reduction operations, whose parallelization requires synchronization.

Specifically, let us go back to the example of the binary tree in Figure 9.10. The forward substitution of the associated linear system:

$$\begin{pmatrix} L_{11} & 0 & 0 \\ 0 & L_{22} & 0 \\ L_{31} & L_{32} & L_{33} \end{pmatrix} \begin{pmatrix} y_1 \\ y_2 \\ y_3 \end{pmatrix} = \begin{pmatrix} b_1 \\ b_2 \\ b_3 \end{pmatrix}$$

involves the following operations, if we decompose b_3 into two local contributions:

– a parallel phase of degree 2 for the forward substitution of the block's first two diagonals, and the calculation of corrections in the third block of the second member:

$$L_{11}y_1 = b_1 \qquad\qquad L_{22}y_2 = b_2$$
$$b_3^{(1)} = b_3^{(1)} - L_{31}y_1 \qquad\qquad b_3^{(2)} = b_3^{(2)} - L_{32}y_2$$

– a non-parallel assembly phase of the second member and forward substitution of the third block diagonal:

$$b_3 = b_3^{(1)} + b_3^{(2)}$$
$$L_{33}y_3 = b_3$$

These are the same steps that we used for the factorization phase. The backward substitution of the system:

$$
\begin{pmatrix} U_{11} & 0 & U_{13} \\ 0 & U_{22} & U_{23} \\ 0 & 0 & U_{33} \end{pmatrix} \begin{pmatrix} x_1 \\ x_2 \\ x_3 \end{pmatrix} = \begin{pmatrix} y_1 \\ y_2 \\ y_3 \end{pmatrix}
$$

is the same as for forward substitution, just in reverse order:

– a non-parallel phase for the backward substitution in the third block diagonal:

$$U_{33}x_3 = y_3$$

– a parallel phase of degree 2 for the calculation of corrections in the first two blocks of the second member, and the backward substitution of the block's first two diagonals:

$$
\begin{array}{c|c}
y_1 = y_1 - U_{13}x_3 & y_2 = y_2 - U_{23}x_3 \\
U_{11}x_1 = y_1 & U_{22}x_2 = y_2
\end{array}
$$

The problem, however, is that in practice the different phases have a granularity much finer than that of the corresponding factorization phases, since the operations involved are simple forward-backward substitutions, or matrix-vector products. All these operations carry out only a single pair of addition-multiplications, by the coefficients of the matrix recovered from memory.

The scalability of the parallelization of forward-backward substitution on sparse linear systems is even less than that of the factorization; even more so than in the case of dense matrices. It is, therefore, imperative to carry out the different forward-backward operations simultaneously when there are multiple second members.

10

Basics of Krylov Subspaces

In this chapter, we will look at iterative methods for solving the following linear system of dimension n:

$$Ax = b \qquad [10.1]$$

where A is an invertible square matrix, using projections in particular subspaces, namely the Krylov subspaces. The Krylov subspaces allow the construction, with simple operations such as matrix-vector products, scalar products and linear combinations of vectors, affine subspaces which are highly relevant to finding approximations of the solution of the linear system [10.1]. The methods, which will be described, can be applied to either real or complex matrices. To simplify the presentation, *a priori*, we will work on a case of a real matrix. Adaptations for complex systems do not present any particular difficulties.

10.1. Krylov subspaces

If x_0 is an approximate starting value of the solution of equation [10.1], the residual vector associated with x_0 is defined as $g_0 = Ax_0 - b$.

DEFINITION 10.1 (Krylov subspace).– *Let us define the Krylov subspace of order p, denoted by $\mathcal{K}_p$, the vector space spanned by g_0 and the first $p - 1$ powers of A:*

$$\mathcal{K}_p = Span\{g_0, Ag_0, A^2 g_0, \ldots, A^{p-1} g_0\}$$

The Krylov subspaces form an increasing family of subspaces, necessarily bounded. We will denote by p_{max}, the maximum dimension of Krylov subspaces, for a given x_0.

LEMMA 10.1.– If $A^p g_0 \in \mathcal{K}_p$, then $A^{p+q} g_0 \in \mathcal{K}_p$ for all $q > 0$.

PROOF 10.1.– The proof is performed by induction. If for $q \geq 0$, $A^p g_0, A^{p+1} g_0, \ldots, A^{p+q} g_0 \in \mathcal{K}_p$, then:

$$A^{p+q} g_0 = \sum_{k=0}^{p-1} \alpha_k A^k g_0,$$

and therefore:

$$A^{p+q+1} g_0 = \sum_{k=0}^{p-2} \alpha_k A^{k+1} g_0 + \alpha_{p-1} A^p g_0$$

$$= \sum_{k=0}^{p-2} \alpha_k A^{k+1} g_0 + \alpha_{p-1} \sum_{k=0}^{p-1} \beta_k A^k g_0$$

$$= \sum_{k=0}^{p-1} \gamma_k A^k g_0$$

$\square$

LEMMA 10.2.– The series of Krylov subspaces $\mathcal{K}_p$ is strictly increasing from 1 to p_{max} and then stagnates from $p = p_{max}$.

PROOF 10.2.– If p is the smallest integer for which $A^p g_0$ is dependent on previous vectors, then the vectors $(g_0, A g_0, A^2 g_0, \ldots, A^{p-1} g_0)$ are linearly independent, and therefore $\mathcal{K}_q$ is of dimension q, for all $q \leq p$. In particular, $\mathcal{K}_p$ is of dimension p.

In addition, $A^p g_0 \in \mathcal{K}_p$ and, by lemma 10.1, all the vectors $A^{p+q} g_0$ belong to $\mathcal{K}_p$, for all $q > 0$, so that $\mathcal{K}_{p+q} = \mathcal{K}_p$, for all $q > 0$.

Thus, we have: $\mathcal{K}_1 \subsetneq \ldots \subsetneq \mathcal{K}_p = \mathcal{K}_{p+q}$, for all $q > 0$. And, by the definition of p_{max}, necessarily $p = p_{max}$.

$\square$

This leads to the following fundamental theorem:

THEOREM 10.1.– The solution of the linear system $Ax = b$ belongs to the affine space $x_0 + \mathcal{K}_{p_{max}}$.

PROOF 10.3.– From the two lemmas, 10.1 and 10.2, the vectors:

$$(g_0, Ag_0, A^2g_0, \ldots, A^{p_{max}-1}g_0)$$

are linearly independent and:

$$A^{p_{max}}g_0 = \sum_{k=0}^{p_{max}-1} \alpha_k A^k g_0 \qquad [10.2]$$

In equation [10.2], the coefficient α_0 is non-zero, otherwise, by multiplying both sides of the equation by A^{-1}, we get:

$$A^{p_{max}-1}g_0 = \sum_{k=1}^{p_{max}-1} \alpha_k A^{k-1} g_0$$

which is impossible, given the property of the independence of the vectors. Dividing the two terms in equation [10.2] by α_0 and by passing the left member to the right, we obtain:

$$g_0 + \sum_{k=1}^{p_{max}-1} \frac{\alpha_k}{\alpha_0} A^k g_0 - \frac{1}{\alpha_0} A^{p_{max}} g_0 = 0 \Leftrightarrow$$

$$Ax_0 - b + \sum_{k=1}^{p_{max}-1} \frac{\alpha_k}{\alpha_0} A^k g_0 - \frac{1}{\alpha_0} A^{p_{max}} g_0 = 0 \Leftrightarrow$$

$$A(x_0 + \sum_{k=1}^{p_{max}-1} \frac{\alpha_k}{\alpha_0} A^{k-1} g_0 - \frac{1}{\alpha_0} A^{p_{max}-1} g_0) = b$$

□

NOTE 10.1.– The equivalences above conversely show that, if $x \in x_0 + \mathcal{K}_p$, then the vectors $(g_0, Ag_0, A^2g_0, \ldots, A^p g_0)$ are linearly dependent. By lemma

10.2, this means that the series of spaces $\mathcal{K}_p$ reached a stagnation point; hence, $\mathcal{K}_p = \mathcal{K}_{p_{max}}$.

10.2. Construction of the Arnoldi basis

In practice, constructing the Krylov subspaces amounts to determining their basis. The natural basis $(g_0, Ag_0, A^2 g_0, \ldots, A^{p-1} g_0)$ can never be used due to its numerical degeneracy. In fact, if the matrix A is diagonalizable with m distinct eigenvalues $\lambda_1, \ldots, \lambda_m$, then:

$$g_0 = \sum_{i=1}^{m} \alpha_i v_i, \quad \text{and} \quad A^p g_0 = \sum_{i=1}^{m} \alpha_i \lambda_i^p v_i$$

The sequence $A^p g_0$ behaves like $\alpha_{max} \lambda_{max}^p v_{max}$, if λ_{max} is the largest eigenvalue. Numerically, as soon as the factor $(\frac{\alpha_{max}}{\alpha_i})(\frac{\lambda_{max}}{\lambda_i})^p$ exceeds the magnitude of 10^r, where r is the number of significant digits in the representation of the real numbers in the machine, the term $\alpha_i \lambda_i^p v_i$ disappears completely, which happens very quickly in practice. For a ratio of 10 between eigenvalues, just 16 iterations are sufficient to reach this point, if we use the conventional representation of real numbers in 64 bits. Therefore, very quickly, the vectors $A^p g_0$ become numerically collinear. We can easily demonstrate the same phenomenon for any matrix, by using the Jordan form. Moreover, according to whether the norms of the eigenvalues are less than or greater than 1, the terms $\alpha_i \lambda_i^p v_i$ become too small or too large to be represented.

The solution to prevent the degeneration of the numerical natural basis of the Krylov subspace consists of implementing an orthonormalization procedure. The Arnoldi basis is thus constructed by applying the modified Gram–Schmidt orthonormalization method to the vectors obtained by successive products of the matrix, for the Euclidean scalar product. The modified Gram–Schmidt process is thus written as:

– initialization of the Arnoldi basis:

$$g_0 = Ax_0 - b$$
$$v_1 = \frac{1}{\|g_0\|} g_0$$

– construction of vector $j + 1$ of the Arnoldi basis:

$w = Av_j$
for $i = 1$ **to** j
　　$\alpha_i = w \cdot v_i$
　　$w = w - \alpha_i v_i$
end for
$v_{j+1} = \frac{1}{\|w\|} w$

If we denote by h_{ij}, the coefficient of the orthogonalization of Av_j with respect to v_i and h_{j+1j}, the norm of the vector w obtained by orthogonalization of vector Av_j with respect to the v_i vectors, the construction of the Arnoldi basis reads:

$$Av_j = \sum_{i=1}^{j+1} h_{ij} v_i \qquad\qquad [10.3]$$

Let V_p be the rectangular matrix with n rows and p columns, for which the columns are the first p vectors of the Arnoldi basis, then the orthonormality of the vectors, in matrix form, is written as:

$$V_p^t V_p = I_p$$

Similarly, equation [10.3] defining the Arnoldi vectors is written as:

$$AV_p = V_{p+1} H_{p+1p} \qquad\qquad [10.4]$$

where the matrix H_{p+1p} is a matrix with $p + 1$ rows and p columns, for which the coefficients h_{ij} are the coefficients of the orthonormalization of equation [10.3], for $i \leq j + 1$, the other coefficients being null.

$$H_{p+1p} = \begin{pmatrix} h_{11} & h_{12} & \vdots & \vdots & h_{1j} & \vdots & h_{1p} \\ h_{21} & h_{22} & \vdots & \vdots & h_{2j} & \vdots & h_{2p} \\ 0 & h_{32} & \vdots & \vdots & h_{3j} & \vdots & h_{3p} \\ \vdots & \ddots & \ddots & \vdots & \vdots & \vdots & \vdots \\ \vdots & & \ddots & \ddots & \vdots & \vdots & \vdots \\ \vdots & & & \ddots & h_{j+1j} & \vdots & h_{j+1p} \\ \vdots & & & & \ddots & \ddots & \vdots \\ 0 & \cdots & \cdots & \cdots & \cdots & 0 & h_{p+1p} \end{pmatrix} \qquad [10.5]$$

The main diagonal block of H_{p+1p} is a square matrix of dimension p, denoted by H_p, which, using equations [10.2] and [10.4], satisfies:

$$H_p = V_p^t A V_p = \begin{pmatrix} h_{11} & h_{12} & \vdots & \vdots & \vdots & h_{1p} \\ h_{21} & h_{22} & \vdots & \vdots & \vdots & h_{2p} \\ 0 & h_{32} & \vdots & \vdots & \vdots & h_{3p} \\ \vdots & \ddots & \ddots & \vdots & \vdots & \vdots \\ \vdots & & \ddots & \ddots & \vdots & \vdots \\ 0 & \cdots & \cdots & 0 & h_{pp-1} & h_{pp} \end{pmatrix} \qquad [10.6]$$

DEFINITION 10.2 (Hessenberg form).– *Such a matrix, for which the inferior triangular part is null, with the exception of the terms located on the first subdiagonal, is called the upper Hessenberg form.*

Equation [10.6] shows that matrix H_p is, in the Arnoldi basis vectors, the matrix of the projection in the Krylov subspace $\mathcal{K}_p$ of the linear application associated with matrix A.

11

Methods with Complete Orthogonalization for Symmetric Positive Definite Matrices

This chapter presents the Krylov methods with complete orthogonalization for symmetric positive definite matrices. For such matrices, the construction of the Arnoldi basis becomes a short recursion, the algorithm of the construction of the Lanczos basis. The Lanczos method is deduced, but it does not allow calculating the approximate solution with a short recursion. Due to the construction of a conjugate base, the conjugate gradient method allows us to arrive at an optimal method with a short recursion. The comparison is made with the gradient method whose convergence rate is easily determined. At the end of this chapter, the principle of preconditioning techniques for symmetric positive definite matrices is introduced, and then the preconditioned conjugate gradient method is detailed.

11.1. Construction of the Lanczos basis for symmetric matrices

In the specific case where matrix A is symmetric, so is matrix H_p, according to equation [10.6]. As it is also an upper Hessenberg matrix, we deduce immediately that it is symmetric tridiagonal.

The algorithm for constructing the Arnoldi basis is enormously simplified, since it is known that the coefficients h_{ij} are zero, if $i < j - 1$ and the coefficient h_{j-1j} is equal to h_{jj-1}, as calculated previously. The resulting algorithm for constructing an orthonormal basis of Krylov subspaces is called the Lanczos algorithm.

– initialization of the Lanczos basis:

$$g_0 = Ax_0 - b$$
$$v_1 = \frac{1}{\|g_0\|} g_0$$

– construction of the vector $j + 1$ of the Lanczos basis:

$$w = Av_j$$
$$h_{j-1j} = h_{jj-1}$$
$$w = w - h_{j-1j}v_{j-1}$$
$$h_{jj} = w \cdot v_j$$
$$w = w - h_{jj}v_j$$
$$h_{j+1j} = \|w\|$$
$$v_{j+1} = \frac{1}{h_{j+1j}} w \backslash \mathrm{vspace}\{-6\mathrm{pt}\}$$

The Lanczos algorithm has a remarkable property, which allows the construction of an orthonormal basis of Krylov subspaces by using a short recursion. It is enough only to have the vectors v_{j-1} and v_j to be able to calculate v_{j+1}, and the computational cost is independent of the iteration number.

11.2. The Lanczos method

Once the basis V_p of the Krylov subspace $\mathcal{K}_p$ at iteration p is determined, we have to determine the approximate solution x_p of system [10.1] in the affine space $x_0 + \mathcal{K}_p$. Since V_p is a basis of $\mathcal{K}_p$, x_p is written as follows, where z_p is a p-dimensional vector:

$$x_p = x_0 + V_p z_p \tag{11.1}$$

The error vector and the corresponding residual are thus written, respectively:

$$e_p = x_p - x = x_0 - x + V_p z_p = e_0 + V_p z_p \tag{11.2}$$

$$g_p = Ax_p - b = Ae_p = Ae_0 + AV_p z_p = g_0 + AV_p z_p \tag{11.3}$$

A Krylov method is defined, on the one hand, by the algorithm for constructing the basis of Krylov subspaces, and, on the other hand, by the optimality criterion chosen to determine the approximate solution x_p. A *priori*, the ideal would be to minimize the error, or the residual, using a suitable norm.

In the case where matrix A is symmetric positive definite, the choice to make for using the Lanczos method is to minimize the standard error for the scalar product associated with A, which consists of minimizing the scalar product of the error and residual vectors, and then, by some means, to control both quantities simultaneously:

$$\mathcal{E}(x_p) = \|x_p - x\|_A^2 = A(x_p - x) \cdot (x_p - x) = g_p \cdot e_p \qquad [11.4]$$

The approximate solution, thus defined, has some very appealing properties.

THEOREM 11.1.– The approximate solution x_p of the Lanczos method is the projection of x in $x_0 + \mathcal{K}_p$, for the scalar product associated with A.

PROOF 11.1.– From equation [11.4], x_p is the element $x_0 + \mathcal{K}_p$, whose distance to x is minimal for the scalar product associated with A. □

COROLLARY 11.1.– The residual vector $g_p = Ax_p - b$ of the Lanczos method is orthogonal to $\mathcal{K}_p$.

PROOF 11.2.– The properties of a projection into an affine space imply:

$$A(x_p - x) \cdot w_p = 0 , \quad \forall w_p \in \mathcal{K}_p \qquad \qquad □$$

We will now show how to calculate x_p in practice. According to equations [11.2] and [11.3], we have:

$$\mathcal{E}(x_p) = A(e_0 + V_p z_p) \cdot (e_0 + V_p z_p)$$
$$= AV_p z_p \cdot V_p z_p + 2\, g_0 \cdot V_p z_p + g_0 \cdot e_0 \qquad [11.5]$$

in such a way that, in order to minimize $\mathcal{E}(x_p)$, it is sufficient to minimize the quantity which depends on z_p in equation [11.5], and is written as:

$$AV_p z_p \cdot V_p z_p + 2\, g_0 \cdot V_p z_p = V_p^t AV_p z_p \cdot z_p + 2\, V_p^t g_0 \cdot z_p$$
$$= 2(\frac{1}{2} V_p^t AV_p z_p \cdot z_p + V_p^t g_0 \cdot z_p) \qquad [11.6]$$

Finally, the problem boils down to minimizing the quantity:

$$\mathcal{J}_p(z_p) = \frac{1}{2}V_p^t A V_p z_p \cdot z_p + V_p^t g_0 \cdot z_p$$

$$= \frac{1}{2}T_p z_p \cdot z_p - y_p \cdot z_p \qquad\qquad [11.7]$$

where $T_p = H_p$ is the tridiagonal symmetric matrix of orthonormalization coefficients calculated with the Lanczos basis of V_p, and y_p is the p-dimensional vector of which the coefficient i is equal to the scalar product $(-v_i \cdot g_0)$.

We are led to a classical minimization problem of finite dimension, for which we will recall the results of existence and uniqueness of the solution.

LEMMA 11.1.– Let A be a symmetric positive definite matrix, the quadratic functional $J(x) = \frac{1}{2}(Ax \cdot x) - (b \cdot x)$ is strictly convex.

PROOF 11.3.– The quadratic functional evaluated at $(\alpha x + (1 - \alpha)y)$ gives:

$$J(\alpha x + (1 - \alpha)y) = \frac{1}{2}\alpha^2(Ax \cdot x) + \alpha(1 - \alpha)(Ax \cdot y)$$

$$+\frac{1}{2}(1 - \alpha)^2(Ay \cdot y) - \alpha(b \cdot x) - (1 - \alpha)(b \cdot y)$$

$$= \alpha J(x) + (1 - \alpha)J(y)$$

$$+ \frac{1}{2}[(\alpha^2 - \alpha)(Ax \cdot x) + 2\alpha(1 - \alpha)(Ax \cdot y)$$

$$+((1 - \alpha)^2 - (1 - \alpha))(Ay \cdot y)]$$

$$= \alpha J(x) + (1 - \alpha)J(y)$$

$$+\frac{1}{2}\alpha(\alpha - 1)[(Ax \cdot x) - 2(Ax \cdot y) + (Ay \cdot y)]$$

Since A is positive definite:

$$(Ax \cdot x) - 2(Ax \cdot y) + (Ay \cdot y) = A(x - y) \cdot (x - y) > 0, \quad \text{if} \quad x \neq y$$

If $\alpha \in]0, 1[$, then $(\alpha(\alpha - 1)) < 0$, and therefore:

$$\tfrac{1}{2}\alpha(\alpha - 1)[(Ax \cdot x) - 2(Ax \cdot y) + (Ay \cdot y)] < 0 \qquad \square$$

THEOREM 11.2.– The functional $\mathcal{J}(x) = \tfrac{1}{2}Ax \cdot x - b \cdot x$ admits an absolute minimum at the point x, such that $Ax = b$.

PROOF 11.4.– $\mathcal{J}$ is strictly convex and bounded from below as $\mathcal{J}(x) \to +\infty$ when $\|x\| \to +\infty$. It is clearly differentiable, and its differential is:

$$DJ(x) \cdot y = Ax \cdot y - b \cdot y = (Ax - b) \cdot y \qquad [11.8]$$

The functional, therefore, has an absolute minimum at a single point where its differential vanishes, that is to say at the point where $(Ax - b)$ is 0. $\quad\square$

NOTE 11.1.– Equation [11.8] shows that the gradient of $\mathcal{J}$ at a point x satisfies:

$$\nabla \mathcal{J}(x) = Ax - b \qquad [11.9]$$

This justifies the notation g_p, for the vector $Ax_p - b$, which is precisely the gradient of the functional $\mathcal{J}$ associated with the matrix of the linear system $Ax = b$, and will be called a *gradient vector* from now on.

COROLLARY 11.2.– The minimum quantity $\mathcal{E}(x_p)$, defined in equation [11.10], is reached at point $x_p = x_0 + V_p z_p$, with z_p being the solution of the system:

$$T_p z_p = y_p \qquad [11.10]$$

PROOF 11.5.– From theorem [11.2] and equations [11.6] and [11.7], it suffices to prove that matrix T_p is positive definite, which immediately follows from the fact that A is as well, and the fact that the columns of V_p form a family tree of vectors. Hence, it follows:

$$(T_p z_p \cdot z_p) = (AV_p z_p \cdot V_p z_p) \geq \alpha \|V_p z_p\|^2 \geq \alpha\beta \|z_p\|^2 \qquad \square$$

The matrix T_p is very easy to factorize since it is tridiagonal symmetric positive definite. In particular, it admits a Crout factorization of the form $T_p = L_p D_p L_p^t$, where L_p is a lower triangular bidiagonal matrix with coefficients equal to 1 on the diagonal. Moreover, as T_{p-1} is the main diagonal block of T_p, the factorization of T_p is calculated immediately from that of T_{p-1}.

$$
T_p = \begin{pmatrix} T_{p-1} & \begin{pmatrix} 0 \\ \vdots \\ 0 \\ t_{p-1p} \end{pmatrix} \\ (0 \ \cdots \ 0 \ t_{pp-1}) & t_{pp} \end{pmatrix}
$$

$$
= \begin{pmatrix} L_{p-1} & \begin{pmatrix} 0 \\ \vdots \\ 0 \\ 0 \end{pmatrix} \\ (0 \ \cdots \ 0 \ l_{pp-1}) & 1 \end{pmatrix} \begin{pmatrix} D_{p-1} L_{p-1}^t & \begin{pmatrix} 0 \\ \vdots \\ 0 \\ u_{p-1p} \end{pmatrix} \\ (0 \ \cdots \ 0 \ 0) & d_p \end{pmatrix}
$$

By identification, $u_{p-1p} = t_{p-1p}$, $l_{pp-1} = t_{pp-1}/d_{p-1}$ and $d_p = t_{pp} - l_{pp-1} u_{p-1p}$.

Similarly, the update of vector y_p requires only the calculation of the final component, $y_p(p) = -(v_p \cdot g_0)$, the first $p-1$ being the same as those of vector y_{p-1}.

Finally, the p-iteration of the Lanczos method involves determining the last component of the vector y_p, calculating a new vector v_{p+1} and completing the Crout factorization of T_p from that of T_{p-1} using the following algorithm:

$$
\begin{aligned}
& y_p(p) = -v_p \cdot g_0 \\
& w = A v_p \\
& w = w - t_{pp-1} v_{p-1} \\
& t_{pp} = w \cdot v_p \\
& w = w - t_{pp} v_p \\
& t_{p+1p} = \|w\| \\
& v_{p+1} = \frac{1}{t_{p+1p}} w \\
& l_{pp-1} = t_{pp-1}/d_{p-1} \\
& d_p = t_{pp} - l_{pp-1} t_{pp-1}
\end{aligned}
$$

To determine the approximate solution x_p, simply solve the linear system [11.10] using the Crout factorization of T_p, and then calculate x_p according to formula [11.1].

The choice of the optimization criterion $\mathcal{E}(x_p)$ of equation [11.4] makes it possible to determine the approximate solution simply by solving a linear system associated with matrix T_p, which is tridiagonal symmetric. Nevertheless, the method suffers from a serious drawback: although the Lanczos basis vectors are calculated by a short recursion, the calculation of the approximate solution requires preserving all the basis vectors. The cost of each iteration increases linearly with the number of iterations, both in terms of the volume of data and the number of arithmetic operations.

11.3. The conjugate gradient method

The Lanczos method would be much more interesting if the updating of the approximate solution could be reached by means of a short recursion. In other words, it would be necessary that the first components of z_p are identical to those of z_{p-1}, which would lead to this type of formula:

$$x_p = x_{p-1} + \alpha_p v_p$$

To arrive at this, we need a W_p basis of the Krylov subspace $\mathcal{K}_p$ for which the matrix projection $W_p^t A W_p$ is diagonal. Thus, the $p-1$ first components of the solution of the optimization problem of order p:

$$W_p^t A W_p x_p = y_p \tag{11.11}$$

would eventually be identical to that of the problem of order $p-1$.

Moreover, we cannot calculate $\mathcal{E}(x_p)$, since the initial error e_0 is obviously unknown. The only way to control the convergence is to calculate the gradient norm, $g_p = A x_p - b$. The stopping criterion of the method is, therefore, based on the non-dimensional residual:

$$\frac{\|A x_p - b\|}{\|b\|} < \epsilon \tag{11.12}$$

In any case, it is necessary to calculate the successive gradients. Now, according to equation [11.3], the vector g_p belongs to $\mathcal{K}_{p+1}$, and we have demonstrated in corollary 11.1, that it is in $\mathcal{K}_p^{\perp}$. By construction, the orthogonal complement of $\mathcal{K}_p$ in $\mathcal{K}_{p+1}$ is the line generated by v_{p+1}, and thus $g_p = \delta v_{p+1}$. Rather than the orthonormal basis vectors v_p, we can use the orthogonal basis vectors of successive gradients. These vectors will tend to zero, but the iterations will, in any case, be stopped by the test defined by equation [11.12] well before the appearance of round-off problems. Thus, let G_p be the rectangular matrix with n rows and p columns, whose columns are the first p gradient vectors, $(g_0, g_1, \ldots, g_{p-1})$. As we have just seen, $G_p = V_p \Delta_p$, with Δ_p being a diagonal matrix. The projection matrix of the basis G_p is also symmetric tridiagonal positive definite:

$$G_p^t A G_p = \Delta_p^t V_p^t A V_p \Delta_p = \Delta_p^t T_p \Delta_p = \tilde{T}_p \qquad [11.13]$$

Thus, it admits a Crout factorization $\tilde{T}_p = \tilde{L}_p \tilde{D}_p \tilde{L}_p^t$. From this, we deduce:

$$G_p^t A G_p = \tilde{L}_p \tilde{D}_p \tilde{L}_p^t \quad \Leftrightarrow \quad \tilde{L}_p^{-1} G_p^t A G_p \tilde{L}_p^{-t} = \tilde{D}_p \qquad [11.14]$$

Equation [11.14] implies that the column vectors of the matrix:

$$W_p = G_p \tilde{L}_p^{-t} \qquad [11.15]$$

which are linear combinations of the column vectors of G_p, form an orthogonal family with the scalar product associated with A. W_p is thus an A-orthogonal basis of $\mathcal{K}_p$.

Since the projection matrix, $W_p^t A W_p$, is diagonal, W_p provides the *ad hoc* basis so that the optimization problem [11.4] can be solved by a short recursion. Moreover, equation [11.15] shows that the vectors of W_p are calculated by means of a short recursion using those of G_p, since:

$$W_p \tilde{L}_p^t = G_p \qquad [11.16]$$

In fact, if, in order to maintain a certain coherence in the indices, we denote by $(w_0, w_1, \ldots, w_{p-1})$ the column vectors of W_p, and by $(-\gamma_0, -\gamma_1, \ldots)$, the subdiagonal coefficients of matrix $\tilde{L}_p$, equation [11.16] means:

$$w_0 = g_0 \quad \text{and} \quad -\gamma_{j-1} w_{j-1} + w_j = g_j, \forall j > 0 \qquad [11.17]$$

The different known relationships between the vectors x_p, g_p and w_p finally allow us to write a new method, without going through the calculations of the Lanczos vectors, nor the Crout factorization of the projection matrix $\tilde{T}_p$. In fact, x_0 being selected, we necessarily have, according to equation [11.17]:

$$g_0 = Ax_0 - b \quad \text{and} \quad w_0 = g_0$$

On account of the properties of the basis W_p, we have:

$$x_p = x_{p-1} + \rho_{p-1} w_{p-1} \quad \Leftrightarrow \quad g_p = g_{p-1} + \rho_{p-1} A w_{p-1} \qquad [11.18]$$

We know that g_p is orthogonal to $\mathcal{K}_p$ and hence in particular to w_{p-1}. This orthogonality relationship defines the coefficient ρ_{p-1} in a unique way, since according to equation [11.18]:

$$g_p \cdot w_{p-1} = g_{p-1} \cdot w_{p-1} + \rho_{p-1} A w_{p-1} \cdot w_{p-1} = 0$$

$$\Leftrightarrow \qquad\qquad [11.19]$$

$$\rho_{p-1} = -\frac{g_{p-1} \cdot w_{p-1}}{A w_{p-1} \cdot w_{p-1}}$$

Finally, according to equation [11.17], the new vector w_p is calculated with the help of w_{p-1} and g_p:

$$w_p = g_p + \gamma_{p-1} w_{p-1}$$

The coefficient γ_{p-1} is determined uniquely by the relationship of A-orthogonality between w_p and $\mathcal{K}_p$, and more particularly between w_p and w_{p-1}:

$$(w_p \cdot A w_{p-1}) = (g_p \cdot A w_{p-1}) + \gamma_{p-1}(w_{p-1} \cdot A w_{p-1}) = 0$$

$$\Leftrightarrow \qquad\qquad [11.20]$$

$$\gamma_{p-1} = -\frac{g_p \cdot A w_{p-1}}{A w_{p-1} \cdot w_{p-1}}$$

The method defined above is the conjugate gradient method, thus named because the basis of the vectors w_p is built by conjugation, i.e. the A-orthogonalization, of the gradient vectors.

- Initialization of the conjugate gradient:

$$g_0 = Ax_0 - b$$
$$w_0 = g_0$$

- Iteration p of the conjugate gradient:

$$v = Aw_{p-1}$$
$$\rho_{p-1} = -(g_{p-1} \cdot w_{p-1})/(v \cdot w_{p-1})$$
$$x_p = x_{p-1} + \rho_{p-1}w_{p-1}$$
$$g_p = g_{p-1} + \rho_{p-1}v$$
if $(g_p \cdot g_p)/(b \cdot b) < \epsilon^2$ **then**
    End
end if
$$\gamma_{p-1} = -(g_p \cdot v)/(v \cdot w_{p-1})$$
$$w_p = g_p + \gamma_{p-1}w_{p-1}$$

At each iteration, it suffices to compute a matrix-vector product, $v = Aw_{p-1}$; four scalar products, $(g_{p-1} \cdot w_{p-1})$, $(v \cdot w_{p-1})$, $(g_p \cdot g_p)$ and $(g_p \cdot v)$; and three linear combinations of vectors, $x_p = x_{p-1} + \rho_{p-1}w_{p-1}$, $g_p = g_{p-1} + \rho_{p-1}v$ and $w_p = g_p - \gamma_{p-1}w_{p-1}$.

Let us note that using the orthogonality and conjugation relationships, we can rewrite the algorithm in the following way:

- Initialization of the conjugate gradient:

$$g_0 = Ax_0 - b$$
$$w_0 = g_0$$
$$\alpha_0 = g_0 \cdot g_0$$

- Iteration p of the conjugate gradient:

$$v = Aw_{p-1}$$
$$\rho_{p-1} = -\alpha_{p-1}/(v \cdot w_{p-1})$$
$$x_p = x_{p-1} + \rho_{p-1}w_{p-1}$$
$$g_p = g_{p-1} + \rho_{p-1}v$$
$$\alpha_p = g_p \cdot g_p$$
if $\alpha_p/(b \cdot b) < \epsilon^2$ **then**
    End
end if
$$\gamma_{p-1} = \alpha_p/\alpha_{p-1}$$
$$w_p = g_p + \gamma_{p-1}w_{p-1}$$

This form enables us to avoid two scalar products with respect to the latter one. In fact, at each iteration, we only have to compute one matrix-vector product $v = Aw_{p-1}$, two scalar products, $(g_p \cdot g_p)$, $(v \cdot w_{p-1})$, as well as three linear combinations $x_p = x_{p-1} + \rho_{p-1}w_{p-1}$, $g_p = g_{p-1} + \rho_{p-1}v$ and $w_p = g_p + \gamma_{p-1}w_{p-1}$.

The conjugate gradient algorithm is optimal in the sense that the different vectors are calculated by a short recursion, and therefore, the cost of iterations is constant. *A priori*, by making only p products by matrix A, we cannot build, in general, a better approximation space than $x_0 + \mathcal{K}_p$, and the approximate solution x_p calculated by this method is the nearest point in the affine space of solution x, in the sense of the scalar product associated with A.

NOTE 11.2.– The conjugate gradient algorithm constructs two bases of the Krylov subspace $\mathcal{K}_p$. The basis of the gradient vectors $(g_0, g_1, \ldots, g_{p-1})$, which are orthogonal, and the basis vectors $(w_0, w_1, \ldots, w_{p-1})$, referred to as "descent directions", which are conjugated – that is to say A-orthogonal. By construction, g_p is orthogonal to $\mathcal{K}_p$ and w_p is A-orthogonal to $\mathcal{K}_p$.

11.4. Comparison with the gradient method

The gradient method is an optimization method applied to the minimization of the functional $\mathcal{J}(x) = \frac{1}{2}(Ax \cdot x) - (b \cdot x)$. Starting from the state x_{p-1} in the direction w_{p-1}, we look for the point $x_p = x_{p-1} + \rho_{p-1}w_{p-1}$, which minimizes $\mathcal{J}$ on the affine line. The function $f(\rho) = \mathcal{J}(x_{p-1} + \rho w_{p-1})$ is the combination of an affine function and a strictly convex function, bounded from below and differentiable. It is thus itself also strictly convex, bounded from below and derivable and reaches its minimum at the point where its derivative vanishes. Its derivative is:

$$f'(\rho) = D\mathcal{J}(x_{p-1} + \rho w_{p-1}) \cdot w_{p-1}$$
$$= \nabla\mathcal{J}(x_{p-1} + \rho w_{p-1}) \cdot w_{p-1}$$
$$= (Ax_{p-1} + \rho Aw_{p-1} - b) \cdot w_{p-1}$$
$$= (g_{p-1} + \rho Aw_{p-1}) \cdot w_{p-1}$$
$$= (g_{p-1} \cdot w_{p-1}) + \rho(Aw_{p-1} \cdot w_{p-1})$$

And therefore, the minimum of f is reached at the point ρ_{p-1}, defined by:

$$f'(\rho_{p-1}) = 0 \iff \rho_{p-1} = -\frac{g_{p-1} \cdot w_{p-1}}{Aw_{p-1} \cdot w_{p-1}}$$

We find the same equation as the one for the conjugate gradient [11.19], which gives two equivalent definitions of ρ_{p-1}: the coefficient such as the g_p gradient is orthogonal to the direction w_{p-1}, and the coefficient for which x_p minimizes $\mathcal{J}$ on the affine line passing by x_{p-1}, in the direction of w_{p-1}.

It remains to define the method of selecting the direction w_{p-1}. The goal is to decrease $\mathcal{J}(x)$ as rapidly as possible. Based on the definition of the differential of $\mathcal{J}$ in equation [11.8], the direction of greatest variation of $\mathcal{J}$ starting from the point x_{p-1} is that of the gradient at this point: $g_{p-1} = Ax_{p-1} - b$.

The gradient method consists of choosing, as the descent direction, $w_{p-1} = g_{p-1}$. The gradient method is *a priori* slower than the conjugate gradient method, since the latter, in ensuring optimization in relation to the A-orthogonal directions, results in calculating the minimum in the entire space generated by the successive directions, while the gradient method performs this optimization only direction by direction and in a certain manner "forgets" the previous iterations.

We can easily show that the gradient method provides convergence of the square of the geometric distance from x to x_p, for the scalar product associated with A, defined in equation [11.4]. In effect, for the gradient method:

$$x_p = x_{p-1} + \rho_{p-1}g_{p-1} \quad \text{with} \quad \rho_{p-1} = -\frac{g_{p-1} \cdot g_{p-1}}{Ag_{p-1} \cdot g_{p-1}}$$

The error vectors and successive gradients satisfy the relations:

$$x_p - x = x_{p-1} - x + \rho_{p-1}g_{p-1} \quad \iff \quad g_p = g_{p-1} + \rho_{p-1}Ag_{p-1}$$

From where:

$$\mathcal{E}(x_p) = A(x_p - x) \cdot (x_p - x) = g_p \cdot A^{-1} g_p$$

$$= (g_{p-1} \cdot A^{-1} g_{p-1}) + 2\rho_{p-1}(g_{p-1} \cdot g_{p-1}) + \rho_{p-1}^2(Ag_{p-1} \cdot g_{p-1})$$

$$= (g_{p-1} \cdot A^{-1} g_{p-1}) - \frac{g_{p-1} \cdot g_{p-1}}{Ag_{p-1} \cdot g_{p-1}}(g_{p-1} \cdot g_{p-1})$$

$$= (g_{p-1} \cdot A^{-1} g_{p-1})\left(1 - \frac{g_{p-1} \cdot g_{p-1}}{Ag_{p-1} \cdot g_{p-1}} \frac{g_{p-1} \cdot g_{p-1}}{g_{p-1} \cdot A^{-1} g_{p-1}}\right)$$

$$= \mathcal{E}(x_{p-1})\left(1 - \frac{g_{p-1} \cdot g_{p-1}}{Ag_{p-1} \cdot g_{p-1}} \frac{g_{p-1} \cdot g_{p-1}}{g_{p-1} \cdot A^{-1} g_{p-1}}\right)$$

To increase the factor on the right of the last line of equation [11.21], we must increase the quantities of the form:

$$\frac{Av \cdot v}{v \cdot v} \leq \frac{\|Av\|\|v\|}{\|v\|^2} \leq \frac{\|Av\|}{\|v\|} \leq \|A\|$$

Equation [11.21] ultimately leads to the following upper bound:

$$\mathcal{E}(x_p) \leq \mathcal{E}(x_{p-1})\left(1 - \frac{1}{\|A\|\|A^{-1}\|}\right)$$

and therefore, by recursion:

$$\mathcal{E}(x_p) \leq \mathcal{E}(x_0)\left(1 - \frac{1}{\|A\|\|A^{-1}\|}\right)^p$$

The quantity $\|A\|\|A^{-1}\| = \kappa(A)$ is the conditioning of matrix A. As we have seen in section 4.2.4 for a symmetric positive definite matrix, the conditioning in the Euclidean norm (or 2-norm) is $\kappa(A) = \lambda_{max}/\lambda_{min}$, where λ_{min} and λ_{max} are the smallest and largest eigenvalues of A.

The estimated rate of convergence of the gradient algorithm is based on the evolution of $\mathcal{E}(x_p)$ from one iteration to another, since the approximate solution, x_p, depends only on the state of x_{p-1}, derived from the previous iteration. The situation is different from the conjugate gradient method, because $\mathcal{E}(x_p)$ is the minimum reached on the entire space $x_0 + \mathcal{K}_p$. More precisely:

$$x_p = x_0 + P_{p-1}(A)g_0 \tag{11.21}$$

where P_{p-1} is the polynomial of degree $p - 1$ for which $\mathcal{E}(x_p)$ is minimum. By using particular polynomials, the Tchebychev polynomials, we can prove the following result concerning the conjugate gradient convergence rate.

THEOREM 11.3.– With the conjugate gradient method, $\mathcal{E}(x_p)$ converges geometrically, with a convergence rate equal to $\left(1 - \dfrac{1}{\sqrt{\kappa(A)}}\right)^2$.

This result will not be reviewed here further, because the proof, which is quite technical, is based on the interpretation of the conjugate gradient method in terms of the construction of an optimal. The choice that was made in this book for the construction methods starting from the Arnoldi basis and of orthogonalization allows for a simpler approach. The result shown above indicates that the conjugate gradient method converges much faster than the gradient method. What is even more remarkable is that a conjugate gradient iteration differs from that of a gradient only by the fact that the descent direction is obtained by orthogonalizing, for the scalar product associated with A, the gradient with respect to the direction of the preceding descent. This combination costs only a scalar product and a linear combination of additional vectors.

11.5. Principle of preconditioning for symmetric positive definite matrices

The key ingredient in theorem 11.3 proof is that the approximate solution at iteration p minimizes the distance from x_p to x among all the vectors written in the form given by equation [11.21]. The same type of convergence result can be obtained for other Krylov methods such as the conjugate gradient. Matrix conditioning thus plays a fundamental role in the convergence speed of a Krylov method.

Preconditioning a linear system consists of replacing it by an equivalent system – a matrix with smaller conditioning – in such a way that the convergence is faster. The basic principle consists of replacing system $Ax = b$ by the system:

$$MAx = Mb \qquad [11.22]$$

where M is an approximation of A^{-1}. We will refer to this as left preconditioning. You can also precondition to the right:

$$AM\tilde{x} = b \qquad [11.23]$$

with $x = M\tilde{x}$.

In the case where matrix A is symmetric positive definite, the preconditioning matrix M must also be one. Nonetheless, a particular problem arises. In fact, matrix MA is no longer symmetrical *a priori*, since $(MA)^t = AM$, unless we can make sure that A and M commute. This is impossible to achieve in practice unless we construct M as a polynomial. As a result, we can no longer apply the conjugate gradient algorithm to the preconditioned systems [11.22] or [11.23].

To preserve the symmetrical character of the system, we will use another approach. If M admits a factorization LL^t, then the eigenvalues of MA and L^tAL are the same. In fact, if λ and v are, respectively, eigenvalue and eigenvectors of MA:

$$MAv = \lambda v \;\Leftrightarrow\; LL^tAv = \lambda v \;\Leftrightarrow\; L^tAL(L^{-1}v) = \lambda(L^{-1}v)$$

Rather than solving system [11.22], we will instead solve:

$$L^tAL\tilde{x} = L^tb \qquad [11.24]$$

with $x = L\tilde{x}$. To an approximate solution $\tilde{x}_p$ of the system [11.24], there corresponds an approximate solution x_p of the initial system [10.1], with $x_p = L\tilde{x}_p$. Similarly, the respective gradients associated with $\tilde{x}_p$ and x_p satisfy the following relationships:

$$\tilde{g}_p = L^tAL\tilde{x}_p - L^tb = L^t(Ax_p - b) = L^tg_p \qquad [11.25]$$

The calculation of vectors $\tilde{x}_p$ and $\tilde{g}_p$ at iteration p of the conjugate gradient on system [11.24] requires the following operations:

$$\begin{aligned}
\tilde{x}_p &= \tilde{x}_{p-1} + \rho_{p-1}\tilde{w}_{p-1} &\Leftrightarrow x_p &= x_{p-1} + \rho_{p-1}L\tilde{w}_{p-1} \\
\tilde{g}_p &= \tilde{g}_{p-1} + \rho_{p-1}L^t AL\tilde{w}_{p-1} &\Leftrightarrow g_p &= g_{p-1} + \rho_{p-1}AL\tilde{w}_{p-1}
\end{aligned} \qquad [11.26]$$

The descent coefficient ρ_{p-1} is defined by:

$$\rho_{p-1} = -\frac{\tilde{g}_{p-1} \cdot \tilde{w}_{p-1}}{L^t AL\tilde{w}_{p-1} \cdot \tilde{w}_{p-1}} = -\frac{L^t g_{p-1} \cdot \tilde{w}_{p-1}}{L^t AL\tilde{w}_{p-1} \cdot \tilde{w}_{p-1}}$$

$$= -\frac{g_{p-1} \cdot L\tilde{w}_{p-1}}{AL\tilde{w}_{p-1} \cdot L\tilde{w}_{p-1}} \qquad [11.27]$$

Equations [11.26] and [11.27] show that the optimization phase carried out on system [11.24] in iteration p of the conjugate gradient algorithm represents an optimization phase of the initial system [10.1], from the point x_{p-1} in the direction $w_{p-1} = L\tilde{w}_{p-1}$.

Similarly, the new descent direction for system [11.24] is calculated using the formula:

$$\begin{aligned}
\tilde{w}_p &= \tilde{g}_p + \gamma_{p-1}\tilde{w}_{p-1} \Leftrightarrow L\tilde{w}_p = LL^t g_p - \gamma_{p-1}L\tilde{w}_{p-1} \\
&\Leftrightarrow \quad w_p = Mg_p + \gamma_{p-1}w_{p-1}
\end{aligned} \qquad [11.28]$$

The coefficient of the conjugation γ_{p-1} is given by the formula:

$$\gamma_{p-1} = -\frac{\tilde{g}_p \cdot L^t AL\tilde{w}_{p-1}}{\tilde{w}_{p-1} \cdot L^t AL\tilde{w}_{p-1}} = -\frac{LL^t g_p \cdot AL\tilde{w}_{p-1}}{L\tilde{w}_{p-1} \cdot AL\tilde{w}_{p-1}}$$

$$= -\frac{Mg_p \cdot Aw_{p-1}}{w_{p-1} \cdot Aw_{p-1}} \qquad [11.29]$$

The conjugation step of the gradient for system [11.24] is interpreted as a conjugation of the "preconditioned gradient" Mg_p, for the descent directions $w_{p-1} = L\tilde{w}_{p-1}$ and $w_p = L\tilde{w}_p$ of system $Ax = b$. The initial descent direction, for its part, satisfies:

$$w_0 = L\tilde{w}_0 = L\tilde{g}_0 = LL^t g_0 = Mg_0$$

Ultimately, it will appear that the conjugate gradient iterations on system [11.24] return to make the optimization iterations on the initial system [10.1], with the directions of descent produced by the conjugation of the preconditioned gradients Mg_p. Therefore, it is unnecessary to perform the LL^t factorization of the preconditioning matrix, since it suffices to know how to calculate the product by M, in order to be able to implement the new algorithm, called a preconditioned conjugate gradient:

– Initialization of the preconditioned conjugate gradient:

$$g_0 = Ax_0 - b$$
$$z_0 = Mg_0$$
$$w_0 = z_0$$
$$\alpha_0 = g_0 \cdot z_0$$

– Iteration p of the preconditioned conjugate gradient:

$$v = Aw_{p-1}$$
$$\rho_{p-1} = -\alpha_{p-1}/(v \cdot w_{p-1})$$
$$x_p = x_{p-1} + \rho_{p-1}w_{p-1}$$
$$g_p = g_{p-1} + \rho_{p-1}v$$
$$z_p = Mg_p$$
$$\alpha_p = g_p \cdot z_p$$
$$\mathbf{if} \ \ \alpha_p/(b \cdot b) < \epsilon^2 \ \ \mathbf{then}$$
$$\quad End$$
$$\mathbf{end} \ \ \mathbf{if}$$
$$\gamma_{p-1} = \alpha_p/\alpha_{p-1}$$
$$w_p = z_p + \gamma_{p-1}w_{p-1}$$

In terms of computational costs, the conjugate gradient requires only one additional product from matrix M at each iteration. Its convergence speed depends on the conditioning of matrix MA.

Exact Orthogonalization Methods for Arbitrary Matrices

By continuing to rely on the Arnoldi basis, this chapter presents exact orthogonalization with iterative methods for arbitrary matrices. This chapter initially describes the GMRES method, and then its variant with restart, the GMRES(m) method. The application of GMRES to symmetric matrices then leads to the MINRES method, for which there is a short recursion, even for non-positive matrices. The ORTHODIR method allows calculating approximate solutions more easily than the GMRES method, but each iteration is more costly. Preconditioning techniques for non-symmetric matrices, to the left and then to right, are presented at the end of this chapter.

12.1. The GMRES method

In the case of an arbitrary matrix A, matrix H_p of equation [10.6] is not tridiagonal. We can no longer hope for a short recursion to build an orthogonal basis of the Krylov subspace $\mathcal{K}_p$. Moreover, A does not define a scalar product, and the optimality criterion $\mathcal{E}(x_p)$ [11.4] is no longer relevant. The logical choice is to minimize the square of the norm of the residual vector, which, unlike the error vector, is effectively computable.

$$\mathcal{R}(x_p) = A(x_p - x) \cdot A(x_p - x)$$

$$= g_p \cdot g_p$$

$$= \|x_p - x\|_A^2$$

$$= A^t A(x_p - x) \cdot (x_p - x) \qquad [12.1]$$

We will find similar properties to those of theorem 11.1 and its corollary 11.1, for the approximate solution that minimizes $\mathcal{R}(x_p)$.

THEOREM 12.1.– The approximate solution x_p that minimizes $\mathcal{R}(x_p)$ in $x_0 + \mathcal{K}_p$ is the projection of x, for the scalar product associated with $A^t A$.

PROOF 12.1.– According to equation [12.1], x_p is the element of $x_0 + \mathcal{K}_p$ whose distance to x is minimal for the scalar product associated with $A^t A$. □

COROLLARY 12.1.– The residual vector $g_p = A x_p - b$ is orthogonal to $A\mathcal{K}_p$.

PROOF 12.2.– The property of a projection into an affine space implies:

$$A^t A(x_p - x) \cdot w_p = A(x_p - x) \cdot A w_p = g_p \cdot A w_p = 0 , \quad \forall w_p \in \mathcal{K}_p.$$

□

We naturally introduced the scalar product associated with matrix $A^t A$ that is symmetric positive definite as long as A is invertible. It might seem logical to replace the initial system given by equation [10.1], by using the same type of approach as for the preconditioning, with an equivalent system associated with a symmetric positive definite matrix, known as a "normal equation".

$$A^t A x = A^t b \tag{12.2}$$

The advantage is that we can apply the conjugate gradient method to this system.

Regrettably, this is most often a very bad idea. In fact, the conditioning of matrix $A^t A$ can be equal to the square of that of matrix A. This is especially obvious in the case of a symmetric matrix. The convergence of the algorithm will be extremely slow if matrix A is not very well conditioned.

To calculate x_p in $x_0 + \mathcal{K}_p$, for the original system given by equation [10.1], we have available the orthonormal Arnoldi basis V_p, while x_p and g_p satisfy equations [11.1] and [11.3], respectively. According to the properties of the Arnoldi basis, and in particular equation [10.4], we have:

$$g_p = A x_p - b = g_0 + A V_p z_p = g_0 + V_{p+1} H_{p+1p} z_p \tag{12.3}$$

Now, the first vector of the Arnoldi basis satisfies $\|g_0\|v_1 = g_0$, which, according to equation [12.3], gives us another way of writing the optimality criterion [12.1]:

$$\mathcal{R}(x_p) = (g_p \cdot g_p) = \|V_{p+1}\left(\|g_0\|e_{p+1}^1 + H_{p+1p}z_p\right)\|^2$$

where e_{p+1}^1 is the first canonical basis vector of dimension $p + 1$, while z_p is a vector of dimension p. And therefore, since the columns of V_{p+1} form an orthonormal family:

$$\mathcal{R}(x_p) = \|\|g_0\|e_{p+1}^1 + H_{p+1p}z_p\|^2 \qquad [12.4]$$

which brings us back to a classic optimization problem in p dimensions, or more precisely, to a "least squares" problem. We want to minimize the norm of a quantity of dimension $p+1$, while we only have a lower number of control parameters, here, specifically the p coefficients of z_p.

To resolve the least squares problem, the technique that is best suited, given the reduced dimension of the problem and the form of a matrix H_{p+1p}, is the Givens "QR" method, which consists of building, by means of matrix plane rotations, an orthogonal matrix Q_{p+1}, such as:

$$Q_{p+1}H_{p+1p} = \begin{pmatrix} R_p \\ (0\cdots 0) \end{pmatrix}$$

where R_p is an upper triangular matrix. Once this factorization is completed, the minimization problem is solved directly. In fact, since matrix R_p is orthogonal:

$$\| \|g_0\|e_{p+1}^1 + H_{p+1p}z_p\| = \| \|g_0\|Q_{p+1}e_{p+1}^1 + Q_{p+1}H_{p+1p}z_p\|$$

If we denote $y_{p+1} = -\|g_0\|Q_{p+1}e_{p+1}^1$, we have:

$$\|g_0\|Q_{p+1}e_{p+1}^1 + Q_{p+1}H_{p+1p}z_p = \begin{pmatrix} \begin{pmatrix} -y_{p+1}(1) \\ \vdots \\ -y_{p+1}(p) \end{pmatrix} + R_p z_p \\ -y_{p+1}(p+1) + \quad 0 \end{pmatrix} \qquad [12.5]$$

According to equation [12.5], it is clear that the minimum is reached when the p first components cancel each other out, that is to say for the z_p solution of the system:

$$R_p z_p = \tilde{y}_p = \begin{pmatrix} y_{p+1}(1) \\ \vdots \\ y_{p+1}(p) \end{pmatrix}$$ [12.6]

Moreover, the minimum value is known without the need to actually solve system [12.5], and is $|y_{p+1}(p+1)|$. By construction, $|y_{p+1}(p+1)|$ is the norm of $g_p = Ax_p - b$, for $x_p = x_0 + V_p z_p$, where z_p is the solution of system [12.5].

Finally, it remains for us to explain the technique for calculating matrix Q_{p+1} to define completely this new Krylov method, called GMRES, an acronym for general minimum residual.

A matrix of Givens rotation is a rotation matrix in a plane defined by two vectors of the canonical basis. For the GMRES method, the only rotations that will be used are in a plane defined by two successive vectors of the canonical basis, of the following form:

$$G^{\theta_k} = \begin{pmatrix} I_{k-1} & 0 & 0 \\ 0 & \begin{pmatrix} \cos(\theta_k) & -\sin(\theta_k) \\ \sin(\theta_k) & \cos(\theta_k) \end{pmatrix} & 0 \\ 0 & 0 & I_{n-k-1} \end{pmatrix}$$

Since only the rows k and $k+1$ of G^{θ_k} are different from matrix I, the rows of the matrix $N = G^{\theta_k} M$ of a number different from k and from $k+1$ are identical to that of A. As for the terms located in the rows k and $k+1$, they are, column-by-column, the result of the product by the rotation of angle θ_k:

$$\begin{pmatrix} n_{kj} \\ n_{k+1j} \end{pmatrix} = \begin{pmatrix} \cos(\theta_k) & -\sin(\theta_k) \\ \sin(\theta_k) & \cos(\theta_k) \end{pmatrix} \begin{pmatrix} m_{kj} \\ m_{k+1j} \end{pmatrix}$$

$$= \begin{pmatrix} \cos(\theta_k)m_{kj} - \sin(\theta_k)m_{k+1j} \\ \sin(\theta_k)m_{kj} + \cos(\theta_k)m_{k+1j} \end{pmatrix}$$

Let us consider the first two rows of matrix H_{p+1p} in equation [10.5]. We look for the Givens rotation G^{θ_1}, which removes the first subdiagonal term, such that:

$$\begin{pmatrix} \cos(\theta_1) & -\sin(\theta_1) \\ \sin(\theta_1) & \cos(\theta_1) \end{pmatrix} \begin{pmatrix} h_{11} \\ h_{21} \end{pmatrix} = \begin{pmatrix} r_{11} \\ 0 \end{pmatrix}$$

In practice, it is not useful to calculate θ_1 explicitly, but only $\cos(\theta_1)$ and $\sin(\theta_1)$, which we will denote by c_1 and s_1, and which must satisfy:

$$c_1^2 + s_1^2 = 1$$
$$s_1 h_{11} + c_1 h_{21} = 0 \qquad\qquad [12.7]$$

Equation [12.7] admits two pairs of solutions that differ in their signs. We choose one of them arbitrarily. Matrix $G^{\theta_1} H_{p+1p}$ differs from H_{p+1p} only in its first two rows. Therefore, it has the same structure, but with a null $(2, 1)$ coefficient.

The construction of matrix Q_{p+1} is made in a recurring manner. If we cancel the subdiagonal terms of the $j - 1$ first columns, we obtain a matrix of the form:

$$\tilde{H}_{p+1p} = \begin{pmatrix} r_{11} & r_{12} & \vdots & r_{1j-1} & r_{1j} & \vdots & r_{1p} \\ 0 & r_{22} & \vdots & r_{2j-1} & r_{2j} & \vdots & r_{2p} \\ 0 & 0 & \vdots & r_{3j-1} & r_{3j} & \vdots & r_{3p} \\ \vdots & \ddots & \ddots & \vdots & \vdots & \vdots & \vdots \\ \vdots & & \ddots & 0 & \tilde{h}_{jj} & \vdots & \tilde{h}_{jp} \\ \vdots & & & 0 & h_{j+1j} & \vdots & h_{j+1p} \\ \vdots & & & & \ddots & \ddots & \vdots \\ 0 & \cdots & \cdots & \cdots & \cdots & 0 & h_{p+1p} \end{pmatrix} \qquad [12.8]$$

To eliminate coefficient h_{j+1j}, we simply multiply the matrix of equation [12.8] to the left by the Givens rotation matrix G^{θ_j}, defined by the factors c_j and s_j, which satisfy the equation:

$$c_j^2 + s_j^2 = 1$$
$$s_j \tilde{h}_{jj} + c_j h_{j+1j} = 0 \qquad\qquad [12.9]$$

This transformation only changes the rows j and $j + 1$ of the matrix. The rows between 1 and j, inclusive, therefore, will not be affected by subsequent transformations, which justifies the notation used in equation [12.8] for matrix $\tilde{H}_{p+1p}$, arising from the first $j-1$ Givens rotations. The coefficients of the first rows of $j - 1$ are those of matrix R of the QR factorization; the coefficients of the rows between $j + 1$ and $p + 1$, inclusive, are still those of the initial matrix H_{p+1p}. Only the coefficients of row j have values different from their initial ones, but they still need to undergo the effects of the Givens rotation $G^{\theta_j}j$. In particular:

$$\begin{pmatrix} c_j & -s_j \\ s_j & c_j \end{pmatrix} \begin{pmatrix} \tilde{h}_{jj} \\ h_{jj+1} \end{pmatrix} = \begin{pmatrix} r_{jj} \\ 0 \end{pmatrix}$$

Matrix H_{p+1p} is obtained, in iteration p, by adding a column to matrix H_{pp-1}. Therefore, the QR factorization of matrix H_{pp-1} gives a partial QR factorization of matrix H_{p+1p}. In fact, if the QR factorization of matrix H_{pp-1} is written:

$$G_p^{\theta_p} \cdots G_p^{\theta_1} H_{pp-1} = \begin{pmatrix} R_{p-1} \\ (0 \cdots 0) \end{pmatrix}$$

where the matrices $G_p^{\theta_k}$ are the matrices of the Givens rotation of dimension p, thus:

$$G_{p+1}^{\theta_{p-1}} \cdots G_{p+1}^{\theta_1} H_{p+1p} = \begin{pmatrix} R_{p-1} & \begin{pmatrix} r_{1p} \\ \vdots \\ r_{p-1p} \\ \tilde{h}_{pp} \end{pmatrix} \\ (0 \cdots 0) & h_{p+1p} \end{pmatrix}$$

In order to complete the QR factorization of matrix H_{p+1p}, it is, therefore, sufficient to apply *a posteriori* the $p - 1$ previous Givens rotations to column p, and then to calculate the G^{θ_p} Givens rotation by determining the two coefficients c_p and s_p such that:

$$c_p^2 + s_p^2 = 1$$
$$s_p \tilde{h}_{pp} + c_p h_{p+1p} = 0$$

[12.10]

Similarly, the $p - 1$ first components of vector $y_{p+1} = -\|g_0\| Q_{p+1} e^1_{p+1}$ are identical to those of vector $y_p = -\|g_0\| Q_p e^1_p$. The last two components are calculated by simply applying the rotation angle θ_p:

$$\begin{pmatrix} y_{p+1}(p) \\ y_{p+1}(p+1) \end{pmatrix} = \begin{pmatrix} c_p & -s_p \\ s_p & c_p \end{pmatrix} \begin{pmatrix} y_p(p) \\ 0 \end{pmatrix}$$

Finally, the GMRES algorithm consists of iteratively calculating the Arnoldi basis of the Krylov subspace, the QR factorization of matrix H and vector y. As we have seen above, $|y_{p+1}(p+1)|$ is equal to $\|g_p\|$. Therefore, it is useless to calculate the approximate solution in each iteration, but only once, when convergence has been reached.

It is now possible to fully detail the implementation of the GMRES algorithm, denoting, respectively, β_p the last coefficient of vector $\tilde{y}_p$, which is equal to $y_{p+1}(p)$; and r_{p+1}, the coefficient $y_{p+1}(p+1)$, whose absolute value is equal to the norm of the residual.

In terms of computer implementation, it is unnecessary to keep matrix H since only the last column is active, and therefore can be stored only temporarily in a working vector. In the algorithm, as it is described below, this vector, denoted α, also serves to calculate the coefficients of column p of R, so that the resultant product from the first $p - 1$ Givens rotations α_p and α_{p+1}, represents, respectively, $\tilde{h}_{pp}$ and h_{p+1p}. Moreover, it is necessary to store only the upper triangular part of matrix R.

– Initialization of GMRES:

$g_0 = Ax_0 - b$
$r_1 = -\|g_0\|$
$v_1 = \frac{1}{\|g_0\|} g_0$

– Construction of vector $p + 1$ of the Arnoldi basis:

$w = Av_p$
for $i = 1$ **to** p
    $\alpha_i = w \cdot v_i$
    $w = w - \alpha_i v_i$
end for
$\alpha_{p+1} = \|w\|$
$v_{j+1} = \frac{1}{\alpha_{p+1}} w$

– Calculation of the product of column p of matrix H, by the first $p-1$ Givens rotations:

for $i = 1$ **to** $p-1$

$$\begin{pmatrix} r_{ip} \\ \alpha_{i+1} \end{pmatrix} = \begin{pmatrix} c_i & -s_i \\ s_i & c_i \end{pmatrix} \begin{pmatrix} \alpha_i \\ \alpha_{i+1} \end{pmatrix}$$

end for

– Calculation of the new Givens rotation, and updating the last column of R and vector y:

$$c_p = \sqrt{\frac{1}{1+(\frac{\alpha_{p+1}}{\alpha_p})^2}}$$

$$s_p = -c_p \frac{\alpha_{p+1}}{\alpha_p}$$

$$\begin{pmatrix} r_{pp} \\ 0 \end{pmatrix} = \begin{pmatrix} c_p & -s_p \\ s_p & c_p \end{pmatrix} \begin{pmatrix} \alpha_p \\ \alpha_{p+1} \end{pmatrix}$$

$$\begin{pmatrix} \beta_p \\ r_{p+1} \end{pmatrix} = \begin{pmatrix} c_p & -s_p \\ s_p & c_p \end{pmatrix} \begin{pmatrix} r_p \\ 0 \end{pmatrix}$$

– Stopping test:

if $|r_{p+1}|/\|b\| < \epsilon$ **then**
End
end if

It is only when the convergence test is satisfied that we effectively solve system [12.6], with $y_{p+1}(i) = \beta_i$, by using the notations of the above algorithm. It is then possible to calculate the approximate solution $x_p = x_0 + V_p z_p$.

We should note that with this method, it is necessary to calculate the Arnoldi vectors $p+1$ to find the optimal solution in the Krylov subspace of dimension p. We will see, in section 12.3, a method called ORTHODIR, which does not exhibit this shift, but in exchange, requires storage of the basis vector products by the matrix.

The main problem with the GMRES method is that it has no short recursion to calculate the Arnoldi basis vectors, all of which must, therefore, be retained, both for orthonormalizing each new vector compared to the previous ones and for calculating the convergence solution. Most often, it is impossible for reasons of memory space and computational costs to carry out more than a certain number of m iterations, set beforehand. If convergence is not reached in m iterations, we calculate the approximate solution x_m, and we restart from x_m as an initial solution. This method is referred to as GMRES(m) in the literature. Unlike the GMRES method, it cannot converge if m is not sufficiently large.

12.2. The case of symmetric matrices: the MINRES method

In the case where matrix A is symmetric, matrix H_{p+1p} is tridiagonal, denoted by T_{p+1p} from now on, and the Arnoldi procedure is transformed into a short recursion: the Lanczos procedure. Since the Givens rotations operate only with the combination of two successive rows, we can easily see that the upper triangular matrix R_p of the QR factorization of T_{p+1p} is of the form:

$$R_p = \begin{pmatrix} r_{11} & r_{12} & 0 \cdots & \cdots & \cdots & 0 \\ 0 & \ddots & \ddots & \ddots & & \vdots \\ \vdots & \ddots & \ddots & \ddots & \ddots & \vdots \\ \vdots & & \ddots & \ddots & \ddots & 0 \\ \vdots & & \ddots & r_{p-2p-2} & r_{p-2p-1} & r_{p-2p} \\ \vdots & & & \ddots & r_{p-1p-1} & r_{p-1p} \\ 0 & \cdots & \cdots & \cdots & 0 & r_{pp} \end{pmatrix} \qquad [12.11]$$

This property is of great practical importance, as it will allow us to recover the approximate solution by using a short recursion. In fact, the solution to the minimization problem of $r(z_p)$ is given by:

$$R_p z_p = \tilde{y}_p \qquad [12.12]$$

where $\tilde{y}_p$ is the vector of the p first components of vector $-\|g_0\|Q_{p+1}e^1_{p+1}$, with Q_{p+1} being the orthogonal matrix, the product of Givens rotations, such that:

$$Q_{p+1}T_{p+1p} = \begin{pmatrix} R_p \\ (0\cdots0) \end{pmatrix}$$

The approximate solution vector in iteration p thus satisfies:

$$x_p = x_0 + V_pR_p^{-1}\tilde{y}_p = x_0 + W_p\tilde{y}_p$$

The column vectors of $W_p = V_pR_p^{-1}$ define a new basis of the Krylov subspace $\mathcal{K}_p$.

The first $p-1$ components of vector $-\|g_0\|Q_{p+1}e^1_{p+1}$ are identical to those of vector $-\|g_0\|Q_pe^1_p$. As we have seen, the last two components are calculated simply by applying the Givens rotation with angle θ_p:

$$\begin{pmatrix} y_{p+1}(p) \\ y_{p+1}(p+1) \end{pmatrix} = \begin{pmatrix} c_p & -s_p \\ s_p & c_p \end{pmatrix} \begin{pmatrix} y_p(p) \\ 0 \end{pmatrix}$$

This means that the successive approximate solutions are calculated in the new basis W_p, by means of a short recursion:

$$x_p = x_0 + W_p\tilde{y}_p = x_0 + W_{p-1}\tilde{y}_{p-1} + y_{p+1}(p)w_p = x_{p-1} + \beta_pw_p$$

The relation $W_pR_p = V_p$ indicates how the new basis vectors are calculated from those of the Lanczos basis. The tridiagonal structure of matrix R_p indicates that this relation is also a short recursion:

$$v_p = r_{p-2p}w_{p-2} + r_{p-1p}w_{p-1} + r_{pp}w_p \Leftrightarrow w_p$$

$$= \frac{1}{r_{pp}}(v_p - r_{p-2p}w_{p-2} - r_{p-1p}w_{p-1})$$

In general, we could make the same basis change, but that would not add anything, because the upper triangular part of matrix R_p of the GMRES method is dense. In this case, the relation between the vectors V_p and W_p is not a short recursion.

Finally, we notice that in order to go from matrix R_{p-1} to matrix R_p, we can just apply Givens rotations to column p of T_{p+1p}, before calculating the new Givens rotation. However, this column has only two non-zero terms, located in rows p and $p+1$. Therefore, only the last two Givens rotations are needed.

This ultimately leads to an algorithm called MINRES, an acronym for "minimal residual", which can be written as follows:

– Initialization of MINRES:

$$g_0 = Ax_0 - b$$
$$r_1 = -\|g_0\|$$
$$v_1 = \frac{1}{\|g_0\|} g_0$$

– Construction of vector $p+1$ of the Lanczos basis:

$$w = Av_p$$
$$t_{p-1p} = t_{pp-1}$$
$$w = w - t_{p-1p}v_{p-1}$$
$$t_{pp} = w \cdot v_p$$
$$w = w - t_{pp}v_p$$
$$t_{p+1p} = \|w\|$$
$$v_{p+1} = \frac{1}{t_{p+1\,p}} w$$

– Application of the last two Givens rotations to column p of T_{p+1p}:

$$\begin{pmatrix} r_{p-2p} \\ \alpha_{p-1} \end{pmatrix} = \begin{pmatrix} c_{p-2} & -s_{p-2} \\ s_{p-2} & c_{p-2} \end{pmatrix} \begin{pmatrix} 0 \\ t_{p-1p} \end{pmatrix}$$
$$\begin{pmatrix} r_{p-1p} \\ \alpha_p \end{pmatrix} = \begin{pmatrix} c_{p-1} & -s_{p-1} \\ s_{p-1} & c_{p-1} \end{pmatrix} \begin{pmatrix} \alpha_{p-1} \\ t_{pp} \end{pmatrix}$$

– Calculation of the new Givens rotation and the updating of column p of R, and of vector y:

$$c_p = \sqrt{\frac{1}{1 + (\frac{t_{p+1p}}{\alpha_p})^2}}$$
$$s_p = -c_p \frac{t_{p+1p}}{\alpha_p}$$
$$\begin{pmatrix} r_{pp} \\ 0 \end{pmatrix} = \begin{pmatrix} c_p & -s_p \\ s_p & c_p \end{pmatrix} \begin{pmatrix} \alpha_p \\ t_{p+1p} \end{pmatrix}$$
$$\begin{pmatrix} \beta_p \\ r_{p+1} \end{pmatrix} = \begin{pmatrix} c_p & -s_p \\ s_p & c_p \end{pmatrix} \begin{pmatrix} r_p \\ 0 \end{pmatrix}$$

– Calculation of the new vector w_p and the approximate solution:

$$w_p = \frac{1}{r_{pp}}(v_p - r_{p-2p}w_{p-2} - r_{p-1p}w_{p-1})$$
$$x_p = x_{p-1} + \beta_p w_p$$

For reasons of readability, the references to matrices T and R were kept in the above algorithm. However, in practice, only the three non-zero coefficients in the active column of these matrices are useful, so that it is unnecessary to keep the successive coefficients in the arrays. The same is true for the coefficients α_i and β_i.

NOTE 12.1.– The MINRES method makes it possible, as does the conjugate gradient method for symmetric positive definite matrices, to obtain the exact minimization of the distance of the approximate solution to the exact solution, for a certain norm, with the help of a short recursion. The difference is that this is the A-error norm, which is minimized in the case of the conjugate gradient method, while it is the norm of the residual in the case of the MINRES method.

The MINRES method is, therefore, the most appropriate method, *a priori*, to solve systems of a positive non-definite symmetric matrix.

12.3. The ORTHODIR method

If it is necessary to systematically determine the approximate solution x_p in each iteration, the GMRES method is ill-suited because it does not allow us to calculate it by a short recursion. According to theorem 12.1, it would need to have a basis $A^t A$-orthogonal of $\mathcal{K}_p$, W_p, so that $W_p^t A^t A W_p$ is diagonal. Given the structure of matrix H_{p+1p}, matrix $H_{p+1p}^t H_{p+1p}$ is dense. Therefore, it is of no interest to use the Arnoldi basis to compute W_p.

To construct an $A^t A$-orthogonal basis of $\mathcal{K}_p$, it is sufficient to apply the procedure of orthonormalization of the modified Gram–Schmidt vectors, obtained by the successive products of the matrix, for the scalar product associated with $A^t A$. This gives us the following algorithm, in which we made sure to calculate only one matrix-vector product per iteration, which obliges us to maintain not only the vectors w_i, but also their matrix products, denoted by Aw_i.

– Initialization, $A^t A$-normalization of g_0:

$$g_0 = Ax_0 - b$$
$$w = g_0$$

$$v = Aw$$
$$w_1 = \frac{1}{\|v\|}w$$
$$Aw_1 = \frac{1}{\|v\|}v$$

– Construction of vector p of the $A^t A$-orthonormal basis:

$$w = Aw_{p-1}$$
$$v = Aw$$
for $i = 1$ **to** $p - 1$
$\quad \alpha_i = v \cdot Aw_i$
$\quad w = w - \alpha_i v_i$
$\quad v = v - \alpha_i Aw_i$
end for
$$w_p = \frac{1}{\|v\|}w$$
$$Aw_p = \frac{1}{\|v\|}v$$

Since the vectors w_i form an orthonormal family for the scalar product associated with matrix $A^t A$, the approximate solution x_p, which minimizes the quantity $\mathcal{R}(x_p)$ defined in equation [12.1], and the vector g_p are calculated by the following formulas:

$$x_p = x_{p-1} + \rho_p w_p$$
$$g_p = g_{p-1} + \rho_p Aw_p$$

The orthogonal property of vector g_p in the subspace $A\mathcal{K}_p$ (demonstrated by [12.1], and the fact that the norm of vector w_p is equal to 1 for the scalar product associated with matrix $A^t A$, immediately gives us a very simple method for calculating the coefficient ρ_p:

$$g_p \cdot Aw_p = 0 \iff g_{p-1} \cdot Aw_p + \rho_p(Aw_p \cdot Aw_p)$$
$$= 0 \iff \rho_p = -g_{p-1} \cdot Aw_p$$

The Krylov method, as thus defined, is known as the ORTHODIR method. By construction, the ORTHODIR method produces the same approximate solutions as the GMRES method.

NOTE 12.2.– The ORTHODIR method allows us to calculate the approximate solution vector and the residual in iteration p without calculating the basis vectors of iteration $p + 1$, as is the case for the GMRES method. However, it requires more storage space and operations because of the need to conserve vectors Aw_i.

12.4. Principle of preconditioning for non-symmetric matrices

For non-symmetric matrices, preconditioning obviously poses no problem for conserving symmetry. Therefore, it is possible to precondition the system $Ax = b$, with the help of matrix M, an approximation of A^{-1}, either to the left, by replacing it with the system:

$$MAx = Mb$$

or to the right, by replacing it with:

$$AM\tilde{x} = b$$

with $x = M\tilde{x}$. In the first case, we apply the Krylov method to the matrix MA, and in the second case, we apply the Krylov method to the matrix AM, and each time the method requires a matrix-vector product, we carry out the two successive products.

However, whether we precondition to the left or to the right, and if the effect on convergence is identical, right preconditioning is usually better in practice. The reason is that the residual of the right preconditioned system is identical to the residual of the initial problem:

$$\|AM\tilde{x}_p - b\| = \|Ax_p - b\|$$

with $x_p = M\tilde{x}_p$. In contrast, the residual of the left preconditioned system does not satisfy the same property:

$$\|MAx_p - Mb\| = \|M(Ax_p - b)\| \neq \|Ax_p - b\|$$

The implementation of left preconditioning will, therefore, require the calculation of non-preconditioned gradients to control the convergence correctly.

In addition, some methods such as the ORTHODIR method will allow, in the case of right preconditioning, using variable preconditioners during the iterations. In fact, the construction method of a basis $(AM)^t(AM)$-orthogonal from vectors $\tilde{w}_i$ amounts to constructing an A^tA-orthogonal basis from vectors w_i, with $w_i = M\tilde{w}_i$. The procedure works the same way when the preconditioner is variable, i.e. if it is applied to vectors $w_i = M_i\tilde{w}_i$.

Through the conservation of vectors $v_i = M_i\tilde{v}_i$, the GMRES method can also be extended to the case of variable right preconditioning. The preconditioner is variable when using an iterative method to calculate a solution of an approximate system, simplified, as a preconditioning. In such a situation, given that the solved system is only an approximation of the exact system, it is clearly not useful to force a very tight convergence. As a result, the operator applied by such a preconditioning varies according to the right-hand side, and all the more so when the stopping criterion is large.

13

Biorthogonalization Methods for Non-symmetric Matrices

For non-symmetric matrices, there are different methods with exact orthogonalization that exhibit short recursions. This chapter focuses on the construction of the Lanczos biorthogonal basis and the induced non-symmetric Lanczos method. The biconjugate BiCG gradient method, which allows finding a short recursion, is constructed from the non-symmetric Lanczos method, with an approach similar to that of which helped find the conjugate gradient, starting from the Lanczos method. Both of the more conventional stabilization methods of BiCG and quasi-minimal residual (QMR) are then presented, as is the BiCGStab method.

13.1. Lanczos biorthogonal basis for non-symmetric matrices

In the case where matrix A is non-symmetric, how can we find a correlation matrix between AV_p and V_{p+1} that is tridiagonal, as is the case for the symmetric Lanczos method, so as to find methods with short recursion? If V_p were an orthonormal basis of the Krylov subspace that satisfied such a property, we would then have:

$$V_p^t A V_p = T_p$$

where T_p is a tridiagonal matrix, but also, by transposition:

$$V_p^t A^t V_p = T_p^t \qquad\qquad [13.1]$$

Equation [13.1] implies that the correlation matrix between $A^t V_p$ and V_{p+1} would also be tridiagonal. This is certainly not feasible in practice, since the relations of orthogonality of the vectors, and the constraint of the short correlation between AV_p and V_{p+1} already allows for defining V_p. If matrix A is non-symmetric, there is no reason for the correlation between $A^t V_p$ and V_{p+1} to also be short, which leads to an impossibility. There are too many constraints.

To satisfy all the constraints, we need not just one, but two families of vectors: V_p and $\widetilde{V}_p$, which, on the one hand, satisfy a biorthogonal relationship:

$$\widetilde{V}_p^t V_p = I_p \qquad\qquad [13.2]$$

and, on the other hand, relations and correlations between AV_p and V_{p+1} and $A^t\widetilde{V}_p$ and $\widetilde{V}_{p+1}$ such that:

$$\begin{aligned}\widetilde{V}_p^t A V_p &= T_p \\ V_p^t A^t \widetilde{V}_p &= T_p^t\end{aligned} \qquad\qquad [13.3]$$

These relationships will be completed by requiring vectors V_p to be normed.

The construction of these biorthogonal bases will, therefore, start as follows:

$$\begin{aligned}g_0 &= A x_0 - b \\ v_1 &= \frac{1}{\|g_0\|} g_0 \\ \widetilde{v}_1 &= \frac{1}{g_0 \cdot v_1} g_0\end{aligned}$$

With this construction, we have $\|v_1\| = 1$ and $\widetilde{v}_1 \cdot v_1 = 1$. Thus, to satisfy the relations of correlations [13.3], we must define v_2 and $\widetilde{v}_2$ so that the following relations are satisfied:

$$Av_1 = \alpha_1 v_1 + \beta_1 v_2$$
$$A^t \tilde{v}_1 = \tilde{\alpha}_1 \tilde{v}_1 + \tilde{\beta}_1 \tilde{v}_2$$
$$\tilde{v}_1 \cdot v_2 = 0$$
$$\tilde{v}_2 \cdot v_1 = 0 \qquad\qquad [13.4]$$
$$\|v_2\| = 1$$
$$\tilde{v}_2 \cdot v_2 = 1$$

From these relations [13.4], it becomes clear that:

$$\tilde{v}_1 \cdot Av_1 = \alpha_1 = A^t \tilde{v}_1 \cdot v_1 = \tilde{\alpha}_1$$

The condition $\|v_2\| = 1$ will determine β_1, while $\tilde{\beta}_1$, which we will denote from now on as γ_1, will be given by the relation $\tilde{v}_2 \cdot v_2 = 1$. Thus, the first iteration of the algorithm for constructing the Lanczos biorthogonal non-symmetric basis will be written:

$$w = Av_1$$
$$\alpha_1 = \tilde{v}_1 \cdot Av_1$$
$$w = w - \alpha_1 v_1$$
$$\beta_1 = \|w\|$$
$$v_2 = \frac{1}{\beta_1} w$$
$$\tilde{w} = A^t \tilde{v}_1$$
$$\tilde{w} = \tilde{w} - \alpha_1 \tilde{v}_1$$
$$\gamma_1 = \tilde{w} \cdot v_2$$
$$\tilde{v}_2 = \frac{1}{\gamma_1} \tilde{w}$$

We can clearly see, when writing this algorithm, the impossibility of the families of vectors V_p and $\tilde{V}_p$ being identical. There is no reason, unless matrix A is symmetric, that the vectors w and $\tilde{w}$ constructed above, are collinear.

Matrix T_p defined by equation [13.3] will, therefore, have the following form:

$$
T_p = \begin{pmatrix}
\alpha_1 & \gamma_1 & 0 & \cdots & \cdots & & 0 \\
\beta_1 & \alpha_2 & \gamma_2 & \ddots & & & \vdots \\
0 & \beta_2 & \ddots & \ddots & \ddots & & \vdots \\
\vdots & \ddots & \ddots & \ddots & \ddots & & 0 \\
\vdots & & \ddots & \ddots & \ddots & & \gamma_{p-1} \\
0 & \cdots & \cdots & 0 & \beta_{p-1} & & \alpha_p
\end{pmatrix}
$$

Similarly, in iteration p, we will construct the vectors v_{p+1} and $\widetilde{v}_{p+1}$ in such a way as to satisfy the relations:

$$Av_p = \gamma_{p-1}v_{p-1} + \alpha_p v_p + \beta_p v_{p+1}$$

$$A^t\widetilde{v}_p = \beta_{p-1}\widetilde{v}_{p-1} + \alpha_p\widetilde{v}_p + \gamma_p\widetilde{v}_{p+1}$$

$$\widetilde{v}_p \cdot v_{p+1} = 0$$

$$\widetilde{v}_{p+1} \cdot v_p = 0$$

$$\|v_{p+1}\| = 1$$

$$\widetilde{v}_{p+1} \cdot v_{p+1} = 1$$

such that the p iteration of the algorithm for constructing the Lanczos biorthogonal non-symmetric basis will be written:

$$w = Av_p$$
$$\alpha_p = \widetilde{v}_p \cdot Av_p$$
$$w = w - \gamma_{p-1}v_{p-1} - \alpha_p v_p \quad (\Rightarrow w \cdot \widetilde{v}_p = 0)$$
$$\beta_p = \|w\|$$
$$v_{p+1} = \frac{1}{\beta_p}w$$
$$\widetilde{w} = A^t\widetilde{v}_p$$
$$\widetilde{w} = \widetilde{w} - \beta_{p-1}\widetilde{v}_{p-1} - \alpha_p\widetilde{v}_p \quad (\Rightarrow \widetilde{w} \cdot v_p = 0)$$
$$\gamma_p = \widetilde{w} \cdot v_{p+1}$$
$$\widetilde{v}_{p+1} = \frac{1}{\gamma_p}\widetilde{w}$$

Suppose that V_p and V_p are rectangular matrices with n rows and p columns, whose columns are the first p vectors (v_j) and $(\widetilde{v}\|j)$; then, the properties of the two bases, thus constructed, are given in the following theorem.

THEOREM 13.1.– The two families of vectors v_j and $\widetilde{v}_j$ are biorthonormal:

$$\widetilde{V}_p^t V_p = I_p$$

and satisfy the property:

$$\widetilde{V}_p^t A V_p = T_p$$

Moreover, the vectors v_j are normed.

PROOF 13.1.– Vectors v_j are normed by construction. In addition, the successive vectors satisfy the recursive relations:

$$\begin{aligned} A v_p &= \gamma_{p-1} v_{p-1} + \alpha_p v_p + \beta_p v_{p+1} \\ A^t \widetilde{v}_p &= \beta_{p-1} \widetilde{v}_{p-1} + \alpha_p \widetilde{v}_p + \gamma_p \widetilde{v}_{p+1} \end{aligned} \qquad [13.5]$$

which implies that to demonstrate the theorem it suffices to prove that the biorthogonality relations [13.2] are satisfied. However, the coefficients α_p, β_p and γ_p are precisely chosen so that:

$$\begin{aligned} \|v_{p+1}\| &= 1 \\ \widetilde{v}_p \cdot v_{p+1} &= 0 \\ \widetilde{v}_{p+1} \cdot v_p &= 0 \\ \widetilde{v}_{p+1} \cdot v_{p+1} &= 1 \end{aligned}$$

It is, therefore, sufficient to prove by recursion on p that $(\widetilde{v}_j . v_{p+1}) = (v_j . \widetilde{v}_{p+1}) = 0$, if $j < p$. However, because of the recursive relations shown in equation [13.5], and by the recursive hypothesis on the biorthogonality of the vectors, we have the following equations:

$$\begin{aligned} \widetilde{v}_j \cdot \beta_p v_{p+1} &= (\widetilde{v}_j \cdot A v_p) - (\widetilde{v}_j \cdot \gamma_{p-1} v_{p-1}) - (\widetilde{v}_j \cdot \alpha_p v_p) \\ &= (A^t \widetilde{v}_j \cdot v_p) - (\widetilde{v}_j \cdot \gamma_{p-1} v_{p-1}) \\ &= (\beta_{j-1} \widetilde{v}_{j-1} + \alpha_j \widetilde{v}_j + \gamma_j \widetilde{v}_{j+1} \cdot v_p) - (\widetilde{v}_j \cdot \gamma_{p-1} v_{p-1}) \\ &= \gamma_j (\widetilde{v}_{j+1} \cdot v_p) - \gamma_{p-1} (\widetilde{v}_j \cdot v_{p-1}) \end{aligned}$$

Suppose that $j < p - 1$, then the two remaining scalar products are null, and if we let $j = p - 1$, then the last line is written as:

$$\gamma_{p-1}(\tilde{v}_p \cdot v_p) - \gamma_{p-1}(\tilde{v}_{p-1} \cdot v_{p-1}) = \gamma_{p-1} - \gamma_{p-1} = 0$$

In the same way:

$$
\begin{aligned}
v_j \cdot \gamma_p \tilde{v}_{p+1} &= (v_j . A^t \tilde{v}_p) - (v_j \cdot \beta_{p-1} \tilde{v}_{p-1}) - (v_j \cdot \alpha_p \tilde{v}_p) \\
&= (A v_j \cdot \tilde{v}_p) - (v_j \cdot \beta_{p-1} \tilde{v}_{p-1}) \\
&= (\gamma_{j-1} v_{j-1} + \alpha_j v_j + \beta_j v_{j+1} \cdot \tilde{v}_p) - (v_j \cdot \gamma_{p-1} \tilde{v}_{p-1}) \\
&= \beta_j (v_{j+1} \cdot \tilde{v}_p) - \beta_{p-1}(v_j \cdot \tilde{v}_{p-1})
\end{aligned}
$$

Suppose that $j < p - 1$, then the two remaining scalar products are null, and if we let $j = p - 1$, then the last line is written as:

$$\beta_{p-1}(v_p \cdot \tilde{v}_p) - \beta_{p-1}(v_{p-1} \cdot \tilde{v}_{p-1}) = \beta_{p-1} - \beta_{p-1} = 0$$

This completes the proof. $\square$

NOTE 13.1.– The algorithm for constructing the non-symmetric Lanczos biorthogonal basis can fail, if vector $A v_p - \gamma_{p-1} v_{p-1} - \alpha_p v_p$ is null, or if the coefficient β_p is 0. Similarly, if vector $A^t \tilde{v}_p - \beta_{p-1} \tilde{v}_{p-1} - \alpha_p \tilde{v}_p$ is null, or if the β_p coefficient is 0. This can happen, for example, if the Krylov subspace:

$$\tilde{\mathcal{K}}_p = \text{Vect}\{g_0, A^t g_0, (A^t)^2 g_0, \ldots, (A^t)^{p-1} g_0\}$$

has reached its maximum dimension, while this is not the case for the Krylov subspace $\mathcal{K}_p = \text{Vect}\{g_0, A g_0, A^2 g_0, \ldots, A^{p-1} g_0\}$. There are other techniques at our disposal to continue the iterations in these cases.

13.2. The non-symmetric Lanczos method

The non-symmetric Lanczos method consists of searching for the approximate solution in the affine space $x_0 + \mathcal{K}_p$. Since V_p is a basis of $\mathcal{K}_p$, x_p is written as follows, where z_p is a p-dimensional vector:

$$x_p = x_0 + V_p z_p$$

The associated gradient is given by the formula:

$$g_p = Ax_p - b = g_0 + AV_p z_p$$

V_p alone does not define an orthonormal basis of $\mathcal{K}_p$. The coefficients of z_p will be determined by a biorthogonal relation:

$$\tilde{V}_p^t g_p = 0 \Leftrightarrow \tilde{V}_p^t AV_p z_p = -\tilde{V}_p^t g_0$$

The z_p coefficients are, therefore, the solution of the tridiagonal system:

$$T_p z_p = -\tilde{V}_p^t g_0$$

a system whose resolution is easy, by performing the Gauss factorization of the tridiagonal T_p matrix.

However, this method, as with the symmetric Lanczos method, has the drawback that the successive approximate solutions are not, contrary to biorthogonal basis vectors, constructed using a short recursion. This necessitates retaining all the v_j vectors, which makes the method costly in terms of computation and storage. As with the symmetric Lanczos method, we will, therefore, try to find new bases for calculating the successive approximate solutions by a short recursion.

13.3. The biconjugate gradient method: BiCG

Of the two relations, which define the gradient of the solution obtained by the Lanczos method:

$$g_p = g_0 + AV_p z_p$$
$$\tilde{V}_p^t g_p = 0$$

we deduce that g_p is collinear to v_{p+1}. Therefore, we can replace the V_p basis vectors by the vectors $(g_0, g_1, \ldots, g_{p-1})$, which define a matrix denoted by G_p, while also retaining the biorthogonal properties and the tridiagonal nature of the correlation matrix between AG_p and G_{p+1}. In matrix form, these properties are written as:

$$\tilde{V}_p^t G_p = D_p$$

$$\tilde{V}_p^t A G_p = T_p$$

where D_p is a diagonal matrix and T_p is a tridiagonal matrix.

Similarly, we can replace the vectors of $\tilde{V}_p$ by the vectors $(\tilde{g}_0, \tilde{g}_1, \ldots, \tilde{g}_{p-1})$, which are collinear to them, while still retaining the biorthogonal properties and the tridiagonal nature of the correlation matrix between $A^t \tilde{G}_p$ and $\tilde{G}_p$. If we denote by D_p the diagonal correlation matrix between $\tilde{G}_p$ and $\tilde{V}_p$, we have:

$$\tilde{G}_p = \tilde{V}_p D_p$$

$$\tilde{G}_p^t A G_p = D_p \tilde{V}_p^t A G_p$$

If T_p and D_p are, respectively, tridiagonal and diagonal matrices, then their product is of the form:

$$D_p T_p = \begin{pmatrix} d_1 a_1 & d_1 c_1 & 0 & \cdots & \cdots & & 0 \\ d_2 b_1 & d_2 a_2 & d_2 c_2 & \ddots & & & \vdots \\ 0 & d_3 b_2 & \ddots & \ddots & \ddots & & \vdots \\ \vdots & \ddots & \ddots & \ddots & \ddots & & 0 \\ \vdots & & \ddots & \ddots & d_{p-1} b_{p-1} & d_{p-1} c_{p-1} \\ 0 & \cdots & \cdots & 0 & d_p b_{p-1} & d_p a_p \end{pmatrix}$$

Whatever the choice of d_1, and hence $\tilde{g}_0 = d_1 \tilde{v}_0$, we can choose the coefficients d_i in such a way that makes the matrix product symmetric. This can be done by having the coefficients d_i satisfy the recursive relation:

$$d_i b_{i-1} = d_{i-1} c_{i-1}$$

The two bases G_p and $\widetilde{G}_p$, thus determined, therefore, satisfy the relations:

$$\widetilde{G}_p^t G_p = D_p$$

$$\widetilde{G}_p^t A G_p = T_p$$

where D_p is a diagonal matrix and T_p is a tridiagonal symmetric matrix.

The G_p and $\widetilde{G}_p$ bases will be easier to calculate than V_p and $\widetilde{V}_p$, due to the symmetric property of the T_p matrix. This property means that vectors AG_p and G_{p+1}, on the one hand, and vectors $A^t\widetilde{G}_p$ and $\widetilde{G}_{p+1}$, on the other hand, are, respectively, connected together by short recursive relations with the same coefficients. Nonetheless, this property does not always give a short recursion for calculating the successive solutions of the Lanczos method. To do this, we must build two new bases W_p and $\widetilde{W}_p$, starting from G_p and $\widetilde{G}_p$, respectively, in such a way so that matrix $\widetilde{W}_p^t A W_p$ is diagonal. As in the conjugate gradient method, we will use the Crout factorization of matrix T_p:

$$\widetilde{G}_p^t A G_p = L_p D_p L_p^t \iff L_p^{-1}\widetilde{G}_p^t A G_p L_p^{-t} = D_p$$

If we define two new families of vectors $(w_0, w_1, \ldots, w_{p-1})$ giving matrix W_p, on the one hand, and $(\widetilde{w}_0, \widetilde{w}_1, \ldots, \widetilde{w}_{p-1})$ giving matrix $\widetilde{W}_p$, on the other hand, by beginning, respectively, from vectors G_p and $\widetilde{G}_p$, by the relations $W_p L_p^t = G_p$ and $\widetilde{W}_p L_p^t = \widetilde{G}_p$ we obtain:

$$\widetilde{W}_p^t A W_p = D_p \qquad\qquad [13.6]$$

The approximate solution vector in iteration p of the Lanczos method, expressed in the new W_p basis:

$$x_p = x_0 + W_p z_p$$

$$g_p = g_0 + A W_p z_p$$

and defined by the biorthogonal relation:

$$\widetilde{W}_p^t g_p = 0 \iff \widetilde{W}_p^t A W_p z_p = -\widetilde{W}_p^t g_0$$

is determined by solving the diagonal system:

$$D_p z_p = -\widetilde{W}_p^t g_0$$

We deduce that the two successive approximate solution vectors satisfy:

$$x_{p+1} = x_p + \rho_p w_p$$

The entire set of relations between the families of vectors G_p and $\widetilde{G}_p$, and W_p and $\widetilde{W}_p$ can be summarized by the following equations:

$$
\begin{aligned}
x_p &= x_{p-1} + \rho_{p-1} w_{p-1} \\
g_p &= g_{p-1} + \rho_{p-1} A w_{p-1} \\
\widetilde{g}_p &= \widetilde{g}_{p-1} + \rho_{p-1} A^t \widetilde{w}_{p-1} \\
w_p &= g_p + \gamma_{p-1} w_{p-1} \\
\widetilde{w}_p &= \widetilde{g}_p + \gamma_{p-1} \widetilde{w}_{p-1}
\end{aligned}
\qquad [13.7]
$$

It is the symmetry of matrix T_p and the fact that T_p is an upper bidiagonal unitary matrix, which allows us to assert that vectors G_p, AG_p and W_p, on the one hand, and $\widetilde{G}_p$, $A^t\widetilde{G}_p$ and $\widetilde{W}_p$, on the other hand, are linked by short recursive relations written in equation [13.7]. It now suffices to define the method, using the biorthogonal relations of vectors G_p and $\widetilde{G}_p$, on the one hand, and W_p and $\widetilde{W}_p$, on the other hand, satisfying between themselves so as to define the two coefficients ρ_p and γ_p. Indeed, by construction, G_p and $\widetilde{G}_p$ form two biorthogonal bases of $\mathcal{K}_p$ and $\widetilde{\mathcal{K}}_p$, while W_p and $\widetilde{W}_p$ form two biconjugate bases, according to equation [13.6]. We deduce:

$$g_p \cdot \widetilde{w}_{p-1} = 0 \Leftrightarrow \rho_{p-1} = -\frac{g_{p-1} \cdot \widetilde{w}_{p-1}}{A w_{p-1} \cdot \widetilde{w}_{p-1}} \qquad [13.8]$$

$$w_p \cdot A^t \widetilde{w}_{p-1} = 0 \Leftrightarrow \gamma_{p-1} = -\frac{g_p \cdot A^t \widetilde{w}_{p-1}}{A w_{p-1} \cdot \widetilde{w}_{p-1}}$$

Equations [13.7] and [13.9] completely define the new algorithm, called the biconjugate gradient method, whose acronym is BiCG.

– Initialization of the biconjugate gradient:

$g_0 = Ax_0 - b$

$w_0 = g_0$

$\widetilde{g}_0 = g_0$

$\widetilde{w}_0 = \widetilde{g}_0$

– Iteration p of the biconjugate gradient:

$v = Aw_{p-1}$

$\widetilde{v} = A^t\widetilde{w}_{p-1}$

$\rho_{p-1} = -(g_{p-1} \cdot \widetilde{w}_{p-1})/(v \cdot \widetilde{w}_{p-1})$

$x_p = x_{p-1} + \rho_{p-1}w_{p-1}$

$g_p = g_{p-1} + \rho_{p-1}v$

$\widetilde{g}_p = \widetilde{g}_{p-1} + \rho_{p-1}\widetilde{v}$

if $(g_p \cdot g_p)/(b.b) < \epsilon^2$ **then**

 End

end if

$\gamma_{p-1} = -(g_p \cdot \widetilde{v})/(v \cdot \widetilde{w}_{p-1})$

$w_p = g_p + \gamma_{p-1}w_{p-1}$

$\widetilde{w}_p = \widetilde{g}_p + \gamma_{p-1}\widetilde{w}_{p-1}$

In each iteration, it suffices to calculate two matrix-vector products, $v = Aw_{p-1}$ and $\widetilde{v} = A^t\widetilde{w}_{p-1}$; four scalar products, $(g_{p-1} \cdot \widetilde{w}_{p-1})$, $(v \cdot \widetilde{w}_{p-1})$, $(g_p \cdot g_p)$ and $(g_p \cdot \widetilde{v})$; and five linear vector combinations, $x_p = x_{p-1} + \rho_{p-1}w_{p-1}$, $g_p = g_{p-1} + \rho_{p-1}v$, $\widetilde{g}_p = \widetilde{g}_{p-1} + \rho_{p-1}\widetilde{v}$, $w_p = g_p + \gamma_{p-1}w_{p-1}$ and $\widetilde{w}_p = \widetilde{g}_p + \gamma_{p-1}\widetilde{w}_{p-1}$.

NOTE 13.2.– The biconjugate gradient algorithm is the proper way to implement the biconjugate Lanczos method. However, as with the last method, it may fail because of a blockage of the procedure for the biorthogonal construction of the bases $\mathcal{K}_p$ and $\widetilde{\mathcal{K}}_p$, or because matrix T_p is not invertible. There are continuation methods for these situations.

13.4. The quasi-minimal residual method: QMR

One of the drawbacks of the BiCG method is that the approximate solution, calculated in iteration p, does not minimize a certain norm of the residual vector g_p, unless the matrix is symmetric positive definite, in which case, we precisely again find the conjugate gradient method. The biorthogonal relation that defines the approximate solution can even lead to strong oscillations of $\|g_p\|$, which are potentially destabilizing for the method. Moreover, as noted in the remark at the end of the preceding section, the method can fail if matrix T_p is not invertible.

Returning to the construction of the non-symmetric Lanczos basis, we have:

$$AV_p = V_{p+1}T_{p+1p}$$

the rectangular matrix with $p+1$ rows and p columns, with T_{p+1p} being equal to:

$$T_{p+1p} = \begin{pmatrix} \alpha_1 & \gamma_1 & 0 & \cdots & \cdots & 0 \\ \beta_1 & \alpha_2 & \gamma_2 & \ddots & & \vdots \\ 0 & \beta_2 & \ddots & \ddots & \ddots & \vdots \\ \vdots & \ddots & \ddots & \ddots & \ddots & 0 \\ \vdots & & \ddots & \ddots & \ddots & \gamma_{p-1} \\ 0 & \cdots & \cdots & 0 & \beta_{p-1} & \alpha_p \\ 0 & \cdots & \cdots & \cdots & 0 & \beta_p \end{pmatrix}$$

The approximate solution, in the form of $x_p = x_0 + V_p z_p$, gives a residual vector of the form:

$$g_p = Ax_p - b = g_0 + V_{p+1}T_{p+1p}z_p = V_{p+1}(\|g_0\|e_{p+1}^1 + T_{p+1p}z_p) \qquad [13.9]$$

where e_{p+1}^1 is the first canonical basis vector of dimension $p+1$.

The vectors of V_{p+1} do not form an orthonormal basis, but they nonetheless have their norms equal to 1. Hence, the idea of defining z_p as the vector that minimizes the quantity:

$$r(z_p) = \| \, \|g_0\|e_{p+1}^1 + T_{p+1p}z_p\|^2 \qquad [13.10]$$

Can we estimate the exact value of the residual norm obtained by this method based on that of the optimal residual in $x_0 + \mathcal{K}_p$, g_p^{opt} that would be obtained if, for example, we were to apply the GMRES method? Let us consider a rectangular matrix V, and the $y = Vx$ vector.

$$y \cdot y = Vx \cdot Vx = V^t Vx \cdot x \qquad [13.11]$$

Matrix $V^t V$ is symmetric positive. Therefore, it admits an orthonormal basis of eigenvectors and its eigenvalues are all positive. The square roots of its eigenvalues are called the singular values of V. They are identical to the V eigenvalues, if these are square and symmetric positive. If the columns of V form a family of orthonormal vectors, $V^t V = I$, and all the singular values of V are equal to 1. From equation [13.11], we can deduce the following bounds:

$$\sigma_{min} \|x\| \leq \|y\| \leq \sigma_{max} \|x\|$$

where σ_{min} and σ_{max} are, respectively, the smallest and largest singular value of V. The ratio $\kappa(V) = \frac{\sigma_{max}}{\sigma_{min}}$ is the conditioning of V. Suppose that g_p is the residual vector obtained for z_p, minimizing the quantity $r(z_p)$, defined in equation [13.10].

THEOREM 13.2.– $\|g_p\| \leq \sqrt{p+1}\ \sqrt{r(z_p)}$ and $\|g_p\| \leq \kappa(V_{p+1}) \|g_p^{opt}\|$.

PROOF 13.2.– From equation [13.9], $\|g_p\| \leq \sigma_{max}\sqrt{r(z_p)}$, with σ_{max} being the maximum singular value of V_{p+1}. As the vectors of V_{p+1} are of a norm equal to 1, all diagonal coefficients of matrix $V_{p+1}^t V_{p+1}$ are equal to 1, and the trace of this matrix is equal to $p+1$. Therefore, its maximum eigenvalue is less than $p+1$, where $\sigma_{max} \leq \sqrt{p+1}$.

Thus, necessarily, the optimal residual vector can be written as:

$$g_p^{opt} = V_{p+1}(\|g_0\|e_{p+1}^1 + T_{p+1p}z_p')$$

We can, therefore, minimize $\|g_p^{opt}\|$ in the following manner:

$$\|g_p^{opt}\| \geq \sigma_{min}\|\ \|g_0\|e_{p+1}^1 + H_{p+1p}z_p'\| \geq \sigma_{min}\sqrt{r(z_p)}$$

Combined with the inequality of $\|g_p\| \leq \sigma_{max}\sqrt{r(z_p)}$, this equation makes it possible to complete the proof. $\qquad\qquad\square$

This theorem justifies the idea that minimizing $r(z_p)$ is reasonable so as to control g_p. However, the conditioning of V_{p+1} cannot be increased, because σ_{min} can be very small.

The method that we just introduced is called the quasi-minimal residual method, or QMR. Its implementation will be very similar to that of the MINRES method. In particular, the problem posed by the least squares minimization of $r(z_p)$ is solved by the QR method using Givens rotations. Moreover, because of the characteristics of the non-symmetric Lanczos method, matrix T_{p+1p} is tridiagonal, even if matrix A is non-symmetric. Since Givens rotations only operate on two successive rows, we can easily see that the upper triangular matrix R_p of the QR factorization of T_{p+1p} is of the form:

$$
R_p =
\begin{pmatrix}
r_{11} & r_{12} & 0 & \cdots & \cdots & \cdots & 0 \\
0 & \ddots & \ddots & \ddots & & & \vdots \\
\vdots & & \ddots & \ddots & \ddots & \ddots & \vdots \\
\vdots & & \ddots & \ddots & \ddots & \ddots & 0 \\
\vdots & & & \ddots & r_{p-2p-2} & r_{p-2p-1} & r_{p-2p} \\
\vdots & & & & \ddots & r_{p-1p-1} & r_{p-1p} \\
0 & \cdots & \cdots & \cdots & \cdots & 0 & r_{pp}
\end{pmatrix}
$$

As in the case of the MINRES method, this property will allow recovery of the approximate solution with the help of a short recursion. In fact, solving the problem of minimization of $r(z_p)$ is given by:

$$
R_p z_p = \tilde{y}_p \tag{13.12}
$$

where $\tilde{y}_p$ is the vector of the first p-components of the vector $-\|g_0\|Q_{p+1}e^1_{p+1}$, Q_{p+1} being the orthogonal matrix, the product of Givens rotations, such that:

$$Q_{p+1}T_{p+1p} = \begin{pmatrix} R_p \\ (0\cdots0) \end{pmatrix}$$

The final component of this vector, r_{p+1}, gives the minimum value of $r(z_p)$. Specifically, if z_p is the solution of system [13.12], then:

$$r_{p+1} = \pm\sqrt{r(z_p)}$$

The approximate solution defined by z_p is, therefore, written as:

$$x_p = x_0 + V_p R_p^{-1}\tilde{y}_p = x_0 + W_p\tilde{y}_p$$

The column vectors of $W_p = V_p R_p^{-1}$ define a new basis of the $\mathcal{K}_p$ Krylov subspace.

The first $p - 1$ components of vector $-\|g_0\|Q_{p+1}e^1_{p+1}$ are identical to those of vector $-\|g_0\|Q_p e^1_p$. The last two components are calculated simply by applying the Givens rotation angle θ_p to the rows p and $p + 1$:

$$\begin{pmatrix} \tilde{y}_p(p) \\ r_{p+1} \end{pmatrix} = \begin{pmatrix} c_p & -s_p \\ s_p & c_p \end{pmatrix}\begin{pmatrix} r_p \\ 0 \end{pmatrix}$$

This means that the successive approximate solutions are calculated in the new W_p basis, by a short recursion:

$$x_p = x_0 + W_p\tilde{y}_p = x_0 + W_{p-1}\tilde{y}_{p-1} + \tilde{y}_p(p)w_p = x_{p-1} + \tilde{y}_p(p)w_p$$

The $W_p R_p = V_p$ relation indicates how the vectors of the new basis are calculated from those of the Lanczos basis. The upper triangular structure, with three non-zero diagonals of matrix R_p, implies that this is also a short recursion relation:

$$v_p = r_{p-2p}w_{p-2} + r_{p-1p}w_{p-1} + r_{pp}w_p$$
$$\Leftrightarrow$$
$$w_p = \frac{1}{r_{pp}}(v_p - r_{p-2p}w_{p-2} - r_{p-1p}w_{p-1})$$

As with the MINRES method, column p of T_{p+1p} has only two non-zero terms, located in rows p and $p+1$. Thus, only the last two Givens rotations are necessary.

Finally, the QMR algorithm is written in the following manner:

– Initialization of QMR:

$$g_0 = Ax_0 - b$$
$$r_1 = -\|g_0\|$$
$$v_1 = \frac{1}{\|g_0\|} g_0$$
$$\tilde{v}_1 = \frac{1}{g_0 \cdot v_1} g_0$$

– Construction of vectors $p+1$ of the non-symmetric biconjugate Lanczos basis:

$$w = Av_p$$
$$w = w - \gamma_{p-1} v_{p-1}$$
$$\alpha_p = \tilde{v}_p \cdot w$$
$$w = w - \alpha_p v_p$$
$$\beta_p = \|w\|$$
$$v_{p+1} = \frac{1}{\beta_p} w$$
$$\tilde{w} = A^t \tilde{v}_p$$
$$\tilde{w} = \tilde{w} - \beta_{p-1} \tilde{v}_{p-1} - \alpha_p \tilde{v}_p$$
$$\gamma_p = \tilde{w} \cdot v_{p+1}$$
$$\tilde{v}_{p+1} = \frac{1}{\gamma_p} \tilde{w}$$

– Application of the last two Givens rotations to column p of T_{p+1p}:

$$\begin{pmatrix} r_{p-2p} \\ \delta_1 \end{pmatrix} = \begin{pmatrix} c_{p-2} & -s_{p-2} \\ s_{p-2} & c_{p-2} \end{pmatrix} \begin{pmatrix} 0 \\ \gamma_{p-1} \end{pmatrix}$$
$$\begin{pmatrix} r_{p-1p} \\ \delta_2 \end{pmatrix} = \begin{pmatrix} c_{p-1} & -s_{p-1} \\ s_{p-1} & c_{p-1} \end{pmatrix} \begin{pmatrix} \delta_1 \\ \alpha_p \end{pmatrix}$$

– Calculation of the new Givens rotation, and updating column p of R, and the y vector:

$$c_p = \sqrt{\frac{1}{1+(\frac{\beta_p}{\delta_2})^2}}$$
$$s_p = -c_p \frac{\beta_p}{\delta_2}$$

$$\begin{pmatrix} r_{pp} \\ 0 \end{pmatrix} = \begin{pmatrix} c_p & -s_p \\ s_p & c_p \end{pmatrix} \begin{pmatrix} \delta_2 \\ \beta_p \end{pmatrix}$$

$$\begin{pmatrix} \rho_p \\ r_{p+1} \end{pmatrix} = \begin{pmatrix} c_p & -s_p \\ s_p & c_p \end{pmatrix} \begin{pmatrix} r_p \\ 0 \end{pmatrix}$$

– Calculation of the new w_p vector and the approximate solution:

$$w_p = \frac{1}{r_{pp}}(v_p - r_{p-2p}w_{p-2} - r_{p-1p}w_{p-1})$$

$$x_p = x_{p-1} + \rho_p w_p$$

NOTE 13.3.– The QMR method has the double advantage of stabilizing BiCG, while maintaining a short recursion, and it does not fail when matrix T_p is singular. This is because the resolution of the problem of minimization of $r(z_p)$ by the Givens rotation method does not require matrix T_{p+1p} to be of rank p.

13.5. The BiCGSTAB

There is another classic way of stabilizing the BiCG method that consists of interspersing an exact minimization step, as in the GMRES or ORTHODIR algorithms, between two iterations of BiCG. Since all these methods consist of determining the residual vectors as optimal polynomials of A applied to g_0, the calculations can be commuted, and with some algebraic transformations, the BiCGSTAB method can actually be written as a simple recursion, alternating minimization and biorthogonalization.

To be specific, in the BiCG method, the gradient vectors and forward substitutions, respectively, form the biorthogonal and biconjugate bases of the $\mathcal{K}_p$ and $\tilde{\mathcal{K}}_p$ Krylov subspaces. By construction, they can be written as:

$$g_p = \phi_p(A)g_0 \quad w_p = \theta_p(A)g_0$$

[13.13]

$$\tilde{g}_p = \phi_p(A^t)\tilde{g}_0 \quad \tilde{w}_p = \theta_p(A^t)\tilde{g}_0$$

where ϕ_p and θ_p are the polynomials of degree p.

Equation [13.7], which defines the BiCG method, leads to the following recursive relations between the polynomial families of ϕ and θ:

$$\phi_0(A) = I$$
$$\phi_p(A) = \phi_{p-1}(A) + \rho_{p-1} A \theta_{p-1}(A)$$

$$\theta_0(A) = I$$
$$\theta_p(A) = \phi_p(A) + \gamma_{p-1}\theta_{p-1}(A)$$

[13.14]

Furthermore, a first iteration of an exact minimization algorithm, such as GMRES and ORTHODIR, consists of calculating an approximation of the solution from a descent direction collinear to the initial residual, so that the new residual is minimal:

$$x_1 = x_0 + \omega g_0$$

By linearity, we deduce a relationship among the successive gradient vectors:

$$g_1 = g_0 + \omega A g_0 = (I + \omega A)g_0$$

with ω being calculated so that $\|g_1\|$ is minimal.

Alternating exact minimization and biconjugation will, therefore, consist of determining a new family of φ polynomials, which satisfy a recursive relation:

$$\varphi_0(A) = I$$
$$\varphi_p(A) = (I + \omega_{p-1}A)\varphi_{p-1}(A)$$

[13.15]

In each iteration, the coefficient ω will be calculated in a way so as to minimize the residual of the method, which finally consists of determining two new families of gradient vectors and modified descent directions:

$$r_p = \varphi_p(A)\phi_p(A)g_0 \quad d_p = \varphi_p(A)\theta_p(A)g_0$$

[13.16]

The regrouping of the polynomial terms derived from minimizations and alternate biorthogonalizations in formulas [13.16] is possible in that the matrices, written as polynomials of A, commute between themselves.

The same argument of commutation allows writing recursive formulas that connect vectors r and p with each other, using equations [13.14] and [13.15]:

$$r_p = \varphi_p(A)\phi_p(A)g_0$$
$$= (I + \omega_{p-1}A)\varphi_{p-1}(A)(\phi_{p-1}(A) + \rho_{p-1}A\theta_{p-1}(A))g_0$$
$$= (I + \omega_{p-1}A)(\varphi_{p-1}(A)\phi_{p-1}(A)g_0 + \rho_{p-1}A\varphi_{p-1}(A)\theta_{p-1}(A))g_0$$
$$= (I + \omega_{p-1}A)(r_{p-1} + \rho_{p-1}Ad_{p-1})$$
$$= r_{p-1} + A(\rho_{p-1}d_{p-1} + \omega_{p-1}(r_{p-1} + \rho_{p-1}Ad_{p-1}))$$
$$d_p = \varphi_p(A)\theta_p(A)g_0$$
$$= \varphi_p(A)(\phi_p(A) + \gamma_{p-1}\theta_{p-1}(A))g_0$$
$$= \varphi_p(A)\phi_p(A)g_0 + \gamma_{p-1}\phi_p(A)\theta_{p-1}(A)g_0$$
$$= \varphi_p(A)\phi_p(A)g_0 + \gamma_{p-1}(I + \omega_{p-1}A)\varphi_{p-1}(A)\theta_{p-1}(A)g_0$$
$$= r_p + \gamma_{p-1}(I + \omega_{p-1}A)d_{p-1}$$

Finally, by introducing vectors $q_p = r_p + \rho_p Ad_p$, the gradient vectors obtained by the BiCG method alone, these recursive relations are written as:

$$r_p = r_{p-1} + A(\rho_{p-1}d_{p-1} + \omega_{p-1}q_{p-1}) \qquad [13.17]$$
$$d_p = r_p + \gamma_{p-1}(d_{p-1} + \omega_{p-1}Ad_{p-1}) \qquad [13.18]$$

Given the definition of the modified r_p gradient in the above equation, the approximate solution vector calculated in iteration p satisfies the recursive relation:

$$x_p = x_{p-1} + \rho_{p-1}d_{p-1} + \omega_{p-1}q_{p-1}$$

Now, it remains for us to determine the three coefficients ω_{p-1}, ρ_{p-1} and γ_{p-1}.

Regarding the ω_{p-1} coefficient, its value must minimize the $\|r_p\|$ residual. Now, equation [13.17] gives:

$$r_p = q_{p-1} + \omega_{p-1} A q_{p-1}$$

and therefore:

$$\|r_p\|^2 = \|q_{p-1}\|^2 + 2\omega_{p-1}(A q_{p-1} \cdot q_{p-1}) + \omega_{p-1}^2 \|A q_{p-1}\|^2$$

The function $f(\omega) = \|q_{p-1}\|^2 + 2\omega(A q_{p-1} \cdot q_{p-1}) + \omega^2 \|A q_{p-1}\|^2$ is a convex function. Its minimum is reached at the point where its derivative cancels itself out. Thus, we can immediately deduce the formula defining ω_{p-1}:

$$\omega_{p-1} = -\frac{A q_{p-1} \cdot q_{p-1}}{\|A q_{p-1}\|^2}$$

This formula is that of a minimization starting from q_{p-1} in the direction q_{p-1}, for the scalar product associated with $A^t A$.

The coefficients, ρ_{p-1} and γ_{p-1}, are in turn, determined by the properties of orthogonality of the BiCG method. These properties are such that the gradients form a biorthogonal family, while the descent directions form a biconjugate family. With the polynomial notations introduced in equation [13.13], these properties are written, for all pairs of the indices $(i, j), i \neq j$:

$$g_i \cdot \tilde{g}_j = \phi_i(A) g_0 \cdot \phi_j(A^t)\tilde{g}_0 = \phi_j(A)\phi_i(A) g_0 \cdot \tilde{g}_0 = 0$$
$$A w_i \cdot \tilde{w}_j = A\theta_i(A) g_0 \cdot \theta_j(A^t)\tilde{g}_0 = A\theta_j(A)\theta_i(A) g_0 \cdot \tilde{g}_0 = 0$$

[13.19]

We deduce from the recursive formulas [13.14] that the ϕ_i and θ_i polynomials are exactly of degree i. Thus, these polynomials form a basis for all the polynomials. Equation [13.19] finally leads to the following orthogonality relations for each index $j \leq i - 1$:

$$A^j \phi_i(A) g_0 \cdot \tilde{g}_0 = 0$$
$$A^{j+1} \theta_i(A) g_0 \cdot \tilde{g}_0 = 0$$

Given the recursive formulas [13.14], the monomial of degree i of the ϕ_i and θ_i polynomials has the coefficient $\alpha_i = \prod_{j=0}^{i-1} \rho_j$. Similarly, the recursive formula [13.15] entails that the φ_i polynomial is of degree i, and that its monomial of degree i has the coefficient $\beta_i = \prod_{j=0}^{i-1} \omega_j$.

With these relations, we can resume the calculation of the ρ_{p-1} coefficient using the BiCG method [13.9], and by reformulating, with the aid of the polynomials ϕ and θ, the calculations of the various scalar products:

$$\begin{aligned}
g_{p-1} \cdot \widetilde{w}_{p-1} &= \phi_{p-1}(A)g_0 \cdot \theta_{p-1}(A^t)\widetilde{g}_0 \\
&= \theta_{p-1}(A)\phi_{p-1}(A)g_0 \cdot \widetilde{g}_0 \\
&= \alpha_{p-1}(A^{p-1}\phi_{p-1}(A)g_0 \cdot \widetilde{g}_0) \\
Aw_{p-1} \cdot \widetilde{w}_{p-1} &= A\theta_{p-1}(A)g_0 \cdot \theta_{p-1}(A^t)\widetilde{g}_0 \\
&= A\theta_{p-1}(A)\theta_{p-1}(A)g_0 \cdot \widetilde{g}_0 \\
&= \alpha_{p-1}(A^p\theta_{p-1}(A)g_0 \cdot \widetilde{g}_0)
\end{aligned} \qquad [13.20]$$

Using the modified vectors of the BiCGSTAB method, we can again find the values of the above scalar products:

$$\begin{aligned}
r_{p-1} \cdot \widetilde{g}_0 &= \varphi_{p-1}(A)\phi_{p-1}(A)g_0 \cdot \widetilde{g}_0 \\
&= \beta_{p-1}(A^{p-1}\phi_{p-1}(A)g_0 \cdot \widetilde{g}_0) \\
Ad_{p-1} \cdot \widetilde{g}_0 &= A\varphi_{p-1}(A)\theta_{p-1}(A)g_0 \cdot \widetilde{g}_0 \\
&= \beta_{p-1}(A^p\theta_{p-1}(A)g_0 \cdot \widetilde{g}_0)
\end{aligned} \qquad [13.21]$$

We immediately deduce, from formulas [13.20] and [13.21], the calculation of ρ_{p-1}, by using the modified vectors:

$$\rho_{p-1} = -\frac{g_{p-1} \cdot \widetilde{w}_{p-1}}{Aw_{p-1} \cdot \widetilde{w}_{p-1}} = -\frac{A^{p-1}\phi_{p-1}(A)g_0 \cdot \widetilde{g}_0}{A^p\theta_{p-1}(A)g_0 \cdot \widetilde{g}_0} = -\frac{r_{p-1} \cdot \widetilde{g}_0}{Ad_{p-1} \cdot \widetilde{g}_0}$$

It is, therefore, possible to calculate the ω_{p-1} and ρ_{p-1} coefficients by means of scalar products among the vectors modified by the BiCGSTAB method. This allows us to calculate the new modified r_p gradient, as well as the γ_{p-1} coefficient, by applying the same methodology that we used previously.

In the context of the BiCG method, we need to calculate the scalar product:

$$\begin{aligned}
g_p \cdot A^t\widetilde{w}_{p-1} &= A\phi_p(A)g_0 \cdot \theta_{p-1}(A^t)\widetilde{g}_0 \\
&= A\theta_{p-1}(A)\phi_p(A)g_0 \cdot \widetilde{g}_0 \\
&= \alpha_{p-1}A^p\phi_p(A)g_0 \cdot \widetilde{g}_0
\end{aligned} \qquad [13.22]$$

We will find this quantity, again by using the modified vectors of the BiCGSTAB method:

$$
\begin{aligned}
r_p \cdot \tilde{g}_0 &= \varphi_p(A)\phi_p(A)g_0 \cdot \tilde{g}_0 \\
&= \beta_p A^p \phi_p(A) g_0 \cdot \tilde{g}_0
\end{aligned}
\qquad [13.23]
$$

Formulas [13.22] and [13.23], added to formulas [13.20] and [13.21], give the calculation of γ_{p-1}, by using the modified vectors:

$$
\gamma_{p-1} = -\frac{g_p \cdot A^t \tilde{w}_{p-1}}{A w_{p-1} \cdot \tilde{w}_{p-1}} = -\frac{A^p \phi_p(A) g_0 \cdot \tilde{g}_0}{A^p \theta_{p-1}(A) g_0 \cdot \tilde{g}_0} = -\frac{1}{w_{p-1}} \frac{r_p \cdot \tilde{g}_0}{A d_{p-1} \cdot \tilde{g}_0}
$$

This ultimately leads to the BiCGSTAB algorithm:

– Initialization:
$$d_0 = g_0$$
$$\tilde{g}_0 = g_0$$
$$r_0 = g_0$$

– Iteration p:
$$\rho_{p-1} = -\frac{r_{p-1} \cdot \tilde{g}_0}{v \cdot \tilde{g}_0}$$
$$q_{p-1} = r_{p-1} + \rho_{p-1} v$$
$$w = A q_{p-1}$$
$$\omega_{p-1} = -\frac{w \cdot q_{p-1}}{\|w\|^2}$$
$$r_p = q_{p-1} + \omega_{p-1} w$$
$$x_p = x_{p-1} + \rho_{p-1} d_{p-1} + \omega_{p-1} q_{p-1}$$
$$\textbf{if } (r_p \cdot r_p)/(b \cdot b) < \epsilon^2 \textbf{ then}$$
$$\qquad End$$
$$\textbf{end if}$$
$$\gamma_{p-1} = -\frac{1}{\omega_{p-1}} \frac{r_p \cdot \tilde{g}_0}{v \cdot \tilde{g}_0}$$
$$d_p = r_p + \gamma_{p-1}(d_{p-1} + \omega_{p-1} v)$$

Note that this method does not require any product by A^t. However, it requires two products by matrix A per iteration. The computational cost per iteration is thus the same as for the BiCG method, while it is, *a priori*, faster and more stable, due to the additional step of exact minimization carried out in each iteration.

NOTE 13.4.– The formulations using polynomials can be used for all Krylov methods. They make it possible to prove the optimal convergence results. They also serve to define continuation strategies during a blockage of the methods, which arise from the non-symmetric Lanczos algorithm.

14

Parallelization of Krylov Methods

The Krylov methods require three types of operations: matrix-vector products, scalar products and linear vector combinations. To parallelize these operations, we must assign parts of the matrices and the vectors to different processes. Partitioning the set of equations is similar to dividing the vectors and the matrix by subsets of rows, which amounts to dividing the rows of the matrix into blocks.

Parallelization of linear combinations is trivial: each process calculates the subvectors assigned to it. For scalar products, each process calculates the contribution of its subvectors, where the assembly of the different contributions is a standard reduction operation.

We are left with the most important part: the matrix-vector product. This point is discussed in detail in this chapter, particularly in the context of substructuring methods for sparse matrices.

14.1. Parallelization of dense matrix-vector product

Partitioning the set of equations leads us to allocate to each process the block of rows that correspond to the parts of the vectors it processes. In Figure 14.1, these terms are shown in black. However, the process that will produce the matrix-vector product $y = Ax$ for this block of rows, *a priori*, only has the corresponding terms of vector x, also indicated in black. In order to achieve this product, the process needs all the x-vector terms. Therefore, it will need to recuperate the terms it lacks, which are indicated in dark gray in Figure 14.1.

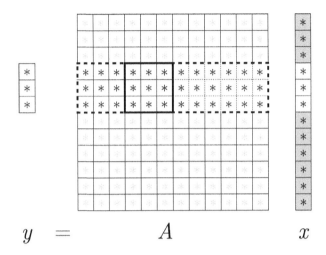

$$y \quad = \quad A \quad\quad\quad x$$

Figure 14.1. *Product by using a block of dense rows*

Since the same applies to all the processes, we will have to reconstruct the full vector x everywhere, by using the scattered data. This is a classic collective exchange process, in which each is both a sender and a receiver, and whose syntax is MPI:

– *MPI_Allgather (local_array, number_of_data_sent, type_of_data_sent, complete_array, number_of_data_received, type_of_data_received, comm).*

The parameters:

number_of_data_sent, and *type_of_data_sent,* and

number_of_data_received, type_of_data_received

respectively, describe the size of the local vector x in each process and its type, that is to say that the process sends, and the size and type of data are received by each process. The *complete_array* contains, in each process, the various local arrays of the same size, arranged one after another as a function of the process number. This presupposes that the size of the local vector x is uniform, and that the first process treats the first subvector, the second process, the second subvector, and so forth – this is obviously the simplest situation.

MPI also enables performing the same type of operation, of reconstituting a global array with local vectors of varying lengths arranged, upon reception, in a different order than the process numbers. The function is called *MPI_Allgatherv*, the suffix *v* meaning variable. The integer parameter *number_of_received_data* is then replaced by two integer arrays of a dimension equal to the number of processes. Parameters *number_of_received_data and shift_of_received_data*, respectively, describe the amount of data received from each process, and the position in which they are stored in the receiving array.

14.2. Parallelization of sparse matrix-vector product based on node sets

We can apply the same procedure as before to sparse matrix-vector products (SMVPs). In this case, a process treats a set of rows of the matrix, and must carry out the product by using its sparse rectangular block. *A priori*, a process only owns the subvectors corresponding to the rows of the matrix allocated to it. To realize its contribution to $y = Ax$, the processes then require the values of vector x for all the columns of its local matrix that have non-zero coefficients. In Figure 14.2, these terms are displayed in dark gray, and the terms in light gray are those that are unnecessary.

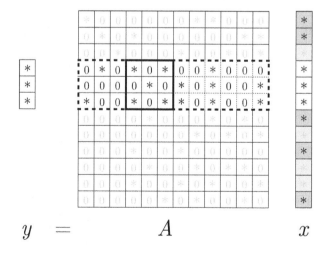

Figure 14.2. *The product by a block of sparse rows*

A priori, this parallelization method allows for a properly balanced degree of parallelism. It is sufficient to assign to the different processes blocks of rows of equal size that are composed of approximately the same number of non-zero coefficients. However, this suffers from a major flaw of granularity for its implementation on a distributed memory system. In effect, the number of $(+, \times)$ pairs of operations to carry out the product by the local sparse matrix is of the order of Cn/p, if n is the dimension of the matrix, p is the number of processors, whereas C is the average number of non-zero entries per row. However, the total number of terms for vector x to recover from other processes, before being able to realize the product, can be of the order of $(p - 1)n/p$, where the local matrix has non-zero coefficients in almost all the columns, as in Figure 14.2.

The amount of data to transfer, therefore, is certainly not small compared to the number of arithmetic operations, unless we find a way to drastically reduce the number of external coefficients of vector x, required to produce the product by the matrix.

The best approach for achieving this is to return to the analysis of the graph of the sparse matrix, and thus, the associated mesh. The set of vertices associated with a local submatrix determines a subgraph. The edges that join the vertices of this subgraph then represent the coefficients of the matrix located in the diagonal block. When we carry out the product by the matrix, the product by the diagonal block requires only the local terms of vector x. However, the off-diagonal coefficients, represented on the graph by the edges that connect the vertices of the local subgraph to the outer vertices, require the corresponding terms of the x vectors.

In Figure 14.3, the edges associated with the local matrix are represented by solid lines, and those that link external vertices to internal vertices are represented by dotted lines.

This analysis clearly shows that the question of minimization transfers is reduced to a problem of dividing the graph of the matrix and, therefore, the mesh. So that the majority of edges are internal, which correspond to the coefficients of the diagonal block, it is necessary that all the local vertices are adjacent to each other, forming a compact submesh. Conversely, the non-local coefficients of the vector required for achieving the product by the block of rows correspond to the outer vertices neighboring the inner vertices, i.e. at the external border of the substructure formed by the local vertices.

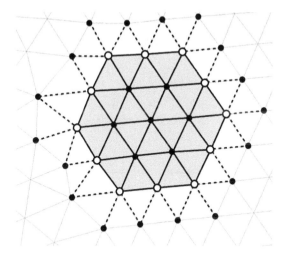

Figure 14.3. *Subgraph associated with a block of rows*

Ultimately, the optimal division is one that partitions the mesh into substructures of the same size, for load balancing, with the smallest possible boundary, so as to limit data transfers. The substructures must be as topologically spherical as possible, since the sphere has the smallest exterior surface for a given volume.

At the end of section 14.3, we will compare the matrix-vector products obtained with the parallelizations based on node and element sets.

14.3. Parallelization of sparse matrix-vector product based on element sets

14.3.1. *Review of the principles of domain decomposition*

Partitioning by the vertices of the mesh, presented in the previous section, does not result in true geometric substructure divisions. Cells that contain vertices from different subsets are required to calculate the interaction coefficients between the vertices in each process that treats the blocks of corresponding rows. The geometric divisions of the spatial domain correspond to an element or cell-based mesh partitioning.

In the case of a division into two, there are two subdomains separated by an interface, as shown in Figure 14.4. The matrix of the overall system then has the following block structure:

$$\begin{pmatrix} A_{11} & 0 & A_{13} \\ 0 & A_{22} & A_{23} \\ A_{31} & A_{32} & A_{33} \end{pmatrix} \tag{14.1}$$

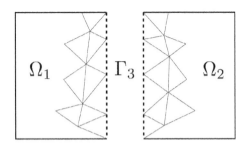

Figure 14.4. *Distinct subdomain meshes*

As we have previously seen in Chapter 9, which discusses the factorization of sparse matrices, the approach for subdomain division is of interest because it leads to a natural parallelization during the matrix formation phase. By assigning the different subdomains to separate processes, they can build the local matrices in parallel:

$$A_1 = \begin{pmatrix} A_{11} & A_{13} \\ A_{31} & A_{33}^{(1)} \end{pmatrix} \qquad A_2 = \begin{pmatrix} A_{22} & A_{23} \\ A_{32} & A_{33}^{(2)} \end{pmatrix} \tag{14.2}$$

Blocks $A_{33}^{(1)}$ and $A_{33}^{(2)}$ represent the interactions between the vertices located on interface Γ_3 integrated in the subdomains Ω_1 and Ω_2, respectively, so that:

$$A_{33} = A_{33}^{(1)} + A_{33}^{(2)}$$

14.3.2. *Matrix-vector product*

After a division into two subdomains, the global matrix-vector product is written as:

$$\begin{pmatrix} y_1 \\ y_2 \\ y_3 \end{pmatrix} = \begin{pmatrix} A_{11} & 0 & A_{13} \\ 0 & A_{22} & A_{23} \\ A_{31} & A_{32} & A_{33} \end{pmatrix} \begin{pmatrix} x_1 \\ x_2 \\ x_3 \end{pmatrix}$$

$$= \begin{pmatrix} A_{11}x_1 + A_{13}x_3 \\ A_{22}x_2 + A_{23}x_3 \\ A_{31}x_1 + A_{32}x_2 + A_{33}x_3 \end{pmatrix}$$

With the local matrices described in equation [14.2], we can calculate the two local matrix-vector products independently:

$$\begin{pmatrix} y_1 \\ y_3^{(1)} \end{pmatrix} = \begin{pmatrix} A_{11}x_1 + A_{13}x_3 \\ A_{31}x_1 + A_{33}^{(1)}x_3 \end{pmatrix}$$

$$\begin{pmatrix} y_2 \\ y_3^{(2)} \end{pmatrix} = \begin{pmatrix} A_{22}x_2 + A_{23}x_3 \\ A_{32}x_2 + A_{33}^{(2)}x_3 \end{pmatrix}$$

[14.3]

Because $A_{33} = A_{33}^{(1)} + A_{33}^{(2)}$, $y_3 = y_3^{(1)} + y_3^{(2)}$, this means that calculating the full matrix-vector product is performed in two steps:

1) the local matrix-vector product;

2) the assembly (sum) on the interface of the local contributions.

The first step involves local data only. The second step requires an exchange of data between processes that treat the subdomains with a common interface.

Let us now consider an important issue. The result on the interface is the same on each subdomain as long as the value of x_3 is the same. Let us suppose that x_3 is the initial value of an iterative method. Even though x_3 is initially continuous on the interface, this equality can be relaxed during the iterations of the solvers due to round-off errors. To illustrate this problem, we study the convergence of the conjugate gradient (CG) method for the solution of the Poisson equation. The example we consider is extreme in the sense that we are going to require a very tight convergence of the CG, down to a residual of 10^{-17}, in order to trigger the effects of round-off errors. Figure 14.5 shows the convergence of CG obtained with one subdomain (sequential mode) and the convergence obtained with 10 subdomains. We can observe that after a descending phase, the residual increases and the method diverges. To explain this phenomenon, we have also plotted the evolution of the maximum difference of the solution on the interfaces between neighbors. We note that this difference follows exactly the value of the residual. To fix this, we have enforced the continuity of the result of the matrix-vector product on the interfaces at each iteration of the CG, by obliging the subdomains to take the minimum interface value. As we can see in the figure, this strategy enables us to control the convergence of the CG. Another option to treat the discontinuity of the solution on the interface consists of performing the assembly operations in the same order on each neighbor. We will then be able to control the convergence of the method, although the convergence in sequential and parallel can be slightly different. Let us note that some engineering codes enforce the interface solution continuity when finalizing the iterative method: this solution is in fact less costly and most of the time sufficient. As we will see at the end of this section, the finite difference (FD) and finite volume (FV) methods do not exhibit this problem because vector x is exchanged rather than y.

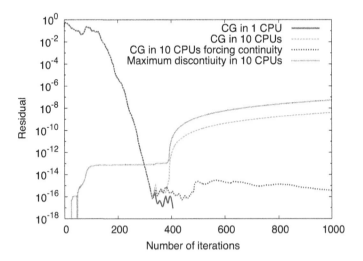

Figure 14.5. *Effect of round-off errors on the convergence of the parallel conjugate gradient method. For a color version of the figure, see www.iste.co.uk/magoules/computing.zip*

14.3.3. *Interface exchanges*

To assemble the contributions of the different subdomains after the local matrix-vector products, each process in charge of a subdomain must know the description of its interfaces. If a subdomain Ω_i has several neighboring subdomains, we denote Γ_{ij} as the interface between Ω_i and Ω_j as described in Figure 14.6. An interface is described simply by the number of neighbors $number\_of\_neighbors$ and the list $list_k$ of equations attached to the nodes or vertices of the interface with subdomain k. Let n_k be the size of the interface with subdomain k, that is the number of nodes multiplied by the number of degrees of freedom per node.

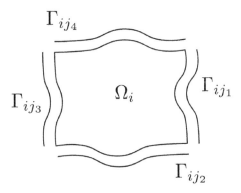

Figure 14.6. *Description of the interfaces*

How should the processes communicate the result of their local matrix-vector products? A first option consists of sending the results by going through the list of neighbors, in the order of their numberings. This simple strategy can affect the scalability, as illustrated in Figure 14.7. In this example, the computational domain is divided into four subdomains, where all the subdomains have to communicate with each other. Subdomain 1 exchanges its local result with subdomains 2, 3 and 4, respectively; subdomain 2 exchanges its local result with subdomains 1, 3 and 4, respectively, and so on. Below the communication scheme, we have depicted a matrix which represents the exchanges that have been carried out during each communication step. The coefficient (i, j) refers to the communication of process i to process j. A "0" indicates that there is no communication (for example, a subdomain does not send anything to itself). A "1" indicates that the message could be sent and received. A cross indicates that process i is blocked because subdomain j could not receive the message as it is already communicating. We see that all messages are exchanged in five communication steps. In order to optimize this communication, we need a communication scheduling (ordering), which can be computed using a graph coloring technique. The rough idea is that in each communication step, we maximize the number of communicating subdomains. The bottom part of the figure shows the optimum scheduling for this particular case, where all the communications can be carried out in three steps. Finally, once we have established the scheduling, we can save an ordered list of neighbors in an array $neighbor(k)$, with $k = 1 \ldots n_k$ and reorder the array $list_k$.

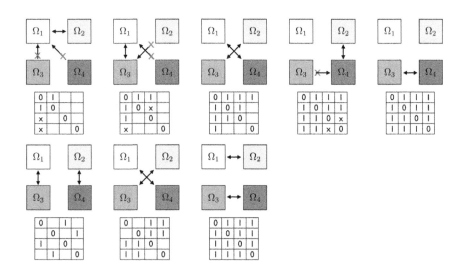

Figure 14.7. *Communication strategies. Top, inefficient strategy. Bottom, optimum strategy*

Let us now describe the exchange procedure. Noting that two subdomains will exchange the same number of data n_k, we will carry out the exchange using the MPI function *MPI_Sendrecv*. From the point of view of each subdomain, the matrix-vector product can be decomposed into three steps:

1) For each neighbor k, save the values of the local $y = Ax$ for all the interface equations in a working array $temp\_send_k$.

```
for  k = 1  to  number_of_neighbors
   for  i = 1  to  n_k
      temp_send_k(i) = y(list_k(i))
end  for
```

2) For each neighbor k, send the working array $temp\_send_k$ and receive the neighbors' contributions in a working array $temp\_recv_k$.

```
for  k = 1  to  number_of_neighbors
   Send   temp_send_k  to  neighbor(k)
   Receive  temp_recv_k  from  neighbor(k)
end  for
```

3) Assemble the contributions received from the neighbors $temp\_recv_k$ to the local components of vector y, corresponding to the interface equations with neighbor k.

```
for  k = 1  to  number_of_neighbors
   for  i = 1  to  n_k
      y(list_k(i)) = y(list_k(i)) + temp_recv_k(i)
   end  for
end  for
```

It is unnecessary for the interface equations to be locally numbered last, as in equations [14.2]. Similarly, it is unnecessary to know the numbering of interface equations in the neighboring subdomains, since only the values of the coefficients of the corresponding indices are exchanged. However, it is necessary that the list of equations $list_j$ of interface Γ_{ij} of subdomain Ω_i are ordered in a manner consistent with the list $list_i$ of interface Γ_{ji} of subdomain Ω_j.

Let us finally note that we can end up with differences between parallel executions using different numbers of processes, as the assembly operations are carried out in different orders. In extreme cases, we can even obtain convergence or divergence of the iterative solver according to the number of processes, as we have already illustrated in Figure 14.5. This may happen, for example, in the case of ill-conditioned systems, especially with algorithms like the CG where the orthogonal basis is not constructed explicitly.

14.3.4. *Asynchronous matrix-vector product with non-blocking communications*

The previous algorithm to compute the matrix-vector product uses blocking communications. The problem with these communications is that the execution of the code cannot continue until the communications are completed. There exists another option which consists of carrying out the communication asynchronously, by using the non-blocking MPI functions *MPI_Isend* to send and *MPI_Irecv* to receive, in order to overlap communication with arithmetic operations. The idea is to start the matrix-vector product for the rows corresponding to the interface nodes, and then perform the communication using these two MPI functions. As they are non-blocking, we can carry out the matrix-vector product of internal nodes at the same time. With the MPI function *MPI_Waitall*, we then block the execution until all communications are completed. Eventually, we can assemble the contributions received in $temp\_recv_k$ into y, just as described in the synchronous exchange algorithm.

14.3.5. *Comparison: parallelization based on node and element sets*

Let us go back to the one-dimensional example described in section 5.3, and in Figures 5.7 and 5.8. Figure 14.8 illustrates the methodologies to compute the sparse matrix-vector product using the parallelization based on node sets, the case of the FD and FV methods, or using the parallelization based on element sets, as in the case of the finite element (FE) method. The coefficients involved in the exchange are indicated in gray. Vectors with no superindex have a global value (the vector is already assembled). In the case of the parallelization based on element sets, the superindex indicates that the value is local to the corresponding subdomain (not assembled yet), and therefore only partial.

We observe that in the three cases, the numbers and sizes of exchanges are the same. In the case of the FD method, the components x_3 and x_4 should be global for the result y_3, computed by subdomain 1 and the result y_4, computed by subdomain 2, to be correct. In the case of FE, the result is only local as each subdomain misses the contribution of its neighbors. The exchange is carried out after obtaining the local result so that, after the assembling step, the result is global in both subdomains. The case of FV is similar to that of FD, as the ownerships of the rows are exclusive. Subdomain 1 requires the value of x_3, while subdomain 2 requires the value of x_2. Summarizing, in the case of FD and FV, the exchange is carried out before the matrix-vector product, and it is carried out after in the case of FE. Let us finally note that for FD and FV, the local matrix is rectangle, while it is square in the case of FE.

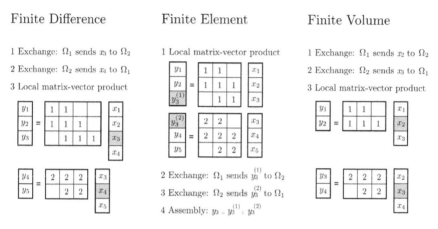

Figure 14.8. *Matrix-vector product. Comparison of FD, FE and FV*

We will end with the comparison between the three discretization methods by commenting on the asynchronous version of the matrix vector-product. As explained before, it consists of overlapping communication and computation, using the non-blocking send and receive of MPI, *MPI_ISend* and *MPI_IRecv*. For the three discretization methods, we note that we can carry out the matrix-vector product for internal nodes and in the meantime exchange the information of the interface/boundary nodes. Let us use subindex b to refer to interface nodes and subindex i to refer to internal nodes. In the case where the communications affect vector x, the asynchronous algorithm reads:

– *MPI_ISend* and *MPI_IRecv* of the interface/boundary values $x|_b$;

– matrix-vector product for the internal nodes $Ax|_i$;

– synchronization with *MPI_Waitall*;

– matrix-vector product for the boundary nodes $Ax|_b$.

In the aforementioned example, for FD, we exchange the values x_3 and x_4 while subdomain 1 carries out the product for rows 1 and 2, and subdomain 2 carries out the product for row 5. After *MPI_Waitall*, subdomain 1 can eventually calculate row 3 and subdomain 2 can eventually calculate row 2. In the case of FE, where communications involve the local and partial results of the matrix-vector product, the algorithm, which was already mentioned earlier in this chapter, reads:

– matrix-vector product for the boundary nodes $y|_b = Ax|_b$;

– *MPI_ISend* and *MPI_IRecv* of $y|_b$ of the interface/boundary values;

– matrix-vector product for the internal nodes $Ax|_i$;

– synchronization with *MPI_Waitall*;

– assembly of the products for the boundary nodes.

In the example under consideration, subdomains 1 and 2 first carry out the local product of row 3. Then, they exchange this result and in the meantime subdomain 1 updates rows 1 and 2 and subdomain 2 updates rows 4 and 5.

14.4. Parallelization of the scalar product

In the case of a parallelization based on node sets, that is the case of FD and FV, the computation of the scalar product is trivial. In a first step, each subdomain computes the scalar product associated with its corresponding rows. The next step consists of a reduction operation which can be carried out with the MPI function $MPI\_Allreduce$.

Unlike the vertex (or node) sets partitioning method, the decomposition method based on elements requires duplicating the vector components associated with the equations of the interfaces. In the case of a partitioning into two subdomains, as shown in Figure 14.4, if we calculate the local scalar products of the two vectors, x and y, we obtain the following results:

$$\begin{pmatrix} x_1 \\ x_3 \end{pmatrix} \cdot \begin{pmatrix} y_1 \\ y_3 \end{pmatrix} = (x_1 \cdot y_1) + (x_3 \cdot y_3)$$

[14.4]

$$\begin{pmatrix} x_2 \\ x_3 \end{pmatrix} \cdot \begin{pmatrix} y_2 \\ y_3 \end{pmatrix} = (x_2 \cdot y_2) + (x_3 \cdot y_3)$$

The sum of two local contributions gives:

$$(x_1 \cdot y_1) + (x_2 \cdot y_2) + 2 (x_3 \cdot y_3)$$

In the case of division into several subdomains, such as in Figure 14.9, it is necessary to find an algorithm that does not duplicate the contributions of the interface nodes to the scalar product. This issue can be solved in different ways. We will now present three of them, referred to by weight, distributivity and ownership.

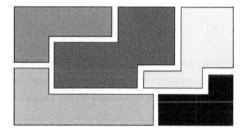

Figure 14.9. *Multi-domain partition*

14.4.1. *By weight*

The idea consists of computing the local-weighted scalar products for each equation by a factor equal to the inverse number of subdomains to which those belong. This factor is determined locally through the lists of equation interfaces. With this technique, the local scalar products of equation [14.4] become:

$$(x_1 \cdot y_1) + \frac{1}{2} (x_3 \cdot y_3) \quad \text{and} \quad (x_2 \cdot y_2) + \frac{1}{2} (x_3 \cdot y_3)$$

The summation of the weighted scalar products gives the correct result.

14.4.2. *By distributivity*

Another method, based on Krylov's methods, is supported by the fact that every time a scalar product is calculated, at least one of the two vectors is the result of a matrix-vector product. Thereby, this vector was first calculated by a local matrix-vector product, like vector y in equation [14.3], and then assembled at the interfaces. The use of unassembled vectors for the calculation of local scalar products gives the following contributions of the two subdomains:

$$(x_1 \cdot y_1) + (x_3 \cdot y_3^{(1)}) \quad \text{and} \quad (x_2 \cdot y_2) + (x_3 \cdot y_3^{(2)})$$

The summation of the two local contributions gives the following result:

$$(x_1 \cdot y_1) + (x_2 \cdot y_2) + x_3 \cdot (y_3^{(1)} + y_3^{(2)}) = x \cdot y$$

This method applies in the case of any multi-domain divisions, as shown in Figure 14.9. It has the advantage of avoiding additional arithmetic operations required for weighting. However, it leads to greater rounding errors, especially when the assembled vector has small coefficients, as is the case of the gradient vector at convergence.

14.4.3. *By ownership*

The third option consists of dividing the interfaces into "own" and "other" parts so that only one equation (one node) belongs to the own interface of only one subdomain. Thereby, the intersection of the own parts of the interfaces of all subdomains is null. The local scalar products are then computed in the following way:

$$(x_1 \cdot y_1) + (x_{3,own}^{(1)} \cdot y_{3,own}^{(1)}) \quad \text{and} \quad (x_2 \cdot y_2) + (x_{3,own}^{(2)} \cdot y_{3,own}^{(2)})$$

In the case of two subdomains, the own interface of one subdomain is the other's interface of the adjacent subdomain. In the case of an arbitrary number of subdomains, the partition of the interfaces can be carried out using the same strategy as the one used to partition the domain (for example, using a partitioner). Using the following reordering of local vectors:

$$v = \begin{pmatrix} v_1 \\ v_{3,own} \\ v_{3,other} \end{pmatrix}$$

we can, therefore, carry out the scalar product looping over the internal and own interface nodes. This numbering can be used as well to perform the asynchronous matrix-vector product in an efficient way.

14.5. Summary of the parallelization of Krylov methods

The coding of a parallel Krylov method based on a message-passing paradigm is quite similar to its sequential version. The additional work in parallel consists of performing the following two types of message exchange:

1) exchange data on the interfaces between neighboring subdomains to assemble the matrix-vector products, as described in sections 14.2 and 14.3;

2) global reduction operations to sum up the different contributions from the subdomains when computing the scalar product.

The exchange of data on the interfaces is carried out using point-to-point functions of MPI. These exchanges are local as a subdomain only exchanges data with its neighbors. The reduction operations involve all the processes and use the MPI function *MPI_Allreduce*. It should be pointed out that these global operations are synchronization points in the code and should be gathered as much as possible.

15

Parallel Preconditioning Methods

In this chapter, we present a few different preconditioning methods. The selection of the preconditioner may be a decisive factor in some applications. Sometimes, even a simple diagonal preconditioner can be sufficient. For other problems, more complex techniques may be chosen to obtain the convergence of the Krylov method. We begin this chapter by studying the simplest preconditioner, the diagonal. We follow with preconditioners based on approximate factorization, which are called incomplete. We then introduce the Schur complement method that relies on an exact local resolution, in the context of subdomain decomposition. This method permits the introduction of projection methods, which are illustrated by algebraic multigrid methods. We then present the additive Schwarz method, also based on local approximations, but with overlap. A special variant of the additive Schwarz method, namely the restricted additive Schwarz method, is also discussed in detail. We conclude the chapter by presenting some preconditioners based on the physics of the problem in play: Gauss–Seidel and linelet. For all these approaches, we discuss parallelization issues.

15.1. Diagonal

When selecting a preconditioner, the user of a scientific code may be tempted to converge the Krylov method as fast as possible, in terms of operations. The choice may, therefore, consist of a complex preconditioner. However, this is not always the best option. Complex preconditioners usually require a high computational and/or communication costs. Depending on the case, this communication can be dominant, and maybe a simpler one, with less communication, would be cheaper in terms of CPU time, despite the fact that it decreases the number of iterations for the Krylov method to converge.

In addition, some applications do not require complex preconditioners. In the case of computational fluid dynamics (CFD), when using a segregated velocity-pressure method (like fractional step), the Krylov method for the momentum equation usually converges well even with a diagonal preconditioner. This equation is often even solved with an explicit method, for sufficiently low time steps. In this case, at each time step, a unique Richardson iteration is solved for the system $Au = b$:

$$u_{p+1} = u_p - M\left(Au_p - b\right)$$

where the preconditioner M is computed as $M = P^{-1}\delta t$, where P is the mass matrix. This matrix can be lumped so that it is diagonal and its inversion is trivial. When the time step is sufficiently small (the time derivative is the dominant term of the equation), matrix M is a good preconditioner for A.

If we want to increase the time step, we could use some iterations of a Krylov method, like GMRES, and use the diagonal as a preconditioner. At the parallelization level, the computation of the diagonal is carried out in the following way:

– compute the local diagonal on each process;

– call the function *MPI_Sendrecv* and assemble the contributions of the neighbors;

– invert the diagonal.

By doing this, on the interface nodes, the coefficient of the diagonal matrix will be the same for all neighbors sharing this node.

Let us go back to the example of Figure 14.8 for the FE method, and let us carry out one Richardson iteration with this diagonal matrix. In the following, the subindex refers to a row and not to an iteration. A and b are known on each subdomain, and let x be an initial solution whose values on the interfaces nodes are the same for all neighboring subdomains, that is $x_3^{(1)} = x_3^{(2)}$. The algorithm is the following:

– Compute the local diagonal d:

$$\Omega_1 : d_1 = A_{11}, \ d_2 = A_{22}, \ d_3^{(1)} = A_{33}^{(1)}$$

$$\Omega_2 : d_4 = A_{44}, \ d_5 = A_{55}, \ d_3^{(2)} = A_{33}^{(2)}.$$

– Exchange $d_3^{(1)}$ and $d_3^{(2)}$ and assemble d in Ω_1 and Ω_2, $d_3 = d_3^{(1)} + d_3^{(2)}$.

– Compute the inverse $invd$ of d.

– Exchange and assemble $b_3 = b_3^{(1)} + b_3^{(2)}$.

– Compute the local matrix-vector product $y = Ax$ and assemble $y_3 = y_3^{(1)} + y_3^{(2)}$.

– Update the solution locally:

$$x_i^* = x_i - (y_i - b_i) \times invd_i$$

with $i = 1, 2, 3$ for Ω_1 and $i = 3, 4, 5$ for Ω_2.

As b_3, y_3 and d_3 were assembled and x_3 has the same initial value in both subdomains, we can easily check that the final solution x^* is the same on the interface node.

15.2. Incomplete factorization methods

15.2.1. *Principle*

Incomplete factorization methods consist of calculating a sparse approximation of the matrix factorization.

The most common approach consists of only calculating the terms that are in the non-zero locations of the initial matrix. That is to say, the lower triangular sparse matrix L and the upper triangular sparse matrix U have non-zero coefficients only at the locations of non-zero coefficients, respectively, in the lower triangular part and the upper triangular part of matrix $A \simeq LU$. This method is denoted by ILU(0).

The ILU(p) method is the one that allows the filling of matrices L and U, with p being a control parameter of the "filling level". We would say that a coefficient of index (i, j) has a filling level equal to 1 if a_{ij} is non-zero in the initial matrix. When calculating the Schur complement using the Gauss factorization method, the operation of updating a coefficient is written as:

$$a_{ij} = a_{ij} - a_{ik} \times a_{kj}$$

If the coefficients (i, k) and (k, j) are of level 1, and if a_{ij} is null in the initial array, then the filling level of the coefficient (i, j) is equal to 2. The ILU(1) method consists of adding all the coefficients of level 2 to the graph of the incomplete factorized matrix.

More generally, null coefficients of matrix A are assigned an initial filling level equal to $+\infty$. Each update of coefficient (i, j) gives to its filling level, the minimum value between its initial value, and the sum of the filling levels of the coefficients (i, k) and (k, j). The ILU(p) method consists of adding to the graph of the incomplete factorized matrix all the coefficients of a level less than or equal to $p + 1$.

The rationale for this approach lies in the fact that, for matrices derived from the discretization by finite element methods or finite difference partial derivative equations of the type of the Laplace equation, the most important numerical terms in the exact factorization are actually in the locations of the non-zero terms of the original matrix. The reason is that local effects, i.e. the interactions between close points in the mesh, are predominant in both the operator and in its inverse.

With the ILU(1) method, we see that we add to the factorized matrix, coefficients corresponding to the interactions between equations situated at a distance of 2 from one another in the sense of the graph of the original matrix. Similarly, the method ILU(p) takes into account interactions between pairs of equations located at a distance of $p + 1$.

In the case of symmetric matrices, the same methodology allows producing incomplete Crout factorizations, or incomplete Cholesky factorizations, for positive definite matrices. From the standpoint of parallelization, the different methods present similar problems.

The implementation of an ILU method consists of applying the exact sparse factorization algorithm, but by only calculating the L and U terms located in a predefined set of placements $\mathcal{S}$, containing the positions of the non-zero coefficients of the initial matrix.

For the first step, the operations will, therefore, be done using the following algorithm:

```
l(1, 1) = 1
u(1, 1) = a(1, 1)
for i = 2 to n
   if (i, 1) ∈ S then
      l(i, 1) = a(i, 1)/u(1, 1)
   end if
end for
for j = 2 to n
   if (1, j) ∈ S then
      u(1, j) = a(1, j)
   end if
end for
for j = 2 to n
   for i = 2 to n
      if (i, j), (i, 1), (1, j) ⊂ S then
         s(i, j) = a(i, j) − l(i, 1) × u(1, j)
      end if
   end for
end for
```

Obviously, in the case of the ILU(0) method, the terms L and U may be substituted by those of A, since the structures of A and LU are the same. In practice, as we must conserve the initial matrix in order to perform matrix-vector products by the Krylov method, the calculation will always be performed in a different data structure.

The following steps are done in the same way, repeating the operation on the incomplete successive Schur complements, stored in the sparse matrix structure.

THEOREM 15.1.– The coefficients of matrix $R = A − LU$ are null for all the indices $(i, j) \in S$.

PROOF 15.1.– It suffices to show that the property is satisfied in the first stage of the algorithm presented above. After this step, we produced a partial incomplete factorization of matrix A. Matrix $L^{(1)}$, resulting from the first stage, contains the first column of the final matrix L, with its other coefficients being those of matrix I. Matrix $U^{(1)}$ contains the first row of the final matrix U and the incomplete Schur complement in its diagonal block, beginning at the second row and second column. By construction, matrix $R^{(1)} = A - L^{(1)}U^{(1)}$ does satisfy the property.

The proof is then easily completed by recursion, since finishing the algorithm consists of applying the same operation to the incomplete successive Schur complements, which are the lower diagonal blocks of the $U^{(k)}$ matrices.   □

The MILU method is a variation of the ILU method, which changes the diagonal terms of matrix U, such that the sum of the coefficients of each row of the product LU is equal to the sum of the coefficients of same row in A. In terms of implementation, only the calculation of the diagonal coefficient of U is changed. MILU factorization does not satisfy the property stated in theorem 15.1.

15.2.2. Parallelization

The parallelization of the incomplete factorization is done using the same techniques as those employed for exact sparse matrices factorization.

Simply, because the filling is restricted *a priori*, the dependencies generated by the different steps of the factorization are weaker, which offers hope for a higher degree of parallelization. However, since we calculate only some of the terms, with a smaller number of operations, the granularity is coarser than in the case of an exact factorization.

Moreover, the numbering that allows parallelization of the incomplete factorization tends toward degrading performance in terms of preconditioning. To illustrate this phenomenon, we will consider the simple case of a tridiagonal matrix.

$$A = \begin{pmatrix} a_{11} & a_{12} & 0 & 0 & \dots \\ a_{21} & a_{22} & a_{23} & 0 & \dots \\ 0 & a_{32} & a_{33} & a_{34} & \dots \\ 0 & 0 & a_{43} & a_{44} & \dots \\ \dots & \dots & \dots & \dots & \dots \end{pmatrix}$$

Exact Gaussian factorization of this matrix does not induce any filling, and leads to the following linear recursion of order 1:

for $i = 1$ **to** n
$$a(i+1, i) = a(i+1, i)/a(i, i)$$
$$a(i+1, i+1) = a(i+1, i+1) - a(i+1, i) \times a(i, i+1)$$
end for

To show the highest level of parallelism for the incomplete factorization of ILU(0) of this matrix, we will use a cyclical-type reduction method, studied in section 3.1.3, which amounts to renumbering the odd equations first, and then the even equations.

With such an "odd-even" renumbering, the initial matrix and the exact factorized matrix have the structure shown in Figure 15.1.

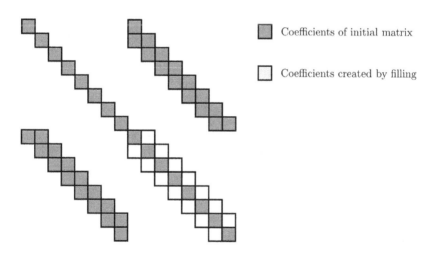

Figure 15.1. *Structure of the renumbered tridiagonal matrix with filling*

Incomplete factorization will ignore the terms created by the filling, so it does not take into account the interactions of coefficients created between the even equations. Thus, it will result in a preconditioning of the same type as if we had independently factored the successive diagonal blocks of dimension 2 in the matrix, with its original numbering, while ignoring the coefficients connecting the various diagonal blocks among one another. This kind of approach is only slightly more numerically efficient than just preconditioning by the inverse of the diagonal matrix.

In the same way, block decomposition leads to calculating the exact inverse of the diagonal blocks, and disregarding the interactions between blocks. Therefore, the smaller the blocks are, the limiting case being that of cycle decomposition, the further incomplete factorization is from exact factorization.

For general matrices, conventional approaches to parallelization are based on divisions into subdomains. Now, more than the incomplete factorization in itself, we must parallelize the forward and backward substitutions, these being the most costly since they are used repeatedly during the Krylov method iterations. In practice, we find ourselves obliged to settle for an incomplete factorization of only the internal subdiagonal blocks of the different local (subdomain) matrices. This reduces the numerical efficiency, which is often already limited, when using this technique of preconditioning.

15.3. Schur complement method

15.3.1. *Optimal local preconditioning*

To improve the purely local approach for determining a preconditioner, we can proceed all the way to exact factorization of the internal diagonal block of the subdomain matrix. In the case of a division into two subdomains, this means factorizing blocks A_{11} and A_{22} of the overall matrix of equation [14.1].

If we have these factorizations on hand, we can ensure the exact resolution of the internal problems. More precisely, given x_3^p, the trace on the interface of an approximate solution in iteration p, we can determine x_1^p and x_2^p to satisfy the local equations:

$$A_{11}x_1^p + A_{13}x_3^p = b_1 \qquad A_{22}x_2^p + A_{23}x_3^p = b_2 \qquad\qquad [15.1]$$

If we are working in the context of a Krylov method, with calculations of the approximate solutions by a short recurrence, as with the conjugate gradient method or the ORTHODIR method, the solution in iteration $p + 1$ is written as:

$$x^{p+1} = x^p + \rho^p w^p$$

For the approximate solution x^{p+1} to satisfy the local equations [15.1], it is sufficient and necessary that the descent direction w^p satisfies the linear equations:

$$A_{11}w_1^p + A_{13}w_3^p = 0 \quad A_{22}w_2^p + A_{23}w_3^p = 0 \qquad [15.2]$$

We can thus construct a method of preconditioning that consists of starting with an initial solution that satisfies the local equations [15.1], and then correcting the given descent direction in each iteration using the non-preconditioned Krylov method, and by determining the internal values by solving equations [15.2].

This kind of preconditioning can be described as locally optimal, in the sense that the gradient is null within each subdomain in each iteration:

$$g_p = \begin{pmatrix} A_{11} & 0 & A_{13} \\ 0 & A_{22} & A_{23} \\ A_{31} & A_{32} & A_{33} \end{pmatrix} \begin{pmatrix} x_1^p \\ x_2^p \\ x_3^p \end{pmatrix} - \begin{pmatrix} b_1 \\ b_2 \\ b_3 \end{pmatrix} = \begin{pmatrix} 0 \\ 0 \\ g_3^p \end{pmatrix} \qquad [15.3]$$

Now, ensuring the nullity of the gradient is the aim of the iterative Krylov method.

15.3.2. *Principle of the Schur complement method*

Taking into account the local equations [15.1], the approximate local solutions x_1^p and x_2^p are given by the equations:

$$x_1^p = -A_{11}^{-1}A_{13}x_3^p + A_{11}^{-1}b_1 \quad x_2^p = -A_{22}^{-1}A_{23}x_3^p + A_{22}^{-1}b_2$$

The component on the interface of the global gradient in equation [15.3] is therefore:

$$\begin{aligned} g_3^p &= A_{31}x_1^p + A_{32}x_2^p + A_{33}x_3^p - b_3 \\ &= \left(A_{33} - A_{31}A_{11}^{-1}A_{13} - A_{32}A_{22}^{-1}A_{23}\right)x_3^p \\ &\quad -(b_3 - A_{31}A_{11}^{-1}b_1 - A_{32}A_{22}^{-1}b_2) \\ &= S_{33}x_3^p - c_3 \end{aligned}$$

Matrix S_{33} is the Schur complement on the interface of the global matrix [14.1]. Similarly, if the descent direction w_p satisfies the local equations [15.2], then its product by the matrix satisfies:

$$v_p = Aw_p = \begin{pmatrix} A_{11} & 0 & A_{13} \\ 0 & A_{22} & A_{23} \\ A_{31} & A_{32} & A_{33} \end{pmatrix} \begin{pmatrix} w_1^p \\ w_2^p \\ w_3^p \end{pmatrix} = \begin{pmatrix} 0 \\ 0 \\ v_3^p \end{pmatrix}$$ [15.4]

with:

$$\begin{aligned} v_3^p &= A_{31}w_1^p + A_{32}w_2^p + A_{33}w_3^p \\ &= \left(A_{33} - A_{31}A_{11}^{-1}A_{13} - A_{32}A_{22}^{-1}A_{23}\right)w_3^p \\ &= S_{33}w_3^p \end{aligned}$$

Let us now consider the global system:

$$\begin{pmatrix} A_{11} & 0 & A_{13} \\ 0 & A_{22} & A_{23} \\ A_{31} & A_{32} & A_{33} \end{pmatrix} \begin{pmatrix} x_1 \\ x_2 \\ x_3 \end{pmatrix} = \begin{pmatrix} b_1 \\ b_2 \\ b_3 \end{pmatrix}$$

In the third row of the system, if we substitute the unknowns, x_1 and x_2, by their values obtained as a function of x_3, using the first two rows of the system we end up with:

$$x_1 = -A_{11}^{-1}A_{13}x_3 + A_{11}^{-1}b_1 \quad x_2 = -A_{22}^{-1}A_{23}x_3 + A_{22}^{-1}b_2$$

This means that the solutions x_1 and x_2 are obtained solving the internal problems by using x_3 as a Dirichlet condition on the interface. In the same way as for the gradient calculation on the interface in equation [15.4], the condensed system on the interface reads:

$$S_{33}x_3 = c_3$$ [15.5]

This means that the component of the global interface gradient, defined in equation [15.3] for the approximate solution x^p, is simply equal, according to equation [15.4], to the gradient at point x_3^p of the condensed system on the interface [15.5].

In the case where matrix A is symmetric positive definite, we can apply the locally optimal preconditioning method to the conjugate gradient algorithm.

In each iteration, the coefficient of optimum descent is, according to equations [15.4] and [15.5]:

$$\rho^p = -(g^p \cdot w^p)/(Aw^p \cdot w^p) = -(g_3^p \cdot w_3^p)/(S_{33}w_3^p \cdot w_3^p)$$

Locally optimal preconditioning consists of calculating the new descent direction using the preconditioned gradient, $v^{p+1} = Mg^{p+1}$, which is obtained by calculating $v_3^{p+1} = g_3^{p+1}$, and in solving the local systems:

$$A_{11}v_1^{p+1} + A_{13}v_3^{p+1} = 0 \quad A_{22}v_2^{p+1} + A_{23}v_3^{p+1} = 0$$

The reconjugation coefficient is, therefore, from equations [15.4] and [15.5]:

$$\gamma^p = (Mg^{p+1} \cdot Aw^p)/(Aw^p \cdot w^p) = (g_3^{p+1} \cdot S_{33}w_3^p)/(S_{33}w_3^p \cdot w_3^p)$$

If we consider the components only on the interface of the different vectors, iteration p of the conjugate gradient with locally optimal preconditioning thus involves the following operations:

1) Matrix-vector product:

$$v_3^p = S_{33}w_3^p$$

2) Calculating the coefficient of optimal descent:

$$\rho^p = -(g_3^p \cdot w_3^p)/(S_{33}w_3^p \cdot w_3^p)$$

3) Updating the solution and the gradient:

$$x_3^{p+1} = x_3^p + \rho^p w_3^p, \quad g_3^{p+1} = g_3^p + \rho^p v_3^p$$

4) Calculating the reconjugation coefficient:

$$\gamma^p = (g_3^{p+1} \cdot S_{33}w_3^p)/(S_{33}w_3^p \cdot w_3^p)$$

5) Determining the new descent direction:

$$w_3^{p+1} = g_3^{p+1} - \gamma^p w_3^p$$

This means that the preconditioned conjugate gradient algorithm, with locally optimal preconditioning applied to the overall system $Ax = b$, is actually equivalent to a conjugate gradient on the condensed interface problem $S_{33}x_3 = b_3$. Due to the nature of the condensed matrix S_{33}, this approach is called the "Schur complement method".

It obviously applies to the case of a decomposition into any number of subdomains. Calculating the preconditioned gradient phase consists of independently solving all the local systems in order to correct the internal values. For the rest, the implementation is identical to that of the classical conjugate gradient.

15.3.3. *Properties of the Schur complement method*

Using the Schur complement method, we carry out the iterations on a condensed problem on the interface without having to actually form matrix S_{33}. Since we use a Krylov method, it suffices to know how to evaluate the product of this matrix, which is done, as is shown by equations [15.2] and [15.5] for the vector w_p, by solving a local problem in each subdomain, followed by a product of the global matrix. Therefore, to implement this, it is enough to carry out the factorization of the diagonal blocks associated with the internal equations of the different subdomains.

What ultimately emerges is a hybrid method, using both direct and iterative methods. It is equivalent to using the direct approach at the local level, and iterative methods globally, i.e. at the interfaces, since the internal equations are always satisfied. Compared to using only a direct method, it is much less costly in the factorization phase. Furthermore, it is as easy to parallelize as the conjugate gradient method, and moreover it has a finer granularity than does the latter, since for both methods, in each iteration the data exchanges are identical, whereas the volume of local computation is significantly greater with the Schurcomplement method. This is because the forward and backward substitutions necessary for local preconditioning require more arithmetic operations than the matrix-vector product, due to filling.

This method can nonetheless be truly interesting only if the increase in the computational cost per iteration is offset by a consequent decrease in the number of iterations; in other words, if the Schur complement conditioning is significantly less than that of the global matrix. Figure 15.2 illustrates this comment. It consists of the solution of the momentum equations of the Navier–Stokes equations (with a fractional step method) using the preconditioned BiCGSTAB method, for the geometry described in section 2.6, which is the brain hemodynamics. The mesh is composed of 19 million elements and is partitioned into 1,920 subdomains. Figure 15.2 shows the convergence of the BiCGSTAB method, during five time steps, which can be easily identified by jumps in the equation residual. A simple diagonal preconditioning is compared to a block (by subdomain) LU preconditioning, the same as the one applied in this section to the conjugate gradient method. In Figure 15.2(a), we observe that the convergence of the block LU preconditioner is six times faster than that of the diagonal one in terms of iterations. However, in terms of CPU time, Figure 15.2(b) shows that the block LU preconditioner is three times slower. Of course, these times greatly depend on the implementation of the local direct solvers, and this example is just an illustration. It is nevertheless significant.

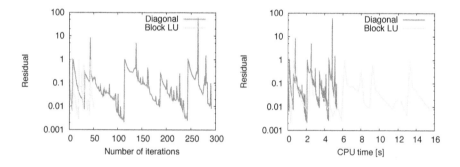

Figure 15.2. *Comparison of diagonal and block LU preconditioners. Number of iterations and CPU time*

Let us now examine the conditioning of the Schur complement. This one cannot be obtained using simple algebraic arguments. We know that for a symmetric positive definite matrix, the conditioning is equal to the ratio between the largest and the smallest eigenvalues. These are given by the following relations:

$$\lambda_{max} = \max_{\|x\|\neq 0} \frac{Ax \cdot x}{x \cdot x} \qquad \lambda_{min} = \min_{\|x\|\neq 0} \frac{Ax \cdot x}{x \cdot x}$$

If we decompose the matrix into four blocks:

$$A = \begin{pmatrix} A_{11} & A_{12} \\ A_{21} & A_{22} \end{pmatrix}$$

Then, we have:

$$\begin{pmatrix} A_{11} & A_{12} \\ A_{21} & A_{22} \end{pmatrix} \begin{pmatrix} 0 \\ x_2 \end{pmatrix} \cdot \begin{pmatrix} 0 \\ x_2 \end{pmatrix} = A_{22} x_2 \cdot x_2$$

We can immediately deduce that the maximum and minimum eigenvalues of block A_{22} are, respectively, smaller and larger than those of A and thus $\kappa(A_{22}) \leq \kappa(A)$. This increase is the best that we can hope for in general. For proof, just consider a matrix of the form:

$$A = \begin{pmatrix} I & 0 \\ 0 & A_{22} \end{pmatrix} \qquad\qquad [15.6]$$

Moreover, if we denote by B the inverse matrix of A, then:

$$AB = \begin{pmatrix} A_{11}B_{11} + A_{12}B_{21} & A_{11}B_{12} + A_{12}B_{22} \\ A_{21}B_{11} + A_{22}B_{21} & A_{21}B_{12} + A_{22}B_{22} \end{pmatrix} = \begin{pmatrix} I & 0 \\ 0 & I \end{pmatrix}$$

which implies:

$$\begin{array}{ll} A_{11}B_{12} + A_{12}B_{22} = 0 & \quad B_{12} = -A_{11}^{-1}A_{12}B_{22} \\ A_{21}B_{12} + A_{22}B_{22} = I & \Leftrightarrow \quad (A_{22} - A_{21}A_{11}^{-1}A_{12})B_{22} = I \end{array}$$

Thus, $B_{22} = (A_{22} - A_{21}A_{11}^{-1}A_{12})^{-1}$, and finally:

$$\kappa(A_{22} - A_{21}A_{11}^{-1}A_{12}) = \kappa(B_{22}) \leq \kappa(B) = \kappa(A)$$

Example 15.6 shows that this increase is the best that we can obtain in general.

A priori, we know that the Schur complement conditioning is less than or equal to that of the full matrix, but we cannot give any upper bound. In the case of a matrix obtained by finite element discretization of a partial elliptic differential equation, we can, nevertheless, show that the Schur complement conditioning on the interface is much better than that of the global matrix. The proof is based on the analysis of partial differential operators. Intuitively, it follows from the fact that the functions that satisfy the local equations form a subspace of sufficiently regular functions, for which the norms of the operators are smaller.

15.4. Algebraic multigrid

15.4.1. *Preconditioning using projection*

We will be working in the context of a linear system with a symmetric positive definite matrix A. In the case of the Schur complement method, if we denote $x_i = R_i x$, R_i is the restriction operator of vector x for the internal equations of subdomain i. Let R be the restriction operator for the internal equations of all p subdomains and A_{ii}, the diagonal block matrix associated with those of subdomain i:

$$R = \begin{pmatrix} R_1 \\ R_2 \\ \cdots \\ R_p \end{pmatrix} \quad R^t A R = \begin{pmatrix} A_{11} & 0 & \cdots & 0 \\ 0 & A_{22} & \cdots & 0 \\ \cdots & \cdots & \cdots & \cdots \\ 0 & \cdots & 0 & A_{pp} \end{pmatrix} \qquad [15.7]$$

The columns of R are the basis vectors associated with the internal equations of the different subdomains. The Schur complement method uses the fact that we know how to easily solve a restricted problem, associated with matrix $R^t A R$, to produce a locally optimal preconditioner.

The same method could be used outside the context of parallelism and the approach by subdomains, if we knew how to identify a small set of equations, which play a key role in the poor conditioning of the matrix. The factorization of matrix $R^t A R$, where R is the restriction to this set of equations, would allow producing a preconditioner that cancels its residual on this set.

More generally, let us consider a small size subspace, whose basis vectors form a rectangular matrix V, so the problem projected onto the subspace is written as:

$$(AV\xi - b \cdot V\zeta) = 0 \ \forall \zeta \ \Leftrightarrow \ V^t A V \xi = V^t b \qquad [15.8]$$

If the rank of V is small, we can calculate and factorize the matrix of the projected problem [15.8], $V^t A V$. Solving this projected problem can provide a "coarse preconditioner", in the sense that it corrects the error only on a small subspace.

So, we will begin from the starting point $x_0 = V \xi_0$, such that ξ_0 is the solution of the projected problem:

$$(AV\xi_0 - b \cdot V\zeta) = 0 \; \forall \zeta \; \Leftrightarrow \; V^t A V \xi_0 = V^t b \qquad [15.9]$$

which means that the initial gradient is orthogonal to the subspace generated by the vectors of V.

Let us assume that the gradient in iteration p satisfies the same property, then the preconditioner will consist of calculating a descent direction by correction of the gradient $w_p = g_p + V \delta_p$, which is an approximation of $A^{-1} g_p$ in a coarse sense:

$$(Aw_p - g_p \cdot V\zeta) = 0 \; \forall \zeta$$
$$\Leftrightarrow \qquad [15.10]$$
$$V^t A V \delta_p = V^t g_p - V^t A g_p = -V^t A g_p$$

which, for w_p, leads to the following orthogonal property:

$$V^t A w_p = V^t g_p = 0 \qquad [15.11]$$

With a descent direction constructed by this preconditioning procedure, the gradient in iteration $p + 1$, $g_{p+1} = g_p + \rho_p A w_p$ will inevitably satisfy the $V^t g_{p+1} = 0$ orthogonal relation. In fact, according to equations [15.10] and [15.11]:

$$V^t g_{p+1} = V^t g_p + \rho_p V^t A w_p = 0 \qquad [15.12]$$

15.4.2. Algebraic construction of a coarse grid

For problems of partial differential equations discretized by finite elements, finite volumes and finite differences methods, a natural approach for identifying a small approximate problem, which allows for the realization of a good preconditioner, consists of constructing a coarser mesh, i.e. one containing fewer elements or cells. Afterward, we project the residual on this coarse mesh to resolve the problem, and then, we interpolate the coarse solution to the initial fine mesh. The main difficulty of this geometric multigrid consists of explicitly constructing the coarse mesh.

In order to generalize this approach to cases of sparse matrices, resulting from unstructured meshes and complex geometries, a purely algebraic methodology has been developed. This methodology is based exclusively on the coarsening of the matrix graph, which makes the method a black box, i.e. almost problem independent. The idea is to coarsen the matrix graph. Although we never end up with an explicit coarse mesh, we will still refer to the coarse mesh in order to illustrate the concepts. This coarse mesh, while being as small as possible, must still contain enough nodes to be able to interpolate a coarse solution on the fine grid, with sufficient accuracy.

The most classic algorithm consists of determining, for each node of the initial graph, the set of nodes to which it is strongly connected:

$$\mathcal{S}_i = \{j \neq i, |a_{ij}| > \tau \max |a_{ik}| , \ 0 < \tau < 1\}$$

The coarsening will ensure that each node of the fine grid has at least one strong connection with one of the nodes of the coarse grid. We refer to as the weight of node i, the number of nodes that are strongly connected to it.

The procedure consists of choosing a maximum-weight node in order to begin building the coarse grid. All the nodes strongly connected to this node are eliminated. The weight of the nodes, strongly connected to those we have just eliminated, is incremented by 1. However, the weight of the nodes, to which the coarse node is strongly connected, is decremented by 1. The operation is then repeated until all the nodes have been determined. Incrementing the weight of strongly connected nodes to those we eliminated allows us to select the following coarse nodes, giving preference to those in the vicinity of the already established coarse grid, so as to frontally advance in the initial graph. This avoids creating coarse areas in all the corners of the initial mesh, which would require us to store numerous coarse nodes in the separation areas.

If the initial grid is a regular Cartesian grid, the coarsening procedure, thus described, allows eliminating one out of two nodes in each direction, as shown in Figure 15.3, in the case of a two-dimensional grid.

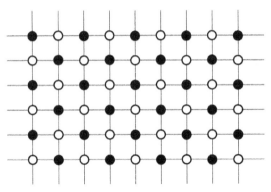

Figure 15.3. *Coarsening of a bidimensional Cartesian grid*

Now, we have to determine the interpolation algorithm and the coarse matrix. The interpolation algorithm will permit us to define the interpolation matrix of a vector defined on the coarse grid, toward the complete vector. Once this matrix P is defined, the coarse matrix becomes the matrix of the projected problem $P^t A P$, at least in the case of the symmetric positive definite matrix A.

We can proceed in several ways, depending on the type of problem from where the considered linear system originates. However, if we want to keep with a very general methodology, there is a purely algebraic approach.

By coarsening, two subsets of nodes were formed. The first, index 1, is for the set of fine nodes that are not in the coarse grid; the second, denoted by index 2, is the set of nodes of the coarse grid. The matrix, therefore, has the following block structure:

$$A = \begin{pmatrix} A_{11} & A_{12} \\ A_{21} & A_{22} \end{pmatrix}$$ [15.13]

The exact relation that allows calculating the values of x_1 as a function of those of x_2 , and using matrix A, is thus:

$$x_1 = -A_{11}^{-1} A_{12} x_2$$ [15.14]

This choice leads to an exact solution method. In fact, the projected problem is none other than the condensed problem, with the elimination of the unknowns in area 1:

$$P = \begin{pmatrix} -A_{11}^{-1}A_{12} \\ I \end{pmatrix}$$
$$P^t AP = A_{22} - A_{21}A_{11}^{-1}A_{12} \qquad [15.15]$$
$$P^t b = b_2 - A_{12}^t A_{11}^{-t}b_1 = b_2 - A_{21}A_{11}^{-1}b_1$$

which gives:

$$P^t APx = P^t b \Leftrightarrow (A_{22} - A_{21}A_{11}^{-1}A_{12})x_2 = b_2 - A_{21}A_{11}^{-1}b_1 \qquad [15.16]$$

The solution to the complete exact problem, $Ax = b$ is, therefore, obtained by doing the following. First, we compute the solution of the initial problem on the fine grid:

$$A_{11}x_1^0 = b_1$$
$$x_2^0 = 0$$

Then, we sum to this solution to the correction coming from the projected problem on the coarse grid [15.16], extended by interpolation on the fine grid, according to the formula [15.14].

Obviously, the transition matrix, thus defined, is dense. Therefore, we make a local approximation that limits the calculations to small subsets of zone 1, which amounts to replacing matrix A_{11} by its diagonal blocks. Typically, each block will be defined by a node, or by a node and its neighbors only.

15.4.3. Algebraic multigrid methods

A single level of coarsening is insufficient to make a problem small enough to be solved at a low cost by using a direct method. Therefore, we must apply several successive coarsening levels.

With several grid levels, the procedure for making a computationally efficient preconditioner consists of carrying out a few iterations of an iterative method at each intermediate level, to slightly reduce the residual, before projecting it onto the coarser grid. Only the problem projected on the coarsest grid is solved exactly by a direct method. Similarly, after each interpolation of the corrected residual of one grid level to a finer level, we again carry out a few iterations of an iterative method. This is the "multigrid" method, characterized as algebraic when successive grids are determined by the methodology presented in section 15.4.2.

There are, therefore, many variants of the multigrid method, depending on the type of iterations performed to reduce the residual on each level of the grid, an operation known as residual "smoothing". This name arises from the fact that, for problems with partial derivatives, it tends to reduce the components of the residual associated with the largest eigenvalues of the system. These in themselves represent, if we conduct a Fourier decomposition analysis, high-frequency components, which are highly oscillatory.

In addition, there are different strategies to pass from one grid to another. The simplest method, which has been described, involves starting from the fine grid and descending from one level to another, until reaching the coarsest grid, on which the problem is solved exactly. Then, we ascend one level at a time, from the coarsest to the finest. This is called a "V-cycle". More complex strategies consist of executing several V-cycles on the coarsest levels, before again ascending to the finest levels, as in the case of a "W-cycle" for three grid levels, illustrated in Figure 15.4.

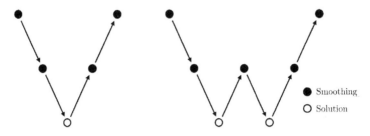

Figure 15.4. *V-cycle and W-cycle for three grid levels*

The analysis of these methods, and the choice of optimal strategies for systems resulting from the discretization of partial differential equations, is based on the properties of the differential equations under consideration, which is a problem that is beyond the scope of this book. In general, these methods cannot really be applied without taking into account the characteristics of the applications being treated.

The methodology used at the level of parallel implementation is that of domain decomposition, which allows for the parallelization of the interpolation phases and the calculation of matrix-vector products on different grid levels. The interpolation phase, always local, only requires a sparse matrix-vector product. However, the granularity tends to gradually decrease as the grid levels become coarser, and direct resolution on the coarsest grid is not easily parallelizable. If this grid is small enough, we can consider explicitly calculating the inverse of the projected matrix, so that the resolution is transformed into a dense matrix-vector product. In terms of the number of arithmetic operations, it costs much more than a forward–backward substitution of the sparse system, but it is easy to parallelize and avoids having an entirely sequential phase in the algorithm, which inevitably limits the scalability.

NOTE 15.1.– The Schur complement method and algebraic multigrid method both include producing preconditioners by projection. In the first case, the projection is localized in the subdomains, which allows solving local problems exactly. Conversely, in the second case, the projection produces a reduced global problem.

The two approaches are, in fact, complementary: one permits constructing an approximate inverse that takes into account the local effects in the system response; the other, instead, favors the capture of the global effects.

Domain decomposition methods combine these two approaches. Since the mid-1980s, they are the object of substantial research. In the following section, we will look at another approach by subdomains, which introduces the concept of overlap.

15.5. The Schwarz additive method of preconditioning

15.5.1. *Principle of the overlap*

For methods that use a local approach, such as the Schur complement method, it is not enough to solve the internal blocks, even in an accurate manner, but we also need to provide conditions for connections between the

264   Parallel Scientific Computing

local solutions, which ensures the transmission of information between subdomains. In the case of the Schur complement method, it is the calculation of the gradient on each interface that allows us to take into account the contributions from the two neighboring subdomains to update the approximate solution value.

Another way to ensure an information transfer between the subdomains is to provide a decomposition with overlap, so that the boundary nodes of one subdomain are found within the neighboring domain. This is the basic principle of an iterative method of resolution called the Schwarz method. The method was published by Schwarz at the end of the 19th Century. In this work, he proposed a method to simplify the solution of the Laplace equation in domains more complex than simple circles or squares, on which analytical solutions can be obtained. With the emergence of parallel computers, this method was given a fresh impetus recently, and is nowadays used to decompose and parallelize the solution of problems on arbitrary geometries.

To illustrate this, we will take as an example, a problem with a tridiagonal matrix, which corresponds to a one-dimensional graph.

$$
\begin{pmatrix}
2 & -1 & 0 & \cdots & 0 \\
-1 & 2 & -1 & \cdots & 0 \\
\vdots & \ddots & \ddots & \ddots & \vdots \\
0 & \cdots & -1 & 2 & -1 \\
0 & \cdots & 0 & -1 & 2
\end{pmatrix}
\begin{pmatrix}
f_1 \\
f_2 \\
\vdots \\
f_{N-1} \\
f_N
\end{pmatrix}
=
\begin{pmatrix}
a \\
0 \\
\vdots \\
0 \\
b
\end{pmatrix}
$$

The solution to this problem is given by the formula $x_i = a + i(b-a)/(n+1)$, $i = 0, 1 \cdots n+1$. This linear system can be derived from the discretization by finite elements or finite differences of the Laplace equation $f''(x) = 0$ on the segment $[0, 1]$, together with the following boundary conditions $f(0) = f_0 = a$ and $f(1) = f_{n+1} = b$. Solution f has a constant derivative. The curve $y = f(x)$ is thus the segment extending from point $(0, a)$ to point $(1, b)$. Figure 15.5(a) shows the solution to the complete problem, in the case where a and b are both equal to 1; the curve $y = f(x)$ is, therefore, a horizontal line.

To apply the Schwarz method, we decompose the set of equations into two overlapping subsets. An iteration of the method consists of successively solving the subproblem associated with each subproblem, taking as boundary conditions the global boundary conditions for the points that are on the boundary of the global domain, and the value of the previous solution in the neighboring subdomain for the boundary points resulting from the decomposition. In the first iteration, the initial value is *a priori* set to 0. The procedure is illustrated in Figure 15.6, which clearly shows that convergence is much faster when the overlap is important, while Figure 15.5(b) shows that in the absence of overlap, the solution is stagnant.

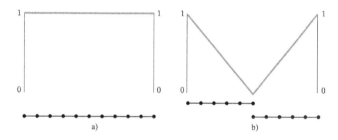

Figure 15.5. *Solutions of the global and local problems, without overlap*

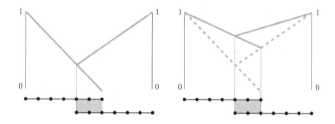

Figure 15.6. *Successive iterations of the Schwarz method*

15.5.2. *Multiplicative versus additive Schwarz methods*

The original Schwarz method presented in the previous section consists of solving alternatively local subproblems by imposing the data from the neighbors as boundary conditions. If we introduce formal operators to describe the successive subdomain resolutions during one iteration of the method, the application of the two operators acts as a product. The method is then referred to as "multiplicative". This method is not parallel, as the solution of one subdomain requires the solution of the other subdomain.

To get rid of the dependence between the local solutions and make the method parallel, we need to introduce as boundary conditions on each subdomain the solution obtained from a previous iteration, as illustrated in Figure 15.7.

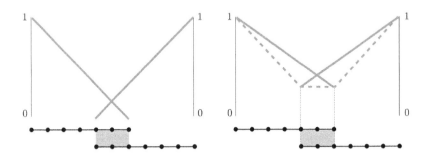

Figure 15.7. *Successive iterations of the additive Schwarz method*

In the overlapping zone, the solutions obtained in both subdomains coexist. Once the linear system is converged, however, both solutions coincide in this zone. It is, therefore, not necessary to explicitly define the solution in the overlapping zone during the iterative process. Using the operator formalism to describe the two resolutions on a single iteration, the simultaneous applications of these two operators act as the addition of operations. This variant of the Schwarz method is then logically referred to as "additive".

If we compare the multiplicative and additive versions of the Schwarz method, we observe that the first one converges faster than the second one, as illustrated by Figures 15.6 and 15.7. However, the additive variant is parallel, for the two local problems can be solved independently during one single operation, contrary to the multiplicative version.

To illustrate this difference, let us go back to the one-dimensional example described previously. Let us divide the segment $[0, 1]$ into $n = 19$ nodes and two subdomains of the same length. In order to construct the overlapping meshes, we add at each overlapping level one node to each subdomain, as shown in Figure 15.8. We denote s as the number of common nodes to both subdomains. In Figure 15.8, we colored the overlapping nodes in light gray, and the interface nodes (where the Dirichlet boundary condition is exchanged between the subdomains) in dark gray. Figure 15.9 compares the convergence of the multiplicative and additive methods. The error is computed as the difference between 1 and the value of the central node of the first subdomain. It can be checked that this value converges toward the solution $f = 1$ more rapidly in the case of the multiplicative Schwarz.

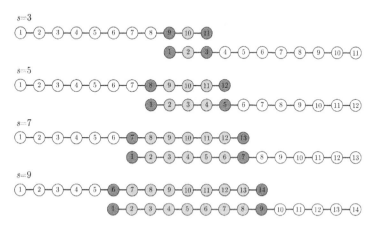

Figure 15.8. *Overlapping meshes with different overlaps s*

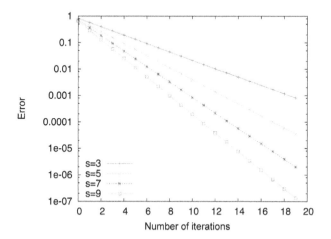

Figure 15.9. *Comparison of the convergences of the multiplicative and additive Schwarz method*

15.5.3. *Additive Schwarz preconditioning*

As with all single-fixed point iterative methods (discussed in section 6.2), an efficient way to use the Schwarz method for solving linear problems is to use it as a preconditioner of a Krylov method. The main feature of the Schwarz method is its reliance on the existence by subdomains; one of the fundamental interests of subdomain approaches is that they allow distributed parallelism. Therefore, the additive Schwarz is the method of choice. The fundamental problem with overlapping approaches resides in the complexity of updating the values on the areas of overlap in an arbitrary mesh decomposition. A methodology to simplify and even avoid this pitfall is to partition the graph of the matrix by vertices (nodes). Let us denote by R_s the restriction operator to the vertex subset Ω_s resulting from the partition. The transposed operator R_s^t is the extension by 0 of a vector defined on the vertices of Ω_s. The overlapping is obtained by adding the neighboring vertices located at a distance δ from Ω_s in order to form a subset of vertices Ω_s^δ. In Figure 15.10, the vertices of the Ω_s subset, and the edges connecting them, are shown in black. The vertices of Ω_s^δ, exterior to Ω_s, are represented in gray. The edges connecting the vertices of Ω_s to its complementary in Ω_s^1, as well as its interconnection edges, are represented by thick gray lines. As suggested by the figure, the construction of Ω_s^1 from Ω_s is carried out using a frontal approach of the matrix graph. Ω_s^2 is constructed in the same way from Ω_s^1. The discontinuous lines of the figure represent the edges which connect the vertices of Ω_s^1 to its complementary in Ω_s^2, as well as the interconnection edges.

We let R_s^δ denote the restriction operator to the subset of vertices Ω_s^δ. The Schwarz additive preconditioner with restriction on the partition is written as:

$$M = \sum_{s=1}^{p} R_s^t R_s R_s^{\delta t} (R_s^\delta A R_s^{\delta t})^{-1} R_s^\delta \qquad [15.17]$$

This means that to calculate vector Mg, we take the restriction of g, $R_s^\delta g$, on each overlapping Ω_s^δ subset, and we solve the linear system associated with the diagonal block of the corresponding matrix $R_s^\delta A R_s^{\delta t} v_s^\delta = R_s^\delta g$. The restriction to the non-overlapping Ω_s subset of the preconditioned vector Mg is the restriction of the vector v_s^δ solution to this system, with $R_s^t R_s R_s^{\delta t}$ being the restriction operator to the vertices of Ω_s of a vector defined on Ω_s^δ.

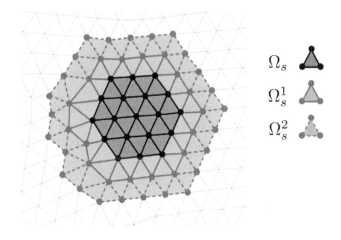

Figure 15.10. *Overlapping (light gray) from a subset defined by a partition by vertices (dark gray)*

Defined in this way, this method allows working by subdomains with a completely assembled matrix, by using only the graph of the matrix. It can, of course, also be based on an approach of decomposition by elements or vertices. It requires the factorization of the overlapping diagonal blocks of the matrix. Compared to the Schur complement method, it is thus substantially more costly at initialization and in each iteration if we use a method of exact local resolution. Moreover, it requires more data transfers since each process must retrieve the values of the vector to precondition from an overlapping interface; necessarily more voluminous than a minimal interface using the cutting of subdomains into elements. However, it can be used with a local inversion approximation, contrary to the Schur complement method.

15.5.4. *Restricted additive Schwarz: parallel implementation*

We now present the Schwarz method with minimum overlap, also referred to as restricted additive Schwarz (RAS). This variant of the Schwarz algorithm has the advantage to almost perfectly adapt to the data structures of parallel codes, in particular to finite element codes, as all the communications are concentrated on the interface nodes. First, we are going to study the equivalence between a preconditioner of Schwarz type and the solution of problems with overlapping subdomains using as Dirichlet boundary condition the solution of the neighboring subdomain.

To illustrate the RAS method, let us consider the example of Figure 15.11, from which we obtain an algebraic system of the form $Ax = b$. Let us first consider a sequential context, although we consider two subdomains. That is we have access to all the data used to assemble all the matrices. We will study the parallel implementation of this algorithm at the end of this section.

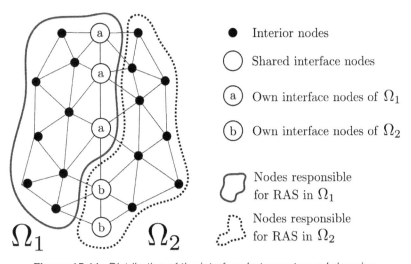

Figure 15.11. *Distribution of the interface between two subdomains*

Let us divide the interface between the two subdomains in own and other parts, as we did in section 14.4. On the one hand, the own interface of subdomain 1 is a and the other interface is b. On the other hand, the own interface of subdomain 2 is b and the other interface is a.

Using the numbering of Figure 15.11, we have $x = (x_1 \ x_a \ x_b \ x_2)^t$, and the monolithic system can be written as:

$$\begin{pmatrix} A_{11} & A_{1a} & A_{1b} & 0 \\ A_{a1} & A_{aa} & A_{ab} & A_{a2} \\ A_{b1} & A_{ba} & A_{bb} & A_{b2} \\ 0 & A_{2a} & A_{2b} & A_{22} \end{pmatrix} \begin{pmatrix} x_1 \\ x_a \\ x_b \\ x_2 \end{pmatrix} = \begin{pmatrix} b_1 \\ b_a \\ b_b \\ b_2 \end{pmatrix}$$

Let us define now two submatrices $\tilde{A}_1$ and $\tilde{A}_2$ such that:

$$\tilde{A}_1 = \begin{pmatrix} A_{11} & A_{1a} & A_{1b} \\ A_{a1} & A_{aa} & A_{ab} \\ A_{b1} & A_{ba} & A_{bb} \end{pmatrix}, \qquad \tilde{A}_2 = \begin{pmatrix} A_{aa} & A_{ab} & A_{a2} \\ A_{ba} & A_{bb} & A_{b2} \\ A_{2a} & A_{2b} & A_{22} \end{pmatrix} \qquad [15.18]$$

The first matrix involves the rows and columns of the global matrix corresponding to subdomain 1 exclusively, while the second matrix involves those of subdomain 2. Let us see now the effect of each submatrix as a preconditioner for the Richardson method to solve the original problem $Ax = b$. We can obtain the following two updates, denoted by subindex 1 or 2 according to the preconditioning matrix considered:

$$\begin{pmatrix} x_1 \\ x_a \\ x_b \\ \hline x_2 \end{pmatrix}_1^{p+1} = \begin{pmatrix} x_1 \\ x_a \\ x_b \\ \hline x_2 \end{pmatrix}^p - \left(\begin{array}{c|c} \tilde{A}_1^{-1} & 0 \\ \hline 0 & 0 \end{array} \right)$$

$$\left[\left(\begin{array}{c|c} & 0 \\ \tilde{A}_1 & A_{a2} \\ & A_{b2} \\ \hline 0\,A_{2a}\,A_{2b} & A_{22} \end{array} \right) \begin{pmatrix} x_1 \\ x_a \\ x_b \\ x_2 \end{pmatrix}^p - \begin{pmatrix} b_1 \\ b_a \\ b_b \\ b_2 \end{pmatrix} \right]$$

$$\begin{pmatrix} x_1 \\ x_a \\ x_b \\ x_2 \end{pmatrix}_2^{p+1} = \begin{pmatrix} x_1 \\ x_a \\ x_b \\ x_2 \end{pmatrix}^p - \left(\begin{array}{c|c} 0 & 0 \\ \hline 0 & \tilde{A}_2^{-1} \end{array} \right)$$

$$\left[\left(\begin{array}{c|c} A_{11} & A_{1a}\,A_{1b}\,0 \\ A_{a1} & \\ \hline A_{b1} & \tilde{A}_2 \\ 0 & \end{array} \right) \begin{pmatrix} x_1 \\ x_a \\ x_b \\ x_2 \end{pmatrix}^p - \begin{pmatrix} b_1 \\ b_a \\ b_b \\ b_2 \end{pmatrix} \right]$$

As can be observed, none of these two equations is sufficient to obtain a global solution to the system: in fact, the first system updates the solution in subdomain 1 (including the interface), while the second system updates the solution of subdomain 2 (including all its interface, the same as subdomain 1).

Let us note that we can rewrite the last two systems as:

$$
\begin{pmatrix} x_1 \\ x_a \\ x_b \\ x_2 \end{pmatrix}^{p+1}_1 = \begin{pmatrix} 0 \\ 0 \\ 0 \\ x_2^p \end{pmatrix} + \left(\frac{\tilde{A}_1^{-1}\left[\begin{pmatrix} b_1 \\ b_a \\ b_b \end{pmatrix} - \begin{pmatrix} 0 \\ A_{a2}x_2^p \\ A_{b2}x_2^p \end{pmatrix} \right]}{0} \right)
$$

$$
\begin{pmatrix} x_1 \\ x_a \\ x_b \\ x_2 \end{pmatrix}^{p+1}_2 = \begin{pmatrix} x_1^p \\ 0 \\ 0 \\ 0 \end{pmatrix} + \left(\frac{0}{\tilde{A}_2^{-1}\left[\begin{pmatrix} b_a \\ b_b \\ b_2 \end{pmatrix} - \begin{pmatrix} A_{a1}x_1^p \\ A_{b1}x_1^p \\ 0 \end{pmatrix} \right]} \right)
$$

By doing this, we can reinterpret both problems in the following way:

– The first equation consists of solving exactly the unknowns (x_1, x_a, x_b) applying as a Dirichlet condition the solution x_2^p obtained from the previous iteration.

– The second equation consists of solving exactly the unknowns (x_2, x_a, x_b) applying as a Dirichlet condition the solution x_1^p obtained from the previous iteration.

We have, therefore, shown the equivalence between the use of $\tilde{A}_1^{-1}$ and $\tilde{A}_2^{-1}$ as preconditioners and the Schwarz method with minimum overlap. In fact, the matrices (A_{a1}, A_{b1}) and (A_{a2}, A_{b2}) connect the interface nodes with the first interior neighboring nodes of subdomains 1 and 2, respectively.

Now, the unknowns on the interface are defined twice, once by each system. If we define R_1^0 as the restriction operator to subdomain 1 and its own interface a, as well as the restriction R_2^0 to subdomain 2 and its own interface b, such that:

$$
R_1^0 = \begin{pmatrix} 1 & 0 & 0 & 0 \\ 0 & 1 & 0 & 0 \\ 0 & 0 & 0 & 0 \\ 0 & 0 & 0 & 0 \end{pmatrix}, \qquad R_2^0 = \begin{pmatrix} 0 & 0 & 0 & 0 \\ 0 & 0 & 0 & 0 \\ 0 & 0 & 1 & 0 \\ 0 & 0 & 0 & 1 \end{pmatrix}
$$

Then, we can define a unique solution in the following way:

$$
\begin{pmatrix} x_1 \\ x_a \\ x_b \\ x_2 \end{pmatrix}^{p+1} = R_1^0 \begin{pmatrix} x_1 \\ x_a \\ x_b \\ x_2 \end{pmatrix}^{p+1}_1 + R_2^0 \begin{pmatrix} x_1 \\ x_a \\ x_b \\ x_2 \end{pmatrix}^{p+1}_2 = \begin{pmatrix} \begin{pmatrix} x_1 \\ x_a \end{pmatrix}_1 \\ \begin{pmatrix} x_b \\ x_2 \end{pmatrix}_2 \end{pmatrix}^{p+1}
\qquad [15.19]
$$

The global solution is, therefore, given by (x_1, x_a), computed in subdomain 1, and by (x_2, x_b), computed in subdomain 2.

Let us examine how to implement this algorithm in a parallel context:

1) In a first step, the two local matrices $\tilde{A}_1$ and $\tilde{A}_2$ are assembled (equation [15.18]). However, in parallel, subdomain 1 can only assemble part of its interface matrices, which we denote by $A_{aa}^{(1)}$, $A_{ab}^{(1)}$ and $A_{bb}^{(1)}$. Subdomain 2 must therefore send its contributions to the interface, represented by matrices $A_{aa}^{(2)}$, $A_{ab}^{(2)}$ and $A_{bb}^{(2)}$. Once this communication is achieved, subdomain 1 can assemble the complete interface matrices: $A_{aa} = A_{aa}^{(1)} + A_{aa}^{(2)}$, etc. The same operation must be carried for subdomain 2. Let us remark that these exchanges are carried out exclusively on the interface nodes.

2) The second operation consists of inverting the two local matrices.

3) The third operation updates the unknowns in each subdomain, using the submatrices $\tilde{A}_1^{-1}$ and $\tilde{A}_2^{-1}$.

4) Eventually, the global solution is defined by equation [15.19]: it corresponds to the solution found on the interior and own interface of each subdomain. In a parallel context, an additional communication is necessary to exchange the updates in order to equalize the interface values: subdomain 1 sends its own interface solution x_a to subdomain 2, and subdomain 2 sends its own interface solution x_b to subdomain 1.

This method can be used as a preconditioner, referred to as C_{RAS}. The preconditioning step consists of solving a system of the form $C_{RAS}x = y$, in the following way: for each subdomain I with internal nodes i and with interface Γ formed by the union if its own interface Γ_{own} and other interface Γ_{oth}:

– Assemble local matrix C'_{RAS}:

$$C'_{RAS} = \begin{pmatrix} A_{ii} & A_{i\Gamma} \\ A_{\Gamma i} & A_{\Gamma\Gamma}^{(I)} \end{pmatrix}.$$

– Exchange the interface contributions between neighbors and assemble the complete preconditioner:

$$C_{RAS} = \begin{pmatrix} A_{ii} & A_{i\Gamma} \\ A_{\Gamma i} & A_{\Gamma\Gamma} \end{pmatrix}.$$

– Invert C_{RAS} exactly or with incomplete factorization.

– Compute $x = C_{RAS}^{-1} y$.

– Exchange $x|_{\Gamma_{own}}$ to equalize to interface solutions.

Before closing the description of the RAS preconditioner, let us outline an important point. In a distributed memory context, complex situations can occur that do not have equivalents in a sequential context. Let us take a look at the example of Figure 15.12. In Figure 15.12, subdomain 2 has two interface nodes (black circles) which are not in its matrix graph. In fact, these two nodes do not share any element of the mesh and therefore are not related through any coefficients in the matrix system. Now, if these nodes belong to the own interface of Ω_2, we will have no mean to assemble the complete local matrix $A_{\Gamma\Gamma}$ of the preconditioner C_{RAS} in this subdomain. One solution to this issue would be to extend the graph of Ω_2 to take into account the relation between its own boundary and all its interface nodes.

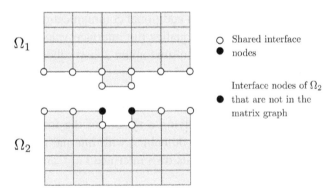

Figure 15.12. *Interface nodes not present in the matrix graph of Ω_2*

15.6. Preconditioners based on the physics

We will now give two examples of preconditioners based on the physics, or the associated numerical method, of the problem under consideration. These are namely the Gauss–Seidel and linelet preconditioners.

15.6.1. *Gauss–Seidel method*

To illustrate this preconditioner, let us take the example of a one-dimensional advection-diffusion equation $f'(x) - \epsilon f''(x) = q$ on the segment $[0, 1]$. Let us discretize these segments by numbering the nodes in increasing order, from 0 to 1. If the diffusion is zero ($\epsilon = 0$), we have a hyperbolic problem for which the information propagates in the direction of the advection, from left to right in this case. Now, if we use a discretization method, such as finite element (FE), finite volume (FV) and finite difference (FD), with an appropriate scheme to stabilize the convection (upwind), we end up with a matrix with the following property: on each row, the only non-zero coefficient apart from the diagonal corresponds to the previous node (the one on the left). That is, we could solve the problem by advancing from node to node, starting from the first node with a Dirichlet condition. This is exactly what would do the GaussSeidel iterative method (see notation in section 6.2):

$$x_{p+1} = x_p - (D - E)^{-1}(Ax_p - b)$$

The solution in this case can be obtained in one single iteration per node. Now, if we increase the diffusion, we distance ourselves from the hyperbolic limit. In a multi-dimensional context, however, if we number the nodes along the advection vector, we can obtain a better convergence than with a simple diagonal preconditioner. In the case where the advection is of the same order as the diffusion, it is more convenient to use the symmetric Gauss–Seidel. This preconditioner consists of carrying out one iteration with matrix $D - E$ and another one with matrix $D - F$. This method is referred to as symmetric successive over relaxation (SSOR) in the literature.

To summarize, we can write the diagonal, Gauss–Seidel and its symmetric version as follows:

– Jacobi: $M = D^{-1}$;

– Gauss–Seidel: $M = (D - E)^{-1}$;

– symmetric Gauss–Seidel: $M = [(D - F)D^{-1}(D - E)]^{-1}$.

Numbering the nodes along the advection can be a hard task. In addition, this numbering may be very inefficient in terms of memory access. At the parallelization level, the interfaces are likely to cut the advection lines. The idea is to use the diagonal (Jacobi) on the interface nodes, and only use the Gauss–Seidel to precondition the interior nodes.

15.6.2. Linelet method

The linelet preconditioner is especially designed for anisotropic meshes, where the dominating coefficients of the matrix are concentrated in the stretching direction. It is a typical case in boundary layers in CFD, where this direction is the normal direction to the wall. Figure 15.13 shows a two-dimensional mesh of such a boundary layer. Now, if we integrate a Laplacian on this mesh, we can observe that in the row of the black node (in FE by using a closed integration rule), the dominating coefficients are those on the columns corresponding to the preceding and following nodes in the normal direction (that is the linelet). In the limit of infinite anisotropy, the other coefficients go to zero and the matrix for the boundary layer nodes ends up tridiagonal.

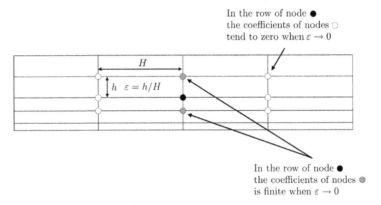

Figure 15.13. *Linelet. The circles are the neighbors of the black node in the matrix graph*

Now, we know how to invert efficiently a tridiagonal matrix. The linelet preconditioner consists, therefore, of assembling for each linelet a tridiagonal matrix and use its inverse as a preconditioner.

The construction of the linelets can be carried out in preprocess, if the mesh is fixed. For Cartesian meshes, their construction is trivial. In the general case, it can be more complex. Each linelet consists of a list of nodes, starting from a wall node and going through the normal direction to it. The linelet stops when anisotropy is no longer significant. As long as parallelization is concerned, we can try to partition the subdomains along the linelets, in order not to cut them off. If this cannot be done, the inverse diagonal can be used on the interface nodes, as was done in the case of the Gauss–Seidel.

Figure 15.14 shows the efficiency of the linelet preconditioner, applied to the deflated conjugate gradient (DCG), for the solution of the thermal turbulent cavity. This preconditioner is compared to the diagonal one applied to the CG and DCG. We observe that, in this case, the CG does not converge.

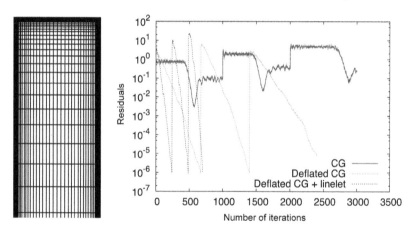

Figure 15.14. *Linelet preconditioner applied to the DCG. Comparison with the CG and DCG with diagonal preconditioner. Left: Mesh. Right: Convergence. For a color version of the figure, see www.iste.co.uk/magoules/computing.zip*

Appendices

A1.1. Parallelization techniques

EXERCISE A1.1.– (Automatic analysis of dependence)

Demonstrate that a necessary condition for a dependence to exist in the loop below is that the greatest common divisor (gcd) of a and c divides $(d - b)$.

```
for  i = 1  to  n
     x(a × i + b) = x(c × i + d) + y(i)
end for
```

EXERCISE A1.2.– (Vectorization and parallelization)

Study the optimization for the vectorization and parallelization on a shared memory computer for the following portion of code:

```
for  i = 1  to  n_i
   for  j = 1  to  n_j
      for  k = 1  to  n_k
         u(i, j, k) = a × u(i, j, k − 1) + b × u(i, j, k) + c × u(i, j, k + 1)
      end for
   end for
end for
```

EXERCISE A1.3.– (Study of loops)

Study, based on the properties of the array $index$, the vectorizability and parallelizability of the following three series of loops:

```
for  i = 1  to  n
    x(index(i)) = c × y(i)
end  for
```

```
for  i = 1  to  n
    x(index(i)) = x(index(i)) + c × y(i)
end  for
```

```
for  i = 1  to  n
    x(i) = x(index(i)) + c × y(i)
end  for
```

EXERCISE A1.4.– (Permutation of loops)

Can the two loops of the following code be permuted?

```
for  i = 2  to  n − 1
    for  j = 1  to  n − 1
        u(i, j) = u(i − 1, j) + u(i, j) + u(i + 1, j)
        u(i, j + 1) = u(i, j)
    end  for
end  for
```

EXERCISE A1.5.– (Study of loops)

Study, based on the properties of the array $index$, the optimization for the vectorization, the parallelization, or both simultaneously, of the three nested loops below:

```
for  k = 1  to  ne
    for  i = 1  to  6
        for  j = 1  to  6
            y(index(i, k)) = y(index(i, k)) + a(i, j, k) × x(index(j, k))
        end  for
    end  for
end  for
```

EXERCISE A1.6.– (Product of distributed parallel matrix-vectors)

We will consider a parallel distributed-memory machine with p processors. We want to achieve the product of a dense matrix of dimension n by a vector $y = Ax$.

The vector x will be initially known and stored by all the processors, and after concluding the matrix-vector multiplication, the resulting vector y has to be totally reconstituted in each of the processors. However, the coefficients of the matrix should not be duplicated.

In the following questions, we will explain the placement of the matrix on the different processors, the arithmetic operations executed by each processor and the transfers of vectors, or the portions of vectors, necessary to reassemble the resulting vector. We will first try to balance the workload and the size of occupied memory in each of the processors. For the transfer phases, we will attempt to either minimize the length of messages, or minimize the number of messages:

1) Describe the parallelization of the matrix-vector multiplication for a block distribution of the matrix by rows or columns.

2) Describe the parallelization of the product of the matrix-vector and the division of the matrix into block matrices.

3) We will now look at the case of a symmetric matrix and where only the inferior triangular part is stored. Lay out the principle for achieving the matrix-vector multiplication on a single processor with this type of storage.

4) Describe the parallelization of the matrix-vector product for a distribution of the lower triangular part of the matrix by blocks of rows or blocks of columns.

5) Describe the parallelization of the matrix-vector product for a division of the lower triangular part of the matrix into a block matrix.

A1.2. Matrix analysis

EXERCISE A1.7.– (Properties of a matrix)

$$\text{Let } a \in \mathbb{R} \text{ and } A = \begin{pmatrix} 1 & a & a \\ a & 1 & a \\ a & a & 1 \end{pmatrix}$$

For which values of a is matrix A positive definite?

EXERCISE A1.8.– (Change of basis)

Let us consider a change of basis matrix B from V with basis $(\tilde{e}_j)_{j=1}^n$ to V with basis $(e_j)_{j=1}^n$. Show that the coefficients of B are given by $b_{ij} = e_i^t \cdot \tilde{e}_j$.

EXERCISE A1.9.– (Eigenvalues of a matrix)

Calculate the eigenvalues of the following matrices:

$$A = \begin{pmatrix} 2 & -1 \\ 1 & 3 \end{pmatrix}, \quad B = \begin{pmatrix} 1 & 2 \\ 1 & 4 \end{pmatrix}, \quad C = \begin{pmatrix} 2 & 0 & 0 \\ 1 & -4 & 0 \\ -3 & 9 & 4 \end{pmatrix}$$

EXERCISE A1.10.– (Eigenvectors of a matrix)

Let A be the matrix defined by:

$$A = \begin{pmatrix} -1 & -2 & 0 \\ -2 & 0 & 2 \\ 0 & 2 & 1 \end{pmatrix}$$

1) Determine the eigenvalues of A and the associated eigenvectors.

2) Why can we choose the eigenvectors such that they form an orthonormal basis?

3) Which interesting property does the change of basis matrix have?

4) Deduce the expression of A^n as a function of n.

EXERCISE A1.11.– (Conditioning of a matrix)

We will now look at the influence of the pivoting strategy in the Gauss elimination procedure.

1) Show that for any matrix $A = (a_{ij})$ of the $(2, 2)$ type, we have:

$$\kappa_2(A) = \sigma + (\sigma^2 - 1)^{\frac{1}{2}} \quad \text{with} \quad \sigma = \frac{\sum_{i,j=1}^2 |a_{ij}|^2}{2|det(A)|}$$

where $|det(A)| = a_{11}a_{22} - a_{12}a_{21}$ is the determinant of A.

2) Calculate the conditioning $\kappa_p(.)$ for $p = 1, 2, \infty$ of upper triangular linear system matrices, obtained after the substitution of u_1 in the second row, by its value obtained as a function of u_2 in the first row, for the system:

$$10^{-4}u_1 + u_2 = 1$$

$$u_1 + u_2 = 2$$

depending on whether you begin by exchanging the two lines, or not. What can we deduce from this?

EXERCISE A1.12.– (The matrix of the Poisson equation)

Let us consider the Poisson equation $f'' = 1$ on the segment $[0, 1]$ with the Dirichlet boundary conditions $f = 0$ at $x = 0, 1$. Let us divide the segment into $N+2$ equally spaced nodes, where the distance between nodes is $h = \frac{1}{N+1}$. By using second-order finite differences (the same system can be obtained using the Finite Element (FE) or Finite Volume (FV) methods), the algebraic system reads:

$$\begin{pmatrix} 2 & -1 & 0 & \cdots & 0 \\ -1 & 2 & -1 & \cdots & 0 \\ \vdots & \ddots & \ddots & \ddots & \vdots \\ 0 & \cdots & -1 & 2 & -1 \\ 0 & \cdots & 0 & -1 & 2 \end{pmatrix} \begin{pmatrix} f_1 \\ f_2 \\ \vdots \\ f_{N-1} \\ f_N \end{pmatrix} = h^2 \begin{pmatrix} 1 \\ 1 \\ \vdots \\ 1 \\ 1 \end{pmatrix}$$

The N eigenvalues λ_i and eigenvectors e_i ($i = 1, 2 \cdots N$) are given by:

$$\lambda_i = 2[1 - \cos(\pi i/(N + 1))]$$

$$e_i(j) = \sqrt{\frac{2}{N + 1}} \sin(\pi i j/(N + 1))$$

1) Compute the conditioning $\kappa_2(A)$ of matrix A as a function of h, for a high value of N. What can we say about the conditioning as the mesh is refined?

2) What relationship do the eigenvalues have with their corresponding eigenvectors (in terms of frequencies)?

A1.3. Direct methods

EXERCISE A1.13.– (Crout factorization of a dense matrix)

1) Write the Crout factorization $A = LDL^t$ of a dense matrix of dimension n, which stores in a one-dimensional array only the coefficients of the lower-triangular part.

2) Consider different ways of writing the program, and the storage of coefficients of the matrix, in order to obtain the most efficient vectorization code.

3) The same question for parallel-vector optimization. What do you deduce from this?

EXERCISE A1.14.– (Block Cholesky factorization)

We will work on a symmetric positive definite matrix K, of dimension $n = r + p$, where r is smaller than p, composed of the following blocks:

$$K = \begin{pmatrix} K_{11} & K_{12} \\ K_{21} & K_{22} \end{pmatrix}$$

with $K_{21} = K_{12}^t$.

1) Prove that the Cholesky factorization $K = LL^t$ of the matrix is given by:

$$L^t = \begin{pmatrix} L_{11}^t & L_{12}^t \\ 0 & L_{22}^t \end{pmatrix}$$

with $L_{11}L_{11}^t = K_{11}$, $L_{12} = L_{11}^{-1}K_{12}$ and $L_{22}L_{22}^t = K_{22} - K_{21}K_{11}^{-1}K_{12}$.

2) Show that we can calculate the factorization of the matrix, by using three subprograms; the first, which computes the Cholesky factorization of a matrix, with a dimension less than or equal to p; the second, which calculates

by successive forward substitutions, of the product $L^{-1}B$, where L is a lower triangular matrix, and B is a rectangular matrix; and the third that calculates a product by the matrix $K = K - B^t B$.

3) Count for the number of arithmetic operations required for each of these subprograms. Prove that the cost of block factorization is the same as for the classical algorithm.

4) Examine the parallelizability of each of these subprograms, determining their granularity in terms of number of arithmetic operations of each parallel zone. Assume that the targeted machine has shared memory, without cache, and thus, we will not take into account the costs of data transfers. Generalize by recurrence this blockwise algorithm, where the matrix dimension is equal to $n = p \times q + r$.

5) We will study the level of parallelism of the algorithm, as a function of q and p. In particular, we consider the case where p is small, and where a granularity of order $p \times p$ is not sufficient to allow for the efficient use of multiple processors.

EXERCISE A1.15.– (Block-wise resolution of a lower triangular system)

We want to solve the linear system $Lx = b$ of dimension $n = p \times q$, where L is a lower triangular matrix decomposed into blocks L_{ij} of dimension p, with $1 \le i \le j \le q$, being the diagonal blocks L_{ii} lower triangular themselves.

1) Determine the blockwise solution algorithm, by decomposing the vectors x and b into subvectors x_i and b_i of dimension p.

2) Determine the two types of computational tasks associated with operations on the matrix blocks and on the subvectors, and calculate their respective costs in terms of the number of arithmetic operations.

3) By denoting $P \ll Q$ the precedence relationship of task P with task Q, which indicates that P must be executed before Q, write the relationships between the occurrences of the tasks involved in the algorithm solution, by indexing the various occurrences by i and j. Write the complete dependence graph if $n = 4$.

4) If the time costs of the tasks P and Q are assumed to be 1 and 2, respectively, determine the minimum parallel execution time. How many processors are necessary to attain this time? What is the efficiency?

EXERCISE A1.16.– (Block calculation of the kernel and the image of a matrix)

Let us consider a symmetric matrix A of dimension n. We want to solve the problem:

$$Ax = b \qquad\qquad\qquad\qquad [A1.1]$$

1) Show that if b belongs to the image of A, system [A1.1] has a unique solution x belonging to the image of A, and that the solutions are all vectors that are written $x + y$, where y is any element of the kernel of A.

2) Show that problem [A1.1] has a solution, if and only if, b belongs to the orthogonal subspace of the kernel of A.

3) Assume that A has a block decomposition of the form:

$$A = \begin{pmatrix} A_{11} & A_{12} \\ A_{21} & A_{22} \end{pmatrix}$$

with $A_{21} = A_{12}^t$. Using block Gauss factorization, show that if the block A_{11} is the same rank as matrix A, and invertible, then: $A_{22} - A_{21}A_{11}^{-1}A_{12} = 0$.

4) Show that the kernel of A is the set of vectors of the form:

$$\begin{pmatrix} -A_{11}^{-1}A_{12}x_2 \\ x_2 \end{pmatrix}$$

If we denote:

$$N = \begin{pmatrix} -A_{11}^{-1}A_{12} \\ I_2 \end{pmatrix}$$

with I_2 being the identity matrix of a dimension equal to that of the kernel, deduce the necessary and sufficient condition for system [A1.1] to admit a solution is: $N^t b = 0$.

5) We denote:

$$A^+ = \begin{pmatrix} A_{11}^{-1} & 0 \\ 0 & 0 \end{pmatrix}$$

Show that if b belongs to the image of A, then all the solutions of system [A1.1] are written as:

$$A^+b + Nx_2$$

6) Explain how to carry out, in practice, the determination of block A_{11} by the symmetrical pivoting of the rows and columns during the factorization of A.

EXERCISE A1.17.– (Crout factorization of a skyline stored matrix)

1) Write the Crout factorization $A = LDL^t$ of a matrix of dimension n, where we store in a one-dimensional array only the coefficients contained in the lower triangular profile.

We will use a pointer, denoted by mua, which for each row designates the address in the storage array of the coefficients of the matrix, the diagonal term of the previous line. Thus, $mua(0) = 0$, and the coefficients of row i contained in the profile are stored at addresses between $mua(i) + 1$ and $mua(i + 1)$ inclusively.

2) Assuming that the profile of the matrix is monotonic, which is to say, if we call the column $index(i)$ the first non-zero term of row i, then the $index$ function is increasing.

Consider different ways of writing the program, and possibly other modes of storage of the matrix's coefficients to obtain the most efficient code possible for vectorization.

3) The same question for parallel-vector optimization. Explain.

EXERCISE A1.18.– (Multifrontal Cholesky factorization)

We will look at a symmetric positive definite matrix K of dimension $N = N_1 + N_2$ decomposed by blocks:

$$K = \begin{pmatrix} K_{11} & K_{12} \\ K_{21} & K_{22} \end{pmatrix}$$

with $K_{21} = K_{12}^t$.

1) Prove that the Cholesky factorization of matrix $K = LL^t$ is defined by:

$$L^t = \begin{pmatrix} L_{11}^t & L_{12}^t \\ 0 & L_{22}^t \end{pmatrix}$$

with $L_{11}L_{11}^t = K_{11}$, $L_{12} = L_{11}^{-1}K_{12}$ and $L_{22}L_{22} = K_{22} - K_{21}K_{11}^{-1}K_{12}$. Prove that: $K_{22} - K_{21}K_{11}^{-1}K_{12} = K_{22} - L_{12}^t L_{12}$.

2) Assume that the graph of the matrix is a grid of $n \times n$ nodes (the case of a problem of finite elements of degree 1, or finite differences of order 1, on a structured mesh in dimension 2).

If we number the nodes in a lexicographic way, what is the form of the matrix? What is its half-width band for a Cholesky factorization?

3) We number the $(n - 2) \times (n - 2)$ internal nodes of the mesh lexicographically, then the $4(n - 1)$ boundary nodes, according to the numbering of their internal neighbors, from the lowest to the greatest. What is the form of the matrix?

4) Determine the number of operations required for the different steps of the Cholesky factorization of the matrix, using block factorization, described in question 1, with the numbering of question 3.

5) Divide the grid into four $n \times n$ subgrids $p \times p$, with p of order $n/2$.

Find the optimal numbering of each subgrid, so as to minimize the number of operations necessary to factorize the matrix, using the block method; the block K_{11} being associated with the internal nodes of different subgrids, and the block K_{22} to the $2n - 1$ nodes situated at the interface between the four subgrids.

Compare the cost of this method with the classical method that uses lexicographic numbering at a single level.

6) Describe the principle of a factorization using this process recursively, with several nested decompositions.

We can produce graphics to illustrate the resulting forms of the matrices. It is necessary to take into account the profiles of different matrix blocks, so as to only calculate the operations that are truly useful.

EXERCISE A1.19.– (Solving linear systems of tridiagonal matrices)

We consider the linear system $Ax = y$, of dimension n, where A is a tridiagonal matrix. The equation i of the system is written as:

$$f_{i-1} \times x_{i-1} + d_i \times x_i + e_i \times x_{i+1} = y_i$$

1) Determine the graph associated with matrix A and then construct the elimination tree of the LU factorization of A. Calculate the factorization cost in terms of the number of arithmetic operations as a function of n. Is it possible to find any parallel operations?

2) For the following, we assume that $n = 2^p - 1$. The "odd-even" method consists of renumbering the equations of the system, so that the equations of the odd indices in the initial numbering are numbered first in the new numbering. Build the elimination tree of the $\tilde{L}\tilde{U}$ factorization of the matrix, referred to as $\tilde{A}$. What can we conclude about the cost of this method, in terms of the number of arithmetic operations and data volume? Is it possible to find any parallel operations?

3) We recursively apply this renumbering to the $2^{p-1} - 1$ last unknowns of matrix $\tilde{A}$. What is the cost of this method for $n = 2^p - 1$? What is the potential parallelism of this method?

EXERCISE A1.20.– (Multisection factorization method of a tridiagonal matrix)

We look at matrix A, which is tridiagonal of dimension n.

1) Write the LU factorization algorithm of matrix A. Determine the elimination tree, the structure of the L and U matrices, and the factorization cost in terms of the number of arithmetic operations. Can the factorization be parallelized?

2) We assume that $n+1$ is divisible by p and we denote $nb = (n+1)/p - 1$. We decompose the unknowns into $2p - 1$ successive subblocks of dimension nb for the odd-numbered subblocks and of dimension 1 for the even-numbered subblocks.

We then renumber the unknowns starting by sequentially numbering the odd-numbered p subblocks of dimension nb and then the $p - 1$ unknowns of separation blocks of dimension 1.

Determine the form of the elimination tree of the matrix with this new numbering (starting with the case wherein $p = 2$).

3) Deduce that we can factorize in parallel the p diagonal blocks of dimension nb associated with the subblocks of unknowns of odd-numbered rank. Determine the cost of their factorization.

4) Describe the algorithm for calculating the Schur complement resulting from the elimination of these p subblocks of unknowns. Determine the calculation cost, while making sure to avoid unnecessary operations. Is this calculation, at least, partially parallelizable?

5) What is the total computational cost of the factorization? What is the potential additional filling resulting from this numbering?

EXERCISE A1.21.– (Block factorization using cyclic reduction)

First part

Assume that the graph of the matrix is a grid of $n \times n$ nodes (the case of a finite element problem of degree 1, or finite differences of order 1, on a structured mesh in dimension 2). We number the nodes of the graph using lexicographic numbering. We will store the lower triangular part of matrix K in band form:

1) Calculate the bandwidth of the matrix.

2) Determine the number of arithmetic operations required to calculate the Cholesky factorization of the matrix.

3) Determine the number of arithmetic operations needed to solve, by forward-backward substitution, the linear system $Kx = b$.

Second part

Throughout the remainder of this problem, we will consider the case of an $n \times n$ square grid. It is decomposed into p bands of equal width n/p (we will always assume that n is greater than p). We number the nodes of the graph in packets; the first packet corresponds to the internal nodes of the first band;

the second packet corresponds to the internal nodes located at the interface between the first two bands; the third block corresponds to the internal nodes located inside the second band and so on.

4) Show that matrix K, therefore, has the following block tridiagonal structure:

$$K = \begin{pmatrix} K_{11} & K_{12} & 0 & 0 & \cdots \\ K_{21} & K_{22} & K_{23} & 0 & \cdots \\ 0 & K_{32} & K_{33} & K_{34} & \cdots \\ 0 & 0 & K_{43} & K_{44} & \cdots \\ \cdots & \cdots & \cdots & \cdots & \cdots \end{pmatrix}$$

with $K_{ij} = K_{ji}^t$.

5) Show that we can eliminate the unknowns x_1, x_3, x_5, etc., associated with the internal node packets of the bands in the system $Kx = b$, and reduce this to a system involving only the unknowns at the interfaces, x_2, x_4, x_6, etc.

6) Prove that this condensed system still has a block tridiagonal structure. Determine the dimensions and values of the matrix blocks in the condensed system, as well as its right-hand side.

7) Determine the number of arithmetic operations required for this condensation, choosing the best lexicographic numbering for the diagonal blocks associated with the internal nodes of the bands K_{11}, K_{33}, K_{55}, etc.

We have just seen a method to reduce a block tridiagonal system, on the order of $2p - 1$ in a system of order p.

8) Show that we can apply the same technique to obtain a new block tridiagonal system of order $p/2$.

9) Determine the new number of arithmetic operations required for this condensation.

10) Prove that we can apply this reduction technique to obtain a dense linear system of dimension n. Determine the total cost in terms of number of arithmetic operations, using this method of factorization of cyclic block reduction, and also indicate the required memory space. Compare this with the classical algorithm studied in questions 1 and 2.

11) Detail the process in the case where $p = 8$ and graphically plot the sequence of operations.

12) Describe the forward-backward substitution algorithm of the system factorized by cyclic reduction, and calculate its cost in terms of number of arithmetic operations. Compare this with the classical algorithm discussed in question 3.

Third part

In this section, we will just study the parallelization of the method in the case where $p = 8$.

13) Consider the parallelization, on a distributed memory machine with p processors, of the cyclic reduction factorization algorithm, and then with the associated forward-backward substitution algorithm.

14) Specify the placement of the different tasks on the processors and the data transfers to perform among the processors, at each step of the calculation.

15) Determine, as a function of n and p, the speedup obtained by the parallelism, in the case where we assume that the communications costs are null.

EXERCISE A1.22.– (Block factorization of a band matrix)

We consider a matrix A, block tridiagonal, composed of p diagonal blocks of dimension lb.

$$
\begin{bmatrix}
A_{11} & A_{12} & 0 & \cdots\cdots & \cdots & 0 \\
A_{21} & A_{22} & A_{22} & 0 & & \vdots \\
0 & A_{32} & \ddots & \ddots & \ddots & \vdots \\
\vdots & 0 & \ddots & \ddots & \ddots & \vdots \\
\vdots & & \ddots & \ddots & \ddots & 0 \\
\vdots & & & \ddots & \ddots & A_{p-1p} \\
0 & \cdots & \cdots\cdots & \cdots & 0 & A_{pp-1} & A_{pp}
\end{bmatrix}
$$

We assume that the upper diagonal blocks $A_{i\,i+1}$ are lower triangular, and that subdiagonal blocks $A_{i+1\,i}$ are upper triangular. The complete matrix A is referred to as band type:

1) Apply the incomplete Gauss factorization of matrix A for the block A_{11}. Deduce a block factorization algorithm. Use this algorithm to prove that the Gauss factorization retains the banded structure.

2) Determine the cost of this block factorization algorithm, by the number of pairs of operations $(+, \times)$, depending on lb and p. Is this cost changed if some of the non-diagonal coefficients of the off-diagonal blocks are null? The same question if some of the coefficients of the diagonal blocks with numbers strictly greater than 1 are null?

3) Study the temporal and spatial location of data during the different phases of the algorithm. Determine which operations can be performed in parallel, and comment on the parallelism granularity that is exhibited.

EXERCISE A1.23.– (Mixed systems)

Consider the following mixed system:

$$\begin{pmatrix} A & B \\ B^t & 0 \end{pmatrix} \begin{pmatrix} x \\ y \end{pmatrix} = \begin{pmatrix} b \\ 0 \end{pmatrix}$$

1) Assume that matrix A is invertible. Show, preferably using a block factorization, that the complete mixed matrix is invertible, if and only if, the matrix $B^t A^{-1} B$ is invertible.

2) We assume that matrix A is symmetric positive definite. Show that matrix $B^t A^{-1} B$ is symmetric and positive. Show that the kernel of $B^t A^{-1} B$ is equal to that of B and that the image of $B^t A^{-1} B$ is equal to the image of B^t.

EXERCISE A1.24.– (Orthogonalization by Crout factorization)

We possess a family of p vectors of dimension n, $(v_j), 1 \le j \le p, p \le n$, from which we want to construct an orthogonal generating family. We denote by V the matrix with n rows and p columns, where column j is equal to vector v_j. We denote $N = V^t V$, where N is a square matrix of dimension p:

1) Show that N is a symmetric positive matrix, and definite, if and only if, the vectors (v_j) are linearly independent.

2) Assume that N is symmetric positive definite. Its Crout factorization is written as $N = LDL^t$. Calculate a family of orthogonal vectors generating $\text{Vect}\{v_1, v_2, \ldots, v_p\}$ from V and L (without using the Gramm–Schmidt algorithm).

3) If the family of vectors (v_j) is of rank $r < p$, show that we can, possibly by simultaneous permutation of the rows and columns of N, construct a main diagonal subblock of N, symmetric positive definite, of dimension r.

4) Deduce a method of calculating an orthogonally generating family from the Crout factorization of N with symmetrical pivoting (that is to say, simultaneous permutation of rows and columns, while retaining the symmetry of the matrix).

5) Compare the computational cost of this method with that of Gramm-Schmidt's method

A1.4. Iterative methods

EXERCISE A1.25.– (Conjugate gradient for a singular system)

Let us consider a symmetric positive matrix A, but not invertible. Show that the conjugate gradient algorithm applied to the system $Ax = b$, where b belongs to the image of A starting from $x_0 = 0$, converges toward the unique solution of the system which belongs to the image of A.

EXERCISE A1.26.– (Krylov methods with full orthogonalization and eigenvalues)

We solve the linear system of dimension n, $Ax = b$, using a Krylov method with full orthogonalization, of the conjugate gradient type, GMRES or ORTHODIR. We assume that the matrix is diagonalizable and we denote by (e_i), a basis of eigenvectors, and by (λ_i), the corresponding eigenvalues. In this basis, the initial gradient is written as:

$$g^0 = Ax^0 - b = \sum_{i=1}^{n} \beta_i e_i$$

1) Consider Λ_p the set of p, $p \leq n$, distinct values taken by the eigenvalues (λ_i), associated with the non-zero coefficients (β_i). Show that the largest dimension of the Krylov subspaces associated with g_0 is equal to p. Deduce that the Krylov method converges in p iterations, at most.

2) Assume that A is symmetric positive definite. The basis of the eigenvectors (e_i) is, therefore, orthonormal. Let Λ be the diagonal matrix

whose i-th diagonal coefficient is equal to λ_i. Demonstrate by changing the basis that by applying the conjugate gradient algorithm to the system $Ax = b$, or to the system $\Lambda\alpha = \beta$, with $x = \sum_{i=1}^{n} \alpha_i e_i$, we obtain the same residuals in each iteration. Deduce an estimate of the speed of convergence of the conjugate gradient method as a function of $\max(\Lambda_p)/\min(\Lambda_p)$.

3) We assume that $x^0 = \sum_{i=1}^{n} \alpha_i^0 e_i$. What can be said about the behavior of the conjugate gradient algorithm if $\alpha_i^0 = \beta_i/\lambda_i$ for certain i indices?

EXERCISE   A1.27.– (Optimal   restart   Krylov   methods   with   full orthogonalization)

Consider the linear system of dimension n, $Ax = b$. We will assume the availability of vectors $(v_i), 1 \leq i \leq p, p \leq n$, and their products by the matrix A, $(Av_i), 1 \leq i \leq p$, such that $(Av_i \cdot Av_j) = 0$ if $i \neq j$:

1) We consider an arbitrary x_0. Determine the approximate solution x_p of the system $Ax = b$ in the space $x_0 + Vect\{v_1, v_2, \ldots, v_p\}$ which minimizes $\|Ax_p - b\|$.

2) Show that if the vectors (Av_i) are not orthogonal, by using an orthogonalization procedure which does not require any calculations produced by matrix A, we can construct p vectors (w_i), such that $(Aw_i \cdot Aw_j) = 0$ if $i \neq j$.

3) Let us consider vector x_p determined in the first question. Demonstrate that $e_p = x_p - x$ is $A^t A$-orthogonal to the space $Vect\{v_1, v_2, \ldots, v_p\}$. What condition must satisfy a descent direction w so that any vector $x_p + \rho w$ satisfies the same property?

4) Describe a preconditioning procedure that makes it possible to retain this property for all the iterations of the applied ORTHODIR method by taking x_p as a starting point.

EXERCISE A1.28.– (GMRES and MinRES methods with a symmetric positive definite preconditioner)

Consider the linear system $Ax = b$. We want to use M, a symmetric positive definite preconditioner. We know that M can be written in the form $M = CC^t$. We consider the system $C^t AC\tilde{x} = \tilde{b}$ with $\tilde{b} = C^t b$. The solution to this system satisfies $C\tilde{x} = x$. If A is symmetric, $C^t AC$ is also symmetric, whereas MA and AM are not symmetric *a priori*.

1) Show that the eigenvalues of $C^t AC$ and MA are the same. What is the relationship between the eigenvectors of the two matrices?

2) Write the procedure for calculating the Arnoldi basis for the problem $C^t AC\tilde{x} = \tilde{b}$. Show that it is equivalent to the construction of a M^{-1}-orthogonal basis of the Krylov subspace for the preconditioned problem $MAx = Mb$.

3) Show that we can write the calculation procedure of the basis directly, using the products of matrices M and A, as well as, obviously, the scalar products and linear combinations.

4) Deduce a short recurrence to calculate the basis in the case where A is symmetric.

5) Describe (without going into the details of the QR factorization of the matrix H_{p+1p}) the GMRES method for the problem $C^t AC\tilde{x} = \tilde{b}$. Deduce a method for calculating an approximate solution of the problem $Ax = b$ using the M^{-1}-orthogonal basis of the Krylov subspace for the preconditioned problem $MAx = Mb$. What minimizes this approximate solution?

6) Deduce a short recurrence resolution method like MinRES for the preconditioned problem $MAx = Mb$, in the case where matrix A is symmetric.

A1.5. Domain decomposition methods

EXERCISE A1.29.– (Dual Schur method, with and without local regularization)

We consider the linear system $Kx = b$, where K is a symmetric positive definite sparse matrix whose graph has been partitioned into two subdomains, Ω_1 and Ω_2, of interface Γ_3, so that the system admits the following division by blocks:

$$
\begin{pmatrix}
K_{11} & 0 & K_{13} \\
0 & K_{22} & K_{23} \\
K_{31} & K_{32} & K_{33}
\end{pmatrix}
\begin{pmatrix}
x_1 \\
x_2 \\
x_3
\end{pmatrix}
=
\begin{pmatrix}
b_1 \\
b_2 \\
b_3
\end{pmatrix}
$$

We introduce an unknown λ defined on interface Γ_3, and we consider the following two local problems:

$$\begin{pmatrix} K_{ii} & K_{i3} \\ K_{3i} & K_{33}^{(i)} \end{pmatrix} \begin{pmatrix} x_i \\ x_3^{(i)} \end{pmatrix} = \begin{pmatrix} b_i \\ b_3^{(i)} \end{pmatrix} + \begin{pmatrix} 0 \\ (-1)^i \lambda \end{pmatrix}$$

where the integer i takes the values 1 and 2. To simplify some formulas, we can posit:

$$K_i = \begin{pmatrix} K_{ii} & K_{i3} \\ K_{3i} & K_{33}^{(i)} \end{pmatrix} \quad \text{and} \quad B_i = (0 \ I)$$

and write the local problems in the form:

$$K_i \begin{pmatrix} x_i \\ x_3^{(i)} \end{pmatrix} = \begin{pmatrix} b_i \\ b_3^{(i)} \end{pmatrix} + (-1)^i B_i^t \lambda$$

Note that we have:

$$x_3^{(i)} = B_i \begin{pmatrix} x_i \\ x_3^{(i)} \end{pmatrix}$$

Part I: Dual Schur method

1) Show that the two local problems, defined above, admit solutions that restrict the solution x of the overall problem, so that for any second member b it is necessary and sufficient to add to the local equations, the compatibility relationships:

$$x_3^{(1)} = x_3^{(2)}$$

and that we have the following relationships:

$$K_{33}^{(1)} + K_{33}^{(2)} = K_{33}$$
$$b_3^{(1)} + b_3^{(2)} = b_3$$

2) Show that if the local matrices K_i are invertible, then we can write that λ is the solution of a condensed problem on the interface, which is obtained by replacing $x_3^{(1)}$ and $x_3^{(2)}$ in the compatibility relationship:

$$x_3^{(1)} = x_3^{(2)}$$

by their values, as a function of λ, obtained by using the local equations:

$$\begin{pmatrix} K_{ii} & K_{i3} \\ K_{3i} & K_{33}^{(i)} \end{pmatrix} \begin{pmatrix} x_i \\ x_3^{(i)} \end{pmatrix} = \begin{pmatrix} b_i \\ b_3^{(i)} \end{pmatrix} + \begin{pmatrix} 0 \\ (-1)^i \lambda \end{pmatrix}$$

or otherwise, with the introduced notations:

$$K_i \begin{pmatrix} x_i \\ x_3^{(i)} \end{pmatrix} = \begin{pmatrix} b_i \\ b_3^{(i)} \end{pmatrix} + (-1)^i B_i^t \lambda$$

Part II: Dual Schur method with local regularization

We will assume that matrix K_1 is positive definite, and matrix K_2 is positive indefinite.

1) Let us suppose that the kernel of K_2 is of dimension 1, and that it is, therefore, sufficient to impose the value of the solution on a single point for the matrix to be invertible. Deduce that if we use a Gauss or Cholesky factorization of matrix K_2, only the last pivot will be null.

2) In each subdomain, we renumber as the last one the same point on the interface Γ_3. What are the signs of the last pivots of the Gauss and Cholesky factorizations for the two subdomain matrices?

3) Deduce that we can modify the blocks $K_{33}^{(i)}$, so that both matrices, K_1 and K_2, are invertible.

Appendix 2

Solutions

A2.1. Parallelization techniques

SOLUTION A2.1.– (Automatic analysis of dependence)

In order for a solution to exist, there must exist two integers $i_1 \neq i_2$ such that:

$$a \times i_1 + b = c \times i_2 + d \quad \Leftrightarrow a \times i_1 - c \times i_2 = d - b$$

SOLUTION A2.2.– (Vectorization and parallelization)

Only the loop over index k has dependencies, both backward and forward. The loop is, therefore, neither parallelizable nor vectorizable. The loops of indices i and j do not have dependencies, and thus are parallelizable and the loop levels are permutable. Therefore, we can take at the exterior level the loop of index j, which is parallelizable, and at the interior level, the loop of index i which is also parallelizable and involves memory accesses of unit increment.

SOLUTION A2.3.– (Study of loops)

The first loop does not have any dependence if $index$ is injective. If this is not the case, the loop has an output dependence which impedes the parallelization, but not vectorization.

There exists a dependence in the second loop if and only if there exist two integers $i_1 \neq i_2$ such that $index(i_1) = index(i_2)$. Therefore, if $index$ is injective in the interval $[1, n]$, the loop does not have any dependence and is, therefore, parallelizable and vectorizable.

In the third loop, we have a dependence if and only if there exist two integers $i_1 \neq i_2$ such that $i_1 = index(i_2)$. Thus, if some of the values of $index([1, n])$ are in $[1, n]$, there is a dependence. However, if $index(i) \geq i$, $\forall i, 1 \leq i \leq n$, the dependence is forward and does not impede vectorization.

SOLUTION A2.4.– (Permutation of loops)

The solution is not trivial, due to the fact that each instance modifies $u(i, j)$ and $u(i, j+1)$ simultaneously. $u(i, j)$ is flow dependent on $u(i-1, j)$ and $u(i+1, j)$, $u(i, j+1)$ is flow dependent on $u(i, j)$, and by combination, $u(i, j+1)$ is flow dependent on $u(i-1, j)$ and $u(i+1, j)$. This last dependence if of type $(i+, j-)$ toward (i, j). It therefore impedes permutation.

SOLUTION A2.5.– (Study of loops)

This series of loops represents an assembly operation of elemental calculations. It consists of a reduction operation and there exists, therefore, forward and backward dependencies with respect to index j. As far as indices i and k are concerned, the existence of dependencies depends on the injectivity of $index$ with respect to them. If $index$ is injective with respect to both, there is no dependence and all loop levels can be permuted. This situation occurs if all elements have been colored in such a way that elements of the same color are disjoint. The two loop levels i and k are, therefore, parallelizable and vectorizable. But, the length of loop i (6) is insufficient for vectorization, as well as for parallelization if the number of processors is greater than 6. It can thus be a better option to parallelize and vectorize the loop of level k only, and unroll the loop i and j to increase the program's speed.

SOLUTION A2.6.– (Product of distributed parallel matrix-vectors)

1) The number of pairs of operations $(+, \times)$ is equal to the number of coefficients of the matrix. The load balance is, therefore, achieved by distributing the same number of rows and columns to each processor. In the case of a block decomposition, each processor computes chunks of the vector which corresponds to its row block. When the operation is done, it is necessary to assemble the result vector, by gathering the different local contributions (*MPI_Allgather* operation). In the case of a column-wise decomposition, each

processor computes a local vector of dimension equal to that of the matrix. The complete result vector is the sum of all local vectors (*MPI_Allreduce* operation). The number of arithmetic operations is the same in both cases. The data volume involved in the exchange operations is *a priori* less in the first case as each process only sends a chunk of its vector to the others, while in the second case, the complete vectors are exchanged.

2) The decomposition in square blocks combines both the row and column decomposition strategies. As for the matrix-matrix vector product, it is necessary to create row and column communicators to relate blocks on the same row or same column. At the end of the local matrix-vector products, the final result is computed on each row by summing up the different local contributions through *MPI_Allreduce* operations on the different chunks of the vector. To assemble the global vector, it is necessary to gather the different chunks of the vector through an *MPI_Allgather* operation on each column.

3) If only the lower triangular part of the matrix is saved, the complete matrix-vector product is computed as follows: compute the product of the lower triangular matrix by vector x, including the diagonal; sum this result to the product of the transpose by x, this time excluding the diagonal.

4) A block decomposition of the lower triangular part is equivalent to a decomposition by columns of the upper triangular part. The product by the lower inferior part is based, therefore, on the row or column block algorithm, and the product by the lower part is based on the algorithm by blocks of columns or rows.

5) In the case of a square block decomposition, each processor which possesses an extra-diagonal block must carry out the direct product and the product by the transposed block. It thus contributes to the product of two blocks of rows and columns. The processors which deal with the diagonal blocks carry out a unique product and thus half of the operations.

A2.2. Matrix analysis

SOLUTION A2.7.– (Properties of a matrix)

For a matrix to be positive definite, an equivalent condition to those expressed in section 4.2.2 is that its principal minors are all positive. For a square matrix of dimension n, the principal minors are the determinants of the set of n matrices A_i, $i = 1, 2, \ldots n$, where A_i is formed by the ith rows and columns of A. In our case:

$$|1| > 0, \qquad \begin{vmatrix} 1 & a \\ a & 1 \end{vmatrix} > 0, \qquad \begin{vmatrix} 1 & a & a \\ a & 1 & a \\ a & a & 1 \end{vmatrix} > 0$$

The second condition implies that $-1 < a < 1$ and the third condition can be written as:

$$2(a + 1/2)(a - 1)^2 > 0$$

which is satisfied if $a \in] - 1/2, 1[\ \cup \ ]1, \infty]$. The combination of both conditions gives that the matrix is positive definite if and only if $a \in] - 1/2, 1[$.

SOLUTION A2.8.– (Change of basis)

Let v be any vector, with components x_i in the basis $(e_i)_{i=1}^n$ and $\tilde{x}_i$ in the basis $(\tilde{e}_i)_{i=1}^n$. We have:

$$v = \sum_{j=1}^n x_j e_j = \sum_{j=1}^n \tilde{x}_j \tilde{e}_j$$

If we multiply this equation by e_i^t:

$$\sum_{j=1}^n x_j e_i^t \cdot e_j = \sum_{j=1}^n \tilde{x}_j e_i^t \cdot \tilde{e}_j$$

If the basis $(e_i)_{i=1}^n$ is orthonormal, $e_i^t \cdot e_j = \delta_{ij}$, and last equation gives:

$$x_i = \sum_{j=1}^n \tilde{x}_j (e_i^t \cdot \tilde{e}_j)$$

and therefore, the change of basis matrix, such that $x = B\tilde{x}$, has coefficients B_{ij} such that $B_{ij} = e_i^t \cdot \tilde{e}_j$.

SOLUTION A2.9.– (Eigenvalues of a matrix)

The eigenvalues are solutions of the following polynomials:

A : $x^2 - 5x + 7 = 0$
B : $x^2 - 5x + 2 = 0$
C : $(2 - x)(-4 - x)(4 - x) = 0$

By solving these systems, we obtain:

A : $\dfrac{1}{2}(5 \pm i\sqrt{3})$

B : $\dfrac{1}{2}(5 \pm \sqrt{17})$

C : $2,\ 4,\ -4$

SOLUTION A2.10.– (Eigenvectors of a matrix)

1) The eigenvalues are solutions of the system $x(9 - x^2) = 0$, that is $\lambda_1 = -3$, $\lambda_2 = 0$, and $\lambda_3 = 3$. The associated normalized eigenvectors are given by:

$$
e_1 = \frac{1}{3}\begin{pmatrix} 2 \\ 2 \\ -1 \end{pmatrix}, \quad
e_2 = \frac{1}{3}\begin{pmatrix} 2 \\ -1 \\ 2 \end{pmatrix}, \quad
e_3 = \frac{1}{3}\begin{pmatrix} -1 \\ 2 \\ 2 \end{pmatrix}
$$

2) Let λ_i and λ_j be two different eigenvalues associated with the eigenvectors e_i and e_j. We have $Ae_i = \lambda_i e_i$ and $Ae_j = \lambda_j e_j$. By using the. fact that A is symmetric:

$$
\begin{aligned}
\lambda_i(e_i \cdot e_j) = (\lambda_i e_i \cdot e_j) &= (Ae_i \cdot e_j) = (e_i \cdot A^t e_j) \\
&= (e_i \cdot Ae_j) = (e_i \cdot \lambda_j e_j) = \lambda_j(e_i \cdot e_j)
\end{aligned}
$$

The eigenvectors thus satisfy the following relation:

$$(\lambda_i - \lambda_j)(e_i \cdot e_j) = 0$$

As $\lambda_i \neq \lambda_j$, $(e_i \cdot e_j) = 0$. The fact that the matrix is symmetric implies, therefore, that the eigenvectors are orthogonal.

3) The change of basis matrix, formed by the eigenvectors, is given by:

$$P = \frac{1}{3} \begin{pmatrix} 2 & 2 & -1 \\ 2 & -1 & 2 \\ -1 & 2 & 2 \end{pmatrix}$$

and is, therefore, orthogonal.

4) We can, therefore, diagonalize the matrix in the following way:

$$A = PDP^{-1}$$

where D is the diagonal matrix formed by the eigenvalues,

$$D = \begin{pmatrix} \lambda_1 & 0 & 0 \\ 0 & \lambda_2 & 0 \\ 0 & 0 & \lambda_3 \end{pmatrix}$$

and therefore:

$$A^n = \overbrace{(PDP^{-1}) \ldots (PDP^{-1})}^{n}$$

Matrix P being orthogonal, we have that $P^{-1} = P^t$ and A^n can be computed in the following way:

$$A^n = PD^n P^t$$

SOLUTION A2.11.– (Conditioning of a matrix)

1) Using the formula [4.1] for a real matrix, and knowing that the spectrum of the inverse matrix is the inverse of the spectrum of the matrix, we have that:

$$\kappa_2(A) = \|A\|_2 \|A^{-1}\|_2 = \frac{\sqrt{\lambda_{max}(A^t A)}}{\sqrt{\lambda_{min}(A^t A)}}$$

Matrix $A^t A$ is given by:

$$A^t A = \begin{pmatrix} a_{11}^2 + a_{21}^2 & a_{11}a_{12} + a_{21}a_{22} \\ a_{11}a_{12} + a_{21}a_{22} & a_{12}^2 + a_{22}^2 \end{pmatrix}$$

and its eigenvalues are:

$$\lambda_{max} = \frac{1}{2}\left(tr(A^t A) + \sqrt{tr^2(A^t A) - 4det(A^t A)} \right)$$

$$\lambda_{min} = \frac{1}{2}\left(tr(A^t A) - \sqrt{tr^2(A^t A) - 4det(A^t A)} \right)$$

where the trace of $A^t A$ and its determinant are:

$$tr(A^t A) = a_{11}^2 + a_{12}^2 + a_{21}^2 + a_{22}^2 = \sum_{i,j=1}^{2} |a_{ij}|^2$$

$$det(A^t A) = det^2(A)$$

Therefore:

$$\frac{\lambda_{max}}{\lambda_{min}} = \frac{1}{4det^2(A)}\left(tr(A^t A) + \sqrt{tr^2(A^t A) - 4det^2(A)} \right)^2$$

Defining $\sigma = \sum_{i,j=1}^{2} |a_{ij}|^2/(2|det(A)|)$, we obtain the results.

2) The LU decomposition is:

$$LU = \begin{pmatrix} 1 & 0 \\ \dfrac{a_{21}}{a_{11}} & 1 \end{pmatrix} \begin{pmatrix} a_{11} & a_{12} \\ 0 & a_{22} - \dfrac{a_{21}}{a_{11}}a_{12} \end{pmatrix}$$

The conditioning of the matrix U of systems 1 and 2 (being system 1 the one containing the 10^{-4} term) is given by:

System 1: $\kappa_2(U) = 10^8$ $\kappa_1(U) = 10^8$ $\kappa_\infty(U) = 10^8$
System 2: $\kappa_2(U) = 2.6$ $\kappa_1(U) = 4.0$ $\kappa_\infty(U) = 4.0$

The exact solution to the problem is: $u_1 = 1.00001$, $u_2 = 0.9998999$. If we use simple precision (4 bytes), the solutions to systems 1 and 2 are:

System 1: $u_1 = 1.00016594$ $u_2 = 0.999899983$

System 2: $u_1 = 1.00009990$ $u_2 = 0.999900043$

We observe that the result of system 1 is much less accurate than that of system 2. The reason is the very low value of the pivot of the first system, equal to 10^{-4}. When writing system 2, we have carried out a row pivoting to avoid a small pivot when starting the factorization. We will study numerical pivoting and its effects in section 7.3.1.

SOLUTION A2.12.– (The matrix of the Poisson equation)

1) The figure below shows the distribution of the eigenvalues for $N = 5, 10, 20$.

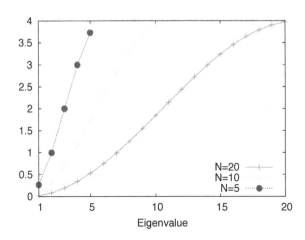

We observe that the minimum eigenvalue decreases with N. We have:

$$\lambda_{min} = 2[1 - \cos(\pi/(N+1))]$$
$$\lambda_{max} = 2[1 - \cos(\pi N/(N+1))]$$

For N large, $\pi N/(N+1) \approx \pi$ and therefore $\lambda_{max} \approx 4$. Using the Taylor series for the sine function, we have $\cos(\pi 1/(N+1)) \approx 1 - \pi^2/2(N+1)^2$

and so that $\lambda_{min} \approx (\pi/(N+1))^2$. The matrix being symmetric, $\kappa_2(A) = \lambda_{max}/\lambda_{min}$:

$$\kappa_2(A) \approx \frac{4}{\pi^2 h^2}$$

We observe that the conditioning is proportional to $1/h^2$. If we do not select a good preconditioning to solve the system with an iterative solver, this implies that as the mesh is refined, the convergence of the solver will be deteriorating.

2) In the figure below, we have drawn the first two and last two eigenvectors for $N = 20$. We observe that the large eigenvalues are associated with high-frequency eigenvectors.

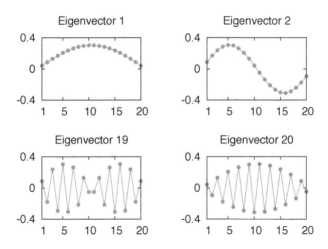

A2.3. Direct methods

SOLUTION A2.13.– (Crout factorization of a dense matrix)

If we store the lower triangular part by rows in an array ℓ, these rows are of increasing length, from 1 to n. The last coefficient of row i, that is the diagonal term, is placed at position $i(i+1)/2$ in the array ℓ. The coefficient l_{ij} is stored at position $\ell(i(i-1)/2+j)$. If we store the matrix by columns, the columns are of decreasing length, from n to 1. The first coefficient of column j, the diagonal, is placed at position $n(n+1)/2-(n-j+1)(n-j+2)/2+1$. The coefficient l_{ij} is then stored at position $n(n+1)/2-(n-j+1)(n-j+2)/2+i-j+1$ in the array ℓ. We can rewrite the Crout's algorithm using the two storing modes just described. At each step, it is necessary to compute the new column of matrix L and then the Schur complement. The calculation of the Schur complement is the most consuming phase. It is carried out with parallelizable loops. It is necessary to place at the interior loop level the loop that gives a regular access to memory with unit increments, that is loop i in the case of a storage by columns, or loop j in the case of a row storage. Unfortunately, the calculation of the new column of L is penalized by irregular accesses to memory in the case of a row storage. The column algorithm should, therefore, be preferred.

SOLUTION A2.14.– (Block Cholesky factorization)

The block Cholesky factorization is deduced from the block LU factorization. The only differences are that we do not only compute half of the blocks and but also the calculation of the Schur complement is carried out by products of upper blocks by lower blocks, these last ones being the transposed of the upper ones. The number of operations is equal to half of number of operations of a non-symmetric Gauss factorization. We should take into account the fact that only the upper triangle of the Schur complement is computed, that is half of the terms.

If the blocks are sufficiently large, we can exploit parallelism at the interior level of the block calculations of products. If this is not the case, we can exploit the possibility of parallelizing the different blocks of the row of blocks, and then the different blocks of the Schur complement, at each step. As in the case of the block LU factorization, the degree of parallelism decreases along the steps. It is twice as low as that of the block LU factorization, as the number of blocks to be computed at each step is twice as low.

SOLUTION A2.15.– (Block-wise resolution of a lower triangular system)

The block forward substitution of the lower triangular system reads:

$$L_{ii}x_i = b_i - \sum_{j=1}^{i-1} L_{ij}x_j = \tilde{b}_i, \quad 1 \le i \le p$$

Step i requires, therefore, $i - 1$ matrix-vector products to compute the right-hand side. Globally, we have p substitutions of lower triangular diagonal blocks which require $q^2/2$ pairs of operations $(+, \times)$ each one, and $p(p-1)/2$ matrix-vector products which cost q^2 pairs of operations $(+, \times)$ each one. We can neglect the time for summing up the different $L_{ij}x_j$ to vector $\tilde{b}_i$.

As far as dependencies are concerned, we can carry out product $l_{ij}x_j$ only when the result of the diagonal system $l_{ii}x_i$ is available. In the same way, we can only solve the diagonal system $L_{ii}x_i = \tilde{b}_i$ when the result of all products $L_{ij}x_j$ for $1 \le j \le i-1$ are available.

SOLUTION A2.16.– (Block calculation of the kernel and the image of a matrix)

For a symmetric matrix, the image and the kernel are orthogonal to each other. Let n_1 and n_2 denote the dimensions of A_{11} and A_{22}, respectively. If A_{11} is invertible, then we can write the block factorization as:

$$\begin{pmatrix} A_{11} & A_{12} \\ A_{21} & A_{22} \end{pmatrix} = \begin{pmatrix} A_{11} & 0 \\ A_{21} & I \end{pmatrix} \begin{pmatrix} I & A_{11}^{-1}A_{12} \\ 0 & A_{22} - A_{21}A_{11}^{-1}A_{12} \end{pmatrix}$$

The rank of the second matrix on the right being equal to that of its upper diagonal block, we deduce that the last block of rows of the matrix is necessarily null and therefore $A_{22} - A_{21}A_{11}^{-1}A_{12} = 0$. We have:

$$\begin{pmatrix} A_{11} & A_{12} \\ A_{21} & A_{22} \end{pmatrix} \begin{pmatrix} -A_{11}^{-1}A_{12} \\ I \end{pmatrix} = \begin{pmatrix} 0 \\ A_{22} - A_{21}A_{11}^{-1}A_{12} \end{pmatrix}$$

The columns of N, of rank equal to n_2, form a basis of the kernel of A and a vector b is in the image if and only if $N^t b = 0$. In practice, we extract block A_{11} of matrix A during the course of the factorization, through a symmetric pivoting. This pivoting consists of renumbering the equations of the system in order to send at the end the equations which correspond to null pivots that appear during the factorization.

SOLUTION A2.17.– (Crout factorization of a skyline stored matrix)

Given the definition of a profile, the lower triangular part must be stored by rows. If $mua(i + 1)$ is the position of the list non-zero term of row i in the array noted by ℓ, that is the diagonal term, the coefficient l_{ij} is stored at position $\ell(mua(i+1) - i + j)$. The first non-zero term of row i is located in column $j_1(i) = i - (mua(i+1) - mua(i)) + 1$. The number of terms of row i contained in the profile is $mua(i+1) - mua(i)$.

To write an efficient code, it is necessary to access to the matrix by row and thus to calculate the coefficients of l row-by-row using only the coefficients of the current row and the preceding rows. The simplest way to write this algorithm consists of using substitutions. If $A = LDL^t$, therefore, we have in row i, for all j such that $j_1(i) \leq j \leq i$:

$$A_{ij} = \sum_{k=1}^{n} L_{ik} D_{kk} L_{kj}^t = \sum_{k=\max(j_1(i),j_1(j))}^{j} L_{ik} D_{kk} L_{jk}$$

We deduce that for all j such that $j_1(i) \leq j \leq i$:

$$L_{ij} D_{jj} = A_{ij} - \sum_{k=\max(j_1(i),j_1(j))}^{j-1} L_{ik} D_{kk} L_{jk}$$

which enables us to compute the coefficients L_{ij}, $j_1(i) \leq j \leq i - 1$, from left to right, and eventually the diagonal coefficient:

$$D_{ii} = A_{ii} - \sum_{k=j_1(i)}^{i-1} L_{ik} D_{kk} L_{ik}$$

To improve the algorithm, we can store the coefficients $l_{ij} d_{jj}$ in a temporal array in such a way to avoid multiplying twice by the diagonal coefficients. Each term l_{ij} is computed through a scalar product of two chunks of rows i and j of matrix L. The different coefficients of the row cannot be computed in parallel as the algorithm is recursive.

If the profile is monotonic, we can store the profile of the lower triangular part by columns without additional cost. We can then apply a classical method by column involving, at each step, the calculation of the new column of L and an actualization of the part of the Schur complement contained in the matrix profile.

SOLUTION A2.18.– (Multifrontal Cholesky factorization)

If we number the nodes lexicographically, the non-zero coefficients end up on lines parallel to the diagonal. More precisely, at row i, these coefficients are located in columns $i - n$, $i - 1$, i, $i + 1$ and $i + n$. The filling obtained during the factorization of the upper triangular part of the matrix will then be contained in the bandwidth n going from column $i - n$ to the diagonal. The Cholesky factorization of a band matrix of dimension dim with half-bandwidth (bandwidth of the lower and upper triangular parts) equal to bw requires $dim \times bw^2/2$ pairs of operations $(+, \times)$. For the matrix under consideration, the cost is, therefore, $n^4/2$ of operations $(+, \times)$.

If we number first the $(n - 2) \times (n - 2)$ internal nodes of the mesh lexicographically, and then the $4(n - 1)$ boundary nodes according to the numbering of the internal neighbors, then we can use the block factorization of the first question. Block K_{11} is of band type with half-bandwidth equal to $n - 2$. Block K_{12} is rectangular, with $(n - 2) \times (n - 2)$ rows and $4(n - 1)$ columns. The number of the first non-zero term of each column is increasing, in such a way that the block has a monotonic column profile. Block $L_{12}^t = L_{11}^{-1} K_{12}$ has, therefore, the same properties, which implies that for each column, it is sufficient to start the resolution from the first non-zero term, which decreases the computational cost.

In the same way, this property can be used to reduce the cost of the computation of matrix $S_{22} = K_{22} - L_{12}^t L_{12}$. Then, we are left with the factorization of the full matrix.

Multifrontal factorization uses this methodology in a recursive way. However, the successive Schur complements are not full but have a block structure which represents a graph of grid type.

SOLUTION A2.19.– (Solving linear systems of tridiagonal matrices)

The graph of the matrix is a vertical line going from 1 to n and containing all the edges $(i, i + 1)$. The same happens with the elimination tree, which implies that the factorization is recursive.

In practice, the factorization at step i consists of computing: $l_i = L_{i+1\,i} = f_i/\tilde{d}_i$, $u_i = U_{i\,i+1} = e_i$ and $S_{i+1\,i+1} = \tilde{d}_{i+1} = d_{i+1} - l_i \times u_i$. Each step thus requires one triplet of operations $(/, \times, -)$.

Using the odd–even numbering, there does not exist any connection between the first p equations, and these are only connected to the last $p - 1$'s. The beginning of the elimination tree is composed of p nodes without connection, located at the same level, which can, therefore, be eliminated in parallel. However, the elimination of an odd node creates a connection between the two even nodes to which it was initially connected. The Schur complement of the resting even nodes is, therefore, a tridiagonal matrix. This creates an additional filling and an extra cost of arithmetic operations. The elimination of each odd node requires two divisions which enable us to compute the two coefficients of L associated with the two even nodes connected to it, and then the computation of a 2×2 block in the Schur complement, that is 10 operations in total. This operation creates two additional non-zero terms in the Schur complement.

The recursive application of this process gives a speedup equal to half the number of remaining nodes at each iteration, but implies an extra cost in terms of storage and computation. The global storage is $5n$ instead of $3n$, and the computational cost is $10n$ instead of $3n$.

SOLUTION A2.20.– (Multisection factorization method of a tridiagonal matrix)

The factorization of a tridiagonal matrix costs $3n$ arithmetic operations. Each one of the p blocks of odd rank and dimension nb is connected with only two separators of even rank and dimension 1. Therefore, we can simultaneously factorize the sublocks of odd rank with dimension nb. Their eliminations create connections between their separators, and then the Schur complement is a tridiagonal matrix.

The cost of the factorization of a tridiagonal block of dimension nb is $3nb$. In order to finish the elimination of the block, it is necessary to compute the Schur complement for the separators. Let us denote the set of internal equations of the block by 1, and the set of two separators by 2. The associated submatrix has a 2×2 block structure: A_{11} is a tridiagonal matrix of dimension nb and A_{22} is the matrix of the two separators of dimension 2, initially diagonal. The computation of block $U_{12} = L_{11}^{-1}A_{12}$ requires two substitutions, one for each column of A_{12}. The first column has only one non-zero coefficient located on its first row, and the second column has only one non-zero coefficient located on its last row. The substitution of the first column creates, therefore, $nb - 1$ new coefficients and requires $2(nb - 1)$ arithmetic operations, for the diagonal coefficients of L_{11} are equal to one. The computation of the second column does not create filling and does require any operation. In the same way, the computation of block $L_{21} = A_{21}U_{11}^{-1}$ creates $nb - 1$ additional terms and requires $2(nb - 1) + nb$ arithmetic operations because the diagonal coefficients of U_{11} are different from 1 and it is necessary to divide by the diagonal coefficient at each step of the backward substitution. The calculation of the product $S_{22} = A_{22} - L_{21}U_{12}$ creates two additional terms in S_{22} and requires $2nb + 6$ arithmetic operations.

The extra cost in terms of storage is of the order of $2n$ coefficients, while the extra cost in terms of operations is of the order of $7n$.

The elimination of the p blocks of dimension nb cannot be parallelized. We are left with the factorization of the Schur complement, which is a tridiagonal matrix of dimension p.

SOLUTION A2.21.– (Block factorization using cyclic reduction)

The half-bandwidth of the matrix $bw = n$. The Cholesky factorization requires $dim \times bw^2/2$ pairs of operations $(+, \times)$, that is $n^4/2$ pairs of operations $(+, \times)$ for the global matrix. The number of coefficients in the lower triangular part is equal to $dim \times bw = n^3$. The cost of both backward and forward substitutions is $2n^3$ pairs of operations $(+, \times)$.

When decomposing the matrix graph in bands of dimension $n/p \times n$, the dimension of each block is n^2/p and its half-bandwidth is n/p. The cost of the factorization of each block is thus equal to n^4/p^3 pairs of operations $(+, \times)$. The total cost of the factorizations of the p blocks is, therefore, equal to n^4/p^2 pairs of operations $(+, \times)$.

In order to finalize the elimination of a block, it is necessary to compute the Schur complement of the two separators. If we denote the set of $n/p \times n$ internal equations of the block by 1 and the set of $2n/p$ for the two separators by 2, the associated submatrix has a 2×2 block structure. The calculation of block $L_{21}^t = L_{11}^{-1}A_{12}$ requires a forward substitution for each column of A_{12}. Matrix A_{12} has a decreasing profile if we place first the columns which correspond to the boundary nodes which are neighbors of interior nodes with lower numbering. Block A_{12} is thus made up of two series of n/p columns, whose first non-zero terms are located on rows $j \times n/p$ and $(j-1) \times n/p+1$ for $n \geq j \geq 1$. The forward substitutions always start with the first non-zero term, so that its total cost is of order n^4/p^2 instead of $2n^4/p^2$ pairs of operations $(+, \times)$. In order to count the number of operations, we must take into account the profile of L_{21} as well as the fact that only the lower triangular part of the Schur complement $S_{22} = A_{22} - L_{21}L_{21}^t$ is computed.

The elimination of the p bands can be carried out in parallel. The Schur complement coming from this elimination is a block tridiagonal matrix. These blocks are full and of dimension n/p. It is composed of $p - 1$ diagonal blocks in $p - 2$ extra-diagonal blocks.

Once more, we can apply a factorization by bands of blocks of this block tridiagonal matrix. The degree of parallelism is less, at most of order $p/2$ in the first step.

The total cost is, therefore, lower to that of the factorization of the complete band matrix.

SOLUTION A2.22.– (Block factorization of a band matrix)

The partial factorization of the matrix requires the factorization of the diagonal block, $A_{11} = L_{11}U_{11}$, the calculation of the non-zero blocks of the first row of U and first column of L, $U_{12} = L_{11}^{-1}A_{12}$ and $L_{21} = A_{21}U_{11}^{-1}$, as well as the calculation of the Schur complement, being L_{21} and U_{12} the only non-zero blocks, only affects the second diagonal block $S_{22} = A_{22} - L_{21}U_{12}$.

By recurrence, we can show that the factorization conserves the block tridiagonal structure. In addition, if A_{12} is the lower triangular part, so U_{12} is as well. Similarly, if A_{21} is an upper triangular, so L_{21} is as well. Therefore, the factorization conserves the band structure.

The calculation of $U_{12} = L_{11}^{-1}A_{12}$ requires lb solutions of lower triangular systems of decreasing dimension, from lb to 1. The cost is, therefore, of order $lb^3/6$ pairs of operations $(+, \times)$. The same occurs with the calculation of $L_{21}^t = U_{11}^{-t}A_{21}^t$. Because blocks L_{21} and U_{12} are upper and lower triangular, respectively, their product only costs $lb^3/3$ pairs of operations $(+, \times)$.

Each of the three operations, factorization of the diagonal block, calculation of both extra-diagonal blocks and calculation of the Schur complement for the following diagonal block, has a cost of $lb^3/3$ pairs of operations $(+, \times)$. The total cost of the factorization is, therefore, of order $p \times lb^3 = dim \times lb^2$ pairs of operations $(+, \times)$. The factorization of the diagonal block has less intrinsic parallelism than the other two operations. The amount of input and output data is at most $2lb^2$. The temporal and spatial localities are good and the granularity depends on lb. If lb is large, the operations can be decomposed into blocks.

SOLUTION A2.23.– (Mixed systems)

If A is invertible, then the mixed system admits the following block factorization:

$$\begin{pmatrix} A & B \\ B^t & 0 \end{pmatrix} = \begin{pmatrix} A & 0 \\ B^t & I \end{pmatrix} \begin{pmatrix} I & A^{-1}B \\ 0 & -B^t A^{-1}B \end{pmatrix}$$

The right-hand side matrix is invertible if and only if $B^t A^{-1}B$ is invertible.

$$B^t A^{-1}Bx \cdot x = A^{-1}Bx \cdot Bx$$

Then, $B^t A^{-1}B$ is symmetric positive definite and so $B^t A^{-1}Bx = 0$ is, if and only if $Bx = 0$. The kernels of $B^t A^{-1}B$ and B are identical. Their images, which are the orthogonal supplement of their kernels, are also identical.

SOLUTION A2.24.– (Orthogonalization by Crout factorization)

$V^t V\alpha \cdot \alpha = ||V\alpha||^2$. N is, therefore, symmetric and positive, and is also definite if the column vectors of V are linearly independent.

If $N = V^t V = LDL^t$, then $L^{-1}V^t V L^{-t} = D$. The family of column vectors of matrix W defined by $WL^t = V$ is orthogonal.

If the vectors V are not independent, we can extract a subset formed by r column vectors of V. The main diagonal subblock of N of dimension r, $N_{11} = V_1^t V_1$, obtained by symmetric permutation of the rows and columns of N during the Crout factorization is of maximum rank. If $N_{11} = L_{11}D_{11}L_{11}^t$, the column vectors of matrix W_1 defined by $W_1 L_{11}^t = V_1$ form an orthogonal family.

In this method, the first step consists of computing $N = V^t V$. It requires $p(p+1)/2$ independent scalar products of dimension n, that is $n(p(p+1)/2)$

pairs of parallelizable operations $(+, \times)$. The second step consists of the Crout factorization of N. It is not parallel but its relative cost is low. The third step consists of solving the system $L^{-t}W^t = V^t$, and requires once more $n(p(p+1)/2)$ pairs of parallelizable operations $(+, \times)$.

The Gramm–Schmidt method requires $p(p-1)/2$ scalar products and linear combinations of vectors, that is 2 times $n(p(p-1)/2)$ pairs of operations $(+, \times)$. The costs are comparable, but the Gramm–Schmidt method is less accurate. We can improve its accuracy using the modified Gramm–Schmidt method, which involves non-parallelizable recursive calculations.

A2.4. Iterative methods

SOLUTION A2.25.– (Conjugate gradient for a singular system)

The image is the orthogonal supplementary of the kernel. If b belongs to the image, the system has a unique solution in this image. If we start with $x_0 = 0$, x_0 is in the image, as well as $g_0 = -b$. Therefore, so is all the Krylov space generated by g_0. The conjugate gradient behaves as if the problems were resolved in the image of A.

SOLUTION A2.26.– (Krylov methods with full orthogonalization and eigenvalues)

By grouping the eigenvectors associated with the same eigenvalue, we have:

$$g_0 = \sum_{i=1}^{p} \gamma_i v_i$$

$$A^k g_0 = \sum_{i=1}^{p} \gamma_i \lambda_i^k v_i$$

The Krylov space is, therefore, included in the space generated by the vectors v_i. Its dimension is lower or equal to p and the method necessarily converges in a number of iterations lower than p.

To perform a change of basis to pass from an orthonormal base to another one is equivalent to perform a change of basis associated with an orthogonal matrix Q. The conjugate gradient applied to the system with change of basis behaves exactly in the same way as the preconditioned system by $Q^t Q = I$.

If some eigenvalues are not in g_0, they will not appear in the successive products by A. The conjugate gradient, therefore, converges as in the case of the reduced system whose conditioning is equal to $\max(\Lambda_p)/\min(\Lambda_p)$.

SOLUTION   A2.27.– (Optimal   restart   Krylov   methods   with   full orthogonalization)

We have $x_p = x_0 = \sum_{i=1}^{p} \rho_{ip} v_i$, with $\rho_{ip} = -(g_0 \cdot Av_i)/(Av_i \cdot Av_i)$. If we apply the Gramm–Schmidt orthogonalization for the scalar product associated with $A^t A$, we obtain:

$$w_j = v_j + \sum_{i=1}^{j-1} \gamma_{ij} w_i$$

$$Aw_j = Av_j + \sum_{i=1}^{j-1} \gamma_{ij} Aw_i$$

where $\gamma_{ij} = (Av_j \cdot Aw_i)/(Aw_i \cdot Aw_i)$. It is, therefore, not necessary to recompute the matrix-vector products if we know vectors v_i and Av_i.

By construction, $(g_p \cdot Av_i) = 0$, $1 \leq i \leq p$. In order to conserve this property, we need that any new descent direction w satisfies $(Aw \cdot Av_i) = 0$, $1 \leq i \leq p$. The preconditioning that permits this consists of orthogonolizing each new descent vector constructed by the ORTHODIR method with respect to the vectors v_i, for the scalar product associated with $A^t A$. As the ORTHODIR method already requires this orthogonolization with respect to the successive descent vectors, it is as if the v_i were the first p descent vectors.

SOLUTION A2.28.– (GMRES and MinRES methods with a symmetric positive definite preconditioner)

We have:

$$C^t AC\tilde{v} = \lambda \tilde{v} \quad \Leftrightarrow \quad CC^t AC\tilde{v} = MAC\tilde{v} = \lambda C\tilde{v}$$

The eigenvectors of MA and $C^t AC$ are related through the equation $v = C\tilde{v}$. The construction of an Arnoldi vector for system $C^t AC$ reads:

$$h_{j+1\,j}\,\tilde{v}_{j+1} = C^t AC\tilde{v}_j + \sum_{i=1}^{j} h_{ij}\tilde{v}_i$$

where $h_{ij} = (C^t AC\tilde{v}_j \cdot \tilde{v}_i)$. The vectors $\tilde{v}_i$ form an orthonormal basis. If we write $v_i = C\tilde{v}_i$, we obtain, multiplying last equation by C:

$$h_{j+1\,j}\,v_{j+1} = MAv_j + \sum_{i=1}^{j} h_{ij}v_i$$

where $h_{ij} = (Av_j \cdot v_i) = (M^{-1}MAv_j \cdot v_i)$ and $(\tilde{v}_j \cdot \tilde{v}_i) = (M^{-1}v_j \cdot v_i)$. The vectors v_i thus form an M^{-1}-orthonormal basis of the Krylov space associated with MA. The only difficulty consists of avoiding the products by M^{-1}. We already saw that we can compute easily the coefficients h_{ij}. We are thus left with the calculation of $h_{j+1\,j}$, which requires computing the M^{-1} auto scalar product (square of the M^{-1} norm) of vector:

$$MAv_j + \sum_{i=1}^{j} h_{ij}v_i$$

Now, we know the value of $(M^{-1}v_j \cdot v_i)$. It is 1 or 0 whether i and j are equal or not. Therefore, we are left with the evaluation of following scalar products: $(M^{-1}MAv_j \cdot v_i) = (Av_j \cdot v_i)$ and $(M^{-1}MAv_j \cdot MAv_j) = (Av_j \cdot MAv_j)$.

To apply the GMRES method to system $C^t AC\tilde{x} = \tilde{b}$ is, therefore, equivalent to applying the GMRES method to the preconditioned system $MAx = Mb$ which minimizes the square of the norm of the preconditioned residual for the scalar product associated with M^{-1}, that is the Euclidean norm of the non-preconditioned residual.

If A is symmetric, then MA is symmetric for the scalar product associated with M^{-1}. Thus, we can apply, as is done for the non-preconditioned case, an algorithm of Lanczos type to construct the vectors v_i with a short recurrence, and a method of MinRes type for the preconditioned problem.

A2.5. Domain decomposition methods

SOLUTION   A2.29.– (Dual   Schur   method,   with   and   without   local regularization)

On the one hand, for the local solutions to be restrictions of the solution of the global system, they must satisfy the compatibility relation: $x_3^{(1)} = x_3^{(2)} = x_3$. On the other hand, the solutions of the local problems imply that the first two rows of the system are satisfied. The last row of this system reads:

$$K_{31}x_1 + K_{32}x_2 + K_{33}x_3 = b_3$$

If we sum the last two rows of the local problems, we obtain:

$$K_{31}x_1 + K_{32}x_2 + K_{33}^{(1)}x_3^{(1)} + K_{33}^{(2)}x_3^{(2)} = b_3^{(1)} + b_3^{(2)}$$

Substituting the compatibility equation into this last equation:

$$K_{31}x_1 + K_{32}x_2 + (K_{33}^{(1)} + K_{33}^{(2)})x_3 = b_3^{(1)} + b_3^{(2)}$$

This equation is identical to the last row of the global system if the partition of the system is such that $K_{33}^{(1)} + K_{33}^{(2)} = K_{33}$ and $b_3^{(1)} + b_3^{(2)} = b_3$. If matrices K_i are invertible, the solutions of the local systems give:

$$\begin{pmatrix} x_i \\ x_3^{(i)} \end{pmatrix} = K_i^{-1} \begin{pmatrix} b_i \\ b_3^{(i)} \end{pmatrix} + (-1)^i K_i^{-1} B_i^t \lambda$$

Now, if we use the fact that:

$$x_3^{(i)} = B_i \begin{pmatrix} x_i \\ x_3^{(i)} \end{pmatrix}$$

and we substitute this equality into equation $x_3^{(1)} - x_3^{(2)} = 0$, we obtain the following equation for λ:

$$(B_1 K_1^{-1} B_1^t + B_2 K_2^{-1} B_2^t)\lambda = B_1 K_1^{-1} \begin{pmatrix} b_1 \\ x_3^{(1)} \end{pmatrix} - B_2 K_2^{-1} \begin{pmatrix} b_2 \\ x_3^{(2)} \end{pmatrix}$$

If matrix K is symmetric positive definite, and knowing that it is sufficient to suppress a row and a column to find an invertible block then, if we carry out the incomplete Cholesky factorization of K, we obtain:

$$\begin{pmatrix} K_{11} & K_{12} \\ K_{21} & K_{22} \end{pmatrix} = \begin{pmatrix} L_{11} & 0 \\ L_{21} & I \end{pmatrix} \begin{pmatrix} L_{11}^t & L_{21}^t \\ 0 & K_{22} - K_{21}K_{11}^{-1}K_{12} \end{pmatrix}$$

The Schur complement $K_{22} - K_{21}K_{11}^{-1}K_{12}$ is a scalar. It is null if matrix K is not definite, and strictly positive if the matrix is positive definite. If we number the two matrices K_1 and K_2 in such a way that the last equation represents the same coefficient of the interface vector x_3, then the Schur complement of K_1 for the last equation is a strictly positive number α, whereas that of K_2 is 0. If we subtract $\alpha/2$ to the last diagonal coefficient of K_1 and sum the same value to that of K_2, the two Schur complements are equal to $\alpha/2$ and the two matrices are positive definite. We keep satisfying the equation $K_{33}^{(1)} + K_{33}^{(2)} = K_{33}$.

Appendix 3

Bibliography and Comments

For further reading, without looking to be exhaustive, here we have selected a fairly comprehensive list of reference works that may well interest our readers. One may be looking for various complementary texts on the concepts we present, or simply be looking for other points of view about the same subject matter. For the convenience of the readers, these references have been classified by topic, and approximately follow the outline of this book.

A3.1. Parallel algorithms

[CAS 08] CASANOVA H., LEGRAND A., ROBERT Y., *Parallel Algorithms*, Chapman & Hall/CRC Press, 2008.

This book perfectly complements the current work. Notably, it approaches parallelism from more of a computer point of view than a numerical one, which allows the readers to understand in detail certain aspects such as the models (PRAM machines, network sorting and scheduling), algorithms (rings of processors, communication and routing, and heterogeneous algorithmic), and pipelines and compilation techniques (vector calculus, systolic architectures, nested loops and automatic parallelization). Each chapter is divided into three sections. The first section consists, in part, of lessons; the second section is made up of tutorial sessions with a series of exercises; and the third section presents detailed corrections and an in-depth discussion of the exercises. This recent version is supplemented by numerous outside parties and takes into account the most current programming paradigms.

[BAR 15] BARNEY B., *Introduction to Parallel Computing*, available at: https://computing.llnl.gov/tutorials/parallel_comp/, 2015.

Introductory webpage to parallel computing: computer architecture, programming models for shared and distributed memory, design of parallel programs. The site also includes some examples such as 2D heat equation whose solution is parallelized with MPI.

A3.2. OpenMP

Numerous works are useful for a better understanding of the principles and functions of OpenMP. Below, we give some details about these references.

[BAU 92] BAUER B.E., *Practical Parallel Programming*, Academic Press, 1992.

This book serves as a general introduction to shared memory parallel programming. It addresses and discusses various notions such as the concepts, difficulties involved, solutions and tools of automatic parallelization. This book does not discuss standard OpenMP, but the essentials of OpenMP, notably the MP directives that preceded OpenMP on SGI computers, from which the developers of OpenMP are largely inspired. Concrete examples written in the C programming language and Fortran are shown in the book. This work teaches programmers to write efficient programs more quickly for parallel computers.

[EIG 01] EIGENMANN R., VOSS M.J., *OpenMP Shared Memory Parallel Programming*, Springer, 2001.

This is a compilation of 15 chapters from papers submitted to the *International Workshop on OpenMP – Applications and Tools* conference that took place in West Lafayette, Indiana, in July 2001. These chapters show state-of-the-art OpenMP distributed memory parallel programming, as well as numerous applications and tools for OpenMP. The chapters are grouped according to the themes presented, such as implementation and optimization, the tools and technologies, experiments and applications, and computer clusters.

[CHA 01] CHANDRA R., MENON R., DAGUM L. *et al.*, *Parallel Programming in OpenMP*, Academic Press, 2001.

This book, which is addressed both to students and experts in parallel programming, is an introduction to OpenMP and focuses particularly on codes written in Fortran 90. The majority of OpenMP directives that are normally used by scientific programmers are described, and at the end of each chapter, exercises are proposed. This book begins with a presentation of OpenMP, and then, through several chapters, introduces and analyzes loop parallelism. Notions of performance, both theoretical and practical, are studied toward the end.

[VOS 03] VOSS M.J. (ed.), *OpenMP Shared Memory Parallel Programming*, Springer, 2003.

This is a compilation of papers submitted to the *International Workshop on OpenMP - Applications and Tools* conference that took place in June 2003, in Toronto, Canada. Twenty chapters describe recent research concerning technologies linked to OpenMP, the different versions of OpenMP, their extensions with clusters and the recent applications and tools for OpenMP.

[BOA 15] The OpenMP API specification for parallel programming, available at: http://openmp.org/wp.

Official webpage of OpenMP. Lots of references, examples and tutorials. The manual can be downloaded here: http://www. openmp.org/mp-documents/OpenMP4.0.0.pdf.

A3.3. MPI

We have selected a few references that illustrate the concepts, functionalities and use of the MPI and MPI-2 libraries.

[FOS 95] FOSTER I., *Designing and Building Parallel Programs*, Addison-Wesley, 1995.

This book is interesting, in that it discusses the methodology to follow when writing parallel programs. As the author indicates, this work is not a manual of programming languages, nor a treatise on algorithms. On the contrary, here, parallel programming is discussed following a methodology where both the costs and performances are taken into consideration. This book is composed of three parts that, respectively, consider: the architecture, tools and resources. The first part is a discussion of the architecture of parallel algorithms, performance analysis and fundamental principles, which are explained using numerous examples. The second part consists of a practical guide to parallel programming tools and performance tools. The third part is composed of numerous bibliographical references.

[PAC 96] PACHECO P.S., *Parallel Programming with MPI*, Morgan Kaufmann Publishers Inc., 1996.

This book is an introduction to parallel programming for systems that use the MPI-1.1 library for programs written in C and Fortran. It is a follow-on to the book User's Guide to MPI. After a general presentation of parallel computing, this work introduces the different notions used by the MPI-1.1 library such as collective communications, point-to-point communications, communicators and input-output. An analysis of performance is discussed afterward, followed by advanced techniques such as the search for errors, parallel algorithms and parallel libraries.

[SNI 98] SNIR M., OTTO S., HUSS-LEDERMAN S. *et al.*, *MPI: The Complete Reference*, The MIT Press, 1998.

Written by the developers of standard MPI, this book is a manual of version MPI 1.1, and is annotated with numerous commentaries. It is also very complementary to [GRO 94]. This work includes advanced discussion of computation and parallel programming, message-passing and libraries for both parallel and distributed computing. There are many examples of commented programs that help to fully understand the notions being presented. Explanations about the choices made by the developers of the libraries, and how the users should implement the available interfaces are also at one's disposal.

[GRO 98] GROPP W., HUSS-LEDERMAN S., LUMSDAINE A. *et al.*, *MPI: The Complete Reference – The MPI-2 Extensions*, vol. 2, 1998.

This book presents the standard specifications of the MPI-2 library. It is annotated with numerous commentaries that permit the understanding of difficult notions, with the choices made by the developers of MPI-2. The way in which to correctly use the various available interfaces is clearly explained and a large number of detailed examples are provided.

[DOW 98] DOWD K., SEVERANCE C., *High Performance Computing*, O'Reilly, 1998.

This work provides a general introduction to modern parallel and vector computing. The architecture of processors, the architecture of memory, programming, optimization, performance evaluation, the comparison of shared memory parallelization (*threads*, Open MP) and message passing (MPI and PVM) are all covered. This book provides a thorough understanding of hardware components, especially the organization of memory that is addressed in Chapter 3.

[GRO 99] GROPP W., LUSK E., SKJELLUM A., *Using MPI: Portable Parallel Programming with the Message Passing Interface*, MIT Press, 1999.

This is a book on the MPI-2 library. The message-passing interface (MPI) library is widely used to solve engineering problems on parallel computers. The first version of MPI-1 has been updated, and the new version, MPI-2, includes numerous options and improvements. Among these are new functions for programs written in C++ and Fortran 90, new types of data and new collective operations. Parallel input-output and the dynamic management of processes are also discussed in detail.

[KAR 03] KARNIADAKIS G.E., KIRBY R.M., *Parallel Scientific Computing in C++ and MPI: A Seamless Approach to Parallel Algorithms and their Implementation*, Cambridge University Press, New York, 2003.

This work is a summary of the use of computer algorithms that use modern programming techniques, most notably parallel programming. First, there is an introduction to the vocabulary commonly used in scientific computing and numerical simulation. Then, it describes the basic notions of computing and programming. The techniques of approximation and the calculation of integrals are discussed, followed by techniques of both explicit and implicit discretization of partial differential equations. The algorithms of solving linear systems, as well as algorithms for the computation of values and eigenvectors, are finally taken up. The illustrated applications cover wavelets, high-level methods, non-symmetric linear systems and the parallelization of algorithms of solving sparse matrix systems.

[FOR 12] MPI: A message-passing interface standard version 3.0, available at: http://www.mpi-forum.org/docs/mpi-3.0/mpi30-report.pdf, 2013.

Manual and example of new MPI-3 standard which includes, among many other features, the very useful non-blocking collective communications.

A3.4. Performance tools

[LAB 05] LABARTA J., GIMÉNEZ J., MARTÍNEZ E. et al., Scalability of Tracing and Visualization Tools, PARCO 2005, available at: http://www.bsc.es/paraver, pp. 869–876, 2005.

[GEI 10] GEIMER M., WOLF F., WYLIE B.J.N. et al., The Scalasca performance toolset architecture, Concurrency and Computation: Practice and Experience, vol. 22, no. 6, pp. 702–719, available at: http://www.scalasca.org, 2010.

We reference here two performance tools, namely Paraver and Scalasca. The readers can find the description of the tools in the articles and webpages mentioned previously, and find the codes in the following ones.

A3.5. Numerical analysis and methods

[DAU 00] DAUTRAY R., LIONS J.L., Mathematical Analysis and Numerical Methods for Science and Technology [Analyse Mathématique et Calcul Numérique pour les Sciences et Techniques], Masson, Paris, vol. 1–9,1984–1988.

The nine books in this series (the first six have been translated into English) have quickly become an indispensable reference for those working in the field of scientific computing. These works are a compilation of numerous articles covering a variety of topics and diverse themes. A different researcher contributes to each one of the various articles.

[BAS 03] BASTIEN J., MARTIN J.-N., Introduction à l'Analyse Numérique: Applications sous Matlab, Dunod, Paris, 2003.

This book presents the basic concepts of numerical analysis illustrated with applications in Matlab. The book introduces the concepts of algorithms and numerical errors. The techniques of polynomial interpolation, integration and derivation are then discussed, followed by methods for solving nonlinear equations and differential equations. The applications presented in the book are also applicable to purely mathematical cases, or related problems, which are often faced in practical engineering.

[QUA 94] QUARTERONI A., VALLI A., *Numerical Approximation of Partial Differential Equations*, Springer-Verlag, 1994.

This books presents the numerical approximations of partial differential equations, with a strong mathematical basis. It covers stability problems, convergence, error estimation, etc. It presents the Galerkin method and its variants, as well as the collocation method. The concepts are mainly applied to the finite element and spectral methods. It deals with advection-diffusion, fluid and hyperbolic problems.

[HIR 07] HIRSCH C., *Numerical Computation of Internal and External Flows: The Fundamentals of Computational Fluid Dynamics*, Butterworth-Heinemann, vol. 1, 2007.

This book presents the different discretization methods used in computational fluid dynamics: finite difference, finite element and finite volume. It covers potential flow equations, invisible flow and Navier–Stokes equations. It includes a code for the solution of simple problems.

A3.6. Finite volume method

[LEV 02] LEVEQUE R.J., *Finite Volume Methods for Hyperbolic Problems*, Cambridge University Press, 2002.

This book presents the governing theory of systems of hyperbolic equations. It is applied to the finite volume method, for the solution of both linear and nonlinear conservative systems. High-order methods are treated as well. The book focuses more on the theory than on the implementation aspects, and the applications are limited to Cartesian meshes.

[VER 07] VERSTEEG H., MALALASEKERA W., *An Introduction to Computational Fluid Dynamics: The Finite Volume Method*, Pearson/Prentice Hall, 2007.

This book is an introduction to the finite volume method and its implementation. The method is applied to the advection-diffusion equation and to the Navier–Stokes equations. Some iterative methods are described for the solution of this last equation (like the SIMPLEX method) as well as the implementation of boundary conditions. The book also discusses the modeling and simulation of turbulent flows.

A3.7. Finite element method

[AXE 01]]AXELSSON O., BARKER V.A., *Finite Element Solution of Boundary Value Problems*, SIAM, Philadelphia, 2001.

This book is an introduction to the finite element method for boundary value problems arising from partial differential equations. This book includes a section related to the theoretical analysis of various methods, and some related to numerical aspects and methods of calculation. The authors first introduce the notion of finite dimensional quadratic functionals, and then the notion of variational formulation of boundary value problems. The Ritz–Galerkin method is then described, followed by the finite element method. The direct and iterative methods for solving linear systems are finally presented. Throughout the book, numerous examples and exercises guide the readers in understanding the concepts presented, and the methods studied.

[CIA 02] CIARLET P.G., *The Finite Element Method for Elliptic Problems*, SIAM, Philadelphia, 2002.

This book presents, in a detailed and pedagogical way, the mathematical basis of the finite element method. This book is an indispensable reference on this subject, and has helped train a large number of students, who have worked toward a Masters or Doctorate degree. To help the readers understand the concepts presented, numerous illustrations are included, and many exercises are provided. This book first presents the general notions of elliptic boundary value problems, and then introduces the finite element method. The finite element methods, consistent with second-order problems, are then presented, as well as other less conventional methods. Discretization methods and error estimates are successively introduced and extensively detailed. From there, applications of nonlinear problems of plates and shells are discussed. A rich bibliography is also available, accompanied by many of the author's comments.

[JOH 87] JOHNSON C., *Numerical Solution of Partial Differential Equations by the Finite Element Method*, Dover Publications, 1987.

This book is an introduction to the finite element method, from a computational mathematics point of view. A good background in the mathematical tools involved in the method is required. It presents numerous applications to different fields of science and engineering.

[LÖH 01] LÖHNER R., *Applied CFD Techniques: An Introduction Based on Finite Element Methods*, John Wiley & Sons, 2001.

This book describes numerical techniques for the solution of computational fluid dynamics problems. It focuses on the efficient implementations of these techniques in simulation codes. It includes various aspects such as data structures, mesh generation, solutions of linear systems, mesh adaptation, the efficient use of the hardware, etc. The book is ideal to programmers in CFD.

A3.8. Matrix analysis

[BEL 97] BELLMAN R., *Introduction to Matrix Analysis*, 2nd ed., SIAM, Philadelphia, 1997.

This book is a useful guide on matrix operations and matrix theory, the functions of matrices, etc. Exercises of varying difficulty, and numerous references to the original articles of the first book's results are indicated. This book introduces the concepts of maximization and minimization. The concepts of vectors, matrices, diagonalization and then matrix reduction are discussed. The functions of matrices, inequalities, circulating matrices, Markov matrices and many other concepts are then discussed in depth.

[HOR 90] HORN R.A., JOHNSON C.R., *Matrix Analysis*, Cambridge University Press, 1990.

This book presents advanced matrix analysis and linear algebra results: vectorial spaces, eigenvalue problems, canonical forms, eigenvalue localization, positive definite matrices, etc. It includes numerous exercises on these topics.

A3.9. Direct methods

[MUM 05] *MUMPS: a MUltifrontal Massively Parallel sparse direct Solver*, CEC ESPRIT IV long term research project – No. 20160 (PARASOL), 2005.

This scientific library implements, for distributed environments, a type of multi-frontal solver. Notably, among the important features of this library are solutions of large linear systems with symmetric positive definite matrices; random matrices; and non-symmetric matrices, whose coefficients are either real or complex. Factorization (respectively, the solution) of the linear system, on one or more processors, is available. As for preconditioning techniques, the user can request a partial factorization, or the Schur complement matrix. To interface with this library using scientific computing codes, several matrix formats can be imported, including, in particular, matrix assembly or the elementary matrices. The source code of this library is written in Fortran 90, and exchanges between processors are based on the MPI library. The source code is optimized, with calls to the BLAS and ScaLAPACK libraries.

A3.10. Iterative methods

[PET 11] *PETSc: portable, extensible toolkit for scientific computation*, Available at: http://www.mcs.anl.gov/petsc, 2012.

This library, extensively used in the scientific community, includes a series of subroutines for the solution of linear systems. It includes direct methods as well as iterative methods (CG, GMRES and BiCGSTAB) and numerous preconditioners (block Jacobi, additive Schwarz, ILU, etc.).

[LAN 96] LANCZOS C., *Linear Differential Operators*, SIAM, Philadelphia, 1996.

This is an outstanding reference work by Lanczos. In accordance with his style, the author describes, in non-mathematical language, some mathematical concepts and illustrates them by numerous examples of applications of the methods and techniques discussed in this book. The work consists of three introductory chapters, which introduce the technical concepts discussed in the remainder of the book. Successively, the subjects of interpolation, harmonic analysis, matrix calculation and boundary value problems are then studied. The readers are exposed to more than 300 problems and exercises concerning the manipulation of differential equations. We are walked through these problems, which are explained and solved, and they help provide a clear path for a student's learning.

[CUL 02] CULLUM J.K., WILLOUGHBY R.A., *Lanczos Algorithms for Large Symmetric Eigenvalue Computations; Vol.I: Theory*, SIAM, Philadelphia, 2002.

This book presents the mathematical foundations and the theories behind the numerical algorithms used to calculate the eigenvalues associated with large-size problems. It is an invaluable source of information about the non-classical Lanczos algorithms, as well as those that are more traditional. Described at length is a comprehensive presentation of the methods, which still today, continue to be the most effective for solving certain large-size eigenvalue problems. Examples, written in Fortran, and a rich documentation accompany each Lanczos algorithm that is discussed.

[MAG 15] MAGOULÈS F., CHEIK AHAMED A.-K., *Alinea: an advanced linear algebra library for massively parallel computations on graphics processing units*, International Journal of High Performance Computing Applications, vol. 29, no. 3, pp. 284–310, 2015.

This paper presents a new effective library implemented both in C++, CUDA and OpenCL language. This library includes several linear algebra operations and numerous algorithms for solving linear systems, with different matrix storage formats, with real and complex arithmetics in single and double precision, on both CPU and GPU devices. The CUDA version includes a self-tuning of the grid, i.e. that the library adapts GPU algorithms upon the hardware characteristics through a threading distribution upon the hardware configuration and the size of the problems. This library shows an interest with a well-balanced compromise on the ease of programming, the efficiency in terms of computing performance and also in terms of energy consumption.

[SAA 03] SAAD Y., *Iterative Methods for Sparse Linear Systems*, 2nd ed., SIAM, Philadelphia, 2003.

This reference work sheds a modern light on iterative algorithms for solving large-size linear systems, in other words, those composed of several millions unknowns. In addition to the many iterative methods that are studied in detail (Jacobi methods, conjugate gradient methods, GMRES methods, etc.), there are clear explanations of multigrid methods, Krylov subspace methods, preconditioning techniques and parallel preconditioners. A relatively recent and comprehensive bibliography is also provided.

[SHE 94] SHEWCHUK J.R., *An introduction to the conjugate gradient method without the agonizing pain*, available at: http://www.cs.cmu.edu/quake-papers/painless-conjugate-gradient.pdf, 1994.

This paper describes the steepest descent and conjugate gradient methods in a very intuitive way, using simple examples and a lot of figures. It also introduces the concept of eigenvectors to study the convergence of these methods.

A3.11. Mesh and graph partitioning

[KAR 15] KARYPIS G., *et al.*, *METIS: serial graph partitioning and fill-reducing matrix ordering*, University of Minnesota, available at: http://glaros.dtc.umn.edu/gkhome/views/metis , 1995–2015.

METIS is a library developed in the George Karypis lab at the University of Minnesota. METIS is a set of programs to partition non-structured graphs, and to renumber the equations of a matrix to reduce fill during factorization. The partitioning is done in such a way that it meets a number of *constraints* and optimizes a number of *objectives*. The most common constraint is to achieve same-size partitions, while the most common objective is to minimize the number of cut edges in the graph. METIS algorithms consist primarily of algorithms for producing graphs by using multilevel partitioning.

[WAL 06] WALSHAW C., *JOSTLE: Graph Partitioning Software*, The University of Greenwich, UK, 1995–2006.

JOSTLE is developed by Chris Walshaw at the University of Greenwich. JOSTLE is a software to partition an unstructured mesh, for example a finite element mesh or finite volume. The major advantage of this program is that it produces high-quality multilevel partitions. First released in 1995, and initially distributed for free, since 2006 JOSTLE is now marketed by NetWorks.

[PEL 08] CHEVALIER C., PELLEGRINI F., *SCOTCH: software package and libraries for sequential and parallel graph partitioning, static mapping and clustering, sequential mesh and hypergraph partitioning, and sequential and parallel sparse matrix block ordering*, LABRI et INRIA Bordeaux Sud-Ouest, available at: http://scotch.gforge.inria.fr , 2008.

SCOTCH and its parallel version PT-SCOTCH are the two libraries developed, just like METIS, for the partition of graphs and the renumbering of sparse matrices. A wrapper enables us to use SCOTCH functions using exactly the same call to the equivalent METIS functions.

[MAG 07] MAGOULÈS F., *Mesh Partitioning and Domain Decomposition Methods*, Saxe-Coburg Publications, 2007.

Mesh-partitioning methods have a strong influence in the convergence of numerical domain decomposition methods, which are very effective for the parallel resolution of very large-sized problems. This book of 13 chapters discusses mesh-partitioning methods and also some domain decomposition methods. Each chapter presents a state-of-the-art method, or a specific algorithm. An extensive bibliography is included at the end of each chapter. The main concepts discussed in this work are multilevel graph partitioning methods, multi-constraint and multi-objective methods, visualization of graph partitioning, substructuring methods, Schur primal and dual methods, domain decomposition methods, FETI, FETI-DP, FETI-H methods, the Schwarz additive algorithm, the Schwarz multiplicative algorithm, the Aitken-Schwarz method, optimized Schwarz methods, mortar element methods, multilevel preconditioning techniques and algebraic preconditioning techniques. The fields of application include fluid mechanics, acoustics and structural engineering.

[BIC 13] BICHOT C.-E., SIARRY P., *Graph Partitioning*, ISTE, London and John Wiley & Sons, New York, 2013.

Optimization of graph partitioning is a theoretical subject with applications in many areas, principally numerical analysis, program mapping onto parallel architectures, image segmentation and VLSI design. The size of graphs to partition has gone from thousands of vertices to millions. This book discusses various methods and tools for resolving graph partitioning problems, presenting both methodological and applied chapters. There are three parts to the book: the first part presents graph partitioning for numerical applications, the second part presents a view of graph partitioning optimization and the third part presents other aspects of graph partitioning. Multilevel, metaheuristics, parallelization or hypergraph methods are also covered. It includes new test graphs and data. The illustrated applications are varied, spanning from air-traffic control to social networks.

A3.12. Domain decomposition methods

[SMI 96] SMITH B.F., BJORSTAD P.E., GROPP W., *Domain Decomposition: Parallel Multilevel Methods for Elliptic Partial Differential Equations*, Cambridge University Press, 1996.

This book is the first, from a chronological point of view, about domain decomposition methods. It introduces, in a simple and pedagogical way, algorithms for domain decomposition. These algorithms are analyzed in detail, and computer implementation is discussed. This is the case of the alternating Schwarz algorithm, which is described first, and two-level preconditioning techniques follow. The generalization of this multilevel preconditioning technique is then discussed. Finally, methods of substructuring are presented. This book also contains a theoretical analysis of the convergence of domain decomposition algorithms, and a study of the particular cases of undefined or non-symmetrical problems.

[QUA 99] QUARTERONI A., VALLI A., *Domain Decomposition Methods for Partial Differential Equations*, Oxford Science Publications, 1999.

This reference book about domain decomposition first presents the basic mathematical concepts of these methods, at the variational level. The analysis of discretized equations is then discussed, followed by the presentation of domain decomposition algorithms at the discrete level. The analysis of these algorithms' convergence is then investigated. Extensions for domain decomposition methods to various boundary value problems are analyzed in detail, especially for convection-diffusion equations, and problems exhibiting a dependency as a function of time.

[TOS 04] TOSELLI A., WIDLUND O., *Domain Decomposition Methods – Algorithms and Theory*, Springer, vol. 34, 2004.

This book presents the principle methods of domain decomposition for finite element approximation, or by spectral elements of partial differential equations. A meticulous and detailed analysis of mathematical and algorithmic aspects of these methods is discussed. This work also reviews overlapping Schwarz methods, two-level preconditioning techniques, substructuring methods, the Schur primal, finite element tearing and interconnecting (FETI) method and the balanced Neumann-Neumann (BNN) method. Spectral element approximation, equations of linear elasticity, and undefined and non-symmetric problems are then examined.

[MAG 10] MAGOULÈS F., *Substructuring Techniques and Domain Decomposition Methods*, Saxe-Coburg Publications, 2010.

Substructuring or domain decomposition methods, in one way or another, have the following components: a partitioner that cuts a mesh into smaller submeshes; a resolution method (direct or iterative, exact or approximate) to determine the solution in each subdomain; interface conditions (strong or weak) to satisfy the continuity of the variables between the subdomains; a resolution method for determining the solution of the problem interface. The difference among these methods lies in the way these components are combined, to best provide an efficient and effective resolution method for the initial problem. A selection of some substructuring and domain decomposition methods is presented. The main topics covered include time decomposition methods, space decomposition methods, multilevel preconditioning techniques, asynchronous iterative methods and multisplitting methods. Various applications are illustrated, and cover fluid mechanics, structural mechanics, biology and finance, among other fields that are reviewed.

Bibliography

[AXE 01] AXELSSON O., BARKER V.A., *Finite Element Solution of Boundary Value Problems*, SIAM, Philadelphia, 2001.

[BAR 15] BARNEY B., Introduction to parallel computing, available at: https://computing.llnl.gov/tutorials/parallelcomp, 2015.

[BAS 03] BASTIEN J., MARTIN J.-N., *Introduction à l'Analyse Numérique. Applications sous Matlab*, Dunod, Paris, 2003.

[BAU 92] BAUER B., *Practical Parallel Programming*, Academic Press, 1992.

[BEL 97] BELLMAN R., *Introduction to Matrix Analysis*, SIAM, Philadelphia, 2nd edition, 1997.

[BIC 13] BICHOT C.-E., SIARRY P., *Graph Partitioning*, ISTE, London and John Wiley & Sons, New York, 2013.

[BOA 15] BOARD O.A.R., The OpenMP API specification for parallel programming, available at: http://openmp.org/wp, 2015.

[CAS 08] CASANOVA H., LEGRAND A., ROBERT Y., *Parallel Algorithms*, Numerical Analysis and Scientific Computing Series, Chapman & Hall/CRC Press, 2008.

[CHA 01] CHANDRA R., MENON R., DAGUM L. *et al.*, *Parallel Programming in OpenMP*, Academic Press, 2001.

[CIA 02] CIARLET P., *The Finite Element Method for Elliptic Problems*, SIAM, Philadelphia, 2002.

[CUL 02] CULLUM J., WILLOUGHBY R., *Lanczos Algorithms for Large Symmetric Eigenvalue Computations. Volume I: Theory*, SIAM, Philadelphia, 2002.

[DAU 00] DAUTRAY R., LIONS J. (eds), *Mathematical Analysis and Numerical Methods for Science and Technology*, vol. 1–9, Springer, 2000.

[DOW 98] DOWD K., SEVERANCE C., *High Performance Computing*, O'Reilly, 2nd edition, 1998.

[EIG 01] EIGENMANN R., VOSS M., (eds.), *OpenMP Shared Memory Parallel Programming*, vol. 2104 of Lecture Notes in Computer Science, International Workshop on OpenMP Applications and Tools, WOMPAT 2001, West Lafayette, IN, USA, Springer July 30–31, 2001.

[FOR 12] FORUM M.P.I., MPI: A message-passing interface standard version 3.0, available at: http://www.mpi-forum.org/docs/mpi-3.0/mpi30-report.pdf, September 2012.

[FOS 95] FOSTER I., *Designing and Building Parallel Programs*, Addison-Wesley, 1995.

[GEI 10] GEIMER M., WOLF F., WYLIE B. *et al.*, "The Scalasca performance toolset architecture", *Concurrency and Computation: Practice and Experience*, vol. 22, no. 6, pp. 702–719, 2010.

[GRO 94] GROPP W., LUSK E., SKJELLUM A., *Using MPI: Portable Parallel Programming with the Message-Passing Interface*, The MIT Press, 1994.

[GRO 98] GROPP W., HUSS-LEDERMAN S., LUMSDAINE A. *et al.*, *MPI: The Complete Reference. The MPI-2 Extensions*, The MIT Press, vol. 2, 1998.

[GRO 99] GROPP W., LUSK E., SKJELLUM A., *Using MPI: Portable Parallel Programming with the Message Passing Interface*, The MIT Press, 2nd edition, ftp://ftp.mcs.anl.gov/pub/mpi/using/UsingMPI.tar.gz, 1999.

[HIR 07] HIRSCH C., *Numerical Computation of Internal and External Flows: The Fundamentals of Computational Fluid Dynamics*, vol. 1, Butterworth-Heinemann, 2007.

[HOR 90] HORN R., JOHNSON C., *Matrix Analysis*, Cambridge University Press, 1990.

[JOH 87] JOHNSON C., *Numerical Solution of Partial Differential Equations by the Finite Element Method*, Dover Publications, 1987.

[KAR 03] KARNIADAKIS G., KIRBY R., *Parallel Scientific Computing in C++ and MPI: A Seamless Approach to Parallel Algorithms and their Implementation*, Cambridge University Press, New York, 2003.

[KAR 15] KARYPIS G., METIS: Serial Graph Partitioning and Fill-reducing Matrix Ordering, available at: http://glaros.dtc.umn.edu/gkhome/views/metis, 1995–2015.

[LAB 05] LABARTA J., GIMENEZ J., MARTÍNEZ E. *et al.*, "Scalability of tracing and visualization tools", *PARCO 2005*, pp. 869–876, 2005.

[LAN 96] LANCZOS C., *Linear Differential Operators*, SIAM, Philadelphia, 1996.

[LEV 02] LEVEQUE R., *Finite Volume Methods for Hyperbolic Problems*, Cambridge University Press, 2002.

[LÖH 01] LÖHNER R., *Applied CFD Techniques: An Introduction Based on Finite Element Methods*, John Wiley & Sons, New York, 2001.

[MAG 07] MAGOULÈS F. (ed.), *Mesh Partitioning Techniques and Domain Decomposition Methods*, Saxe-Coburg Publications, Stirlingshire, UK, 2007.

[MAG 10] MAGOULÈS F. (ed.), *Substructuring Techniques and Domain Decomposition Methods*, Saxe-Coburg Publications, Stirlingshire, UK, 2010.

[MAG 15] MAGOULÈS F., AHAMED A.-K.C., "Alinea: an advanced linear algebra library for massively parallel computations on graphics processing units", *International Journal of High Performance Computing Applications*, vol. 29, no. 3, pp. 284–310, 2015.

[MUM 05] MUMPS TEAM, MUMPS: a MUltifrontal Massively Parallel sparse direct Solver, available at: http://mumps.enseeiht.fr, 2005.

[PAC 96] PACHECO P., *Parallel Programming with MPI*, Morgan Kaufmann Publishers Inc., 1996.

[PEL 08] PELLEGRINI F., CHEVALIER C., SCOTCH: Software package and libraries for sequential and parallel graph partitioning, static mapping and clustering, sequential mesh and hypergraph partitioning, and sequential and parallel sparse matrix block ordering, Report , LABRI – INRIA Bordeaux Sud-Ouest, available at: http://scotch.gforge.inria.fr, 2008.

[PET 11] PETSC TEAM, Portable, Extensible Toolkit for Scientific Computation, Available at: http://www.mcs.anl.gov/petsc, 2011.

[QUA 94] QUARTERONI A., VALLI A., *Numerical Approximation of Partial Differential Equations*, Springer-Verlag, 1994.

[QUA 99] QUARTERONI A., VALLI A., *Domain Decomposition Methods for Partial Differential Equations*, Oxford Science Publications, 1999.

[SAA 03] SAAD Y., *Iterative Methods for Sparse Linear Systems*, SIAM, Philadelphia, 2nd edition, 2003.

[SHE 94] SHEWCHUK J., An introduction to the conjugate gradient method without the agonizing pain, Available at: http://www.cs.cmu.edu/quake-papers/painless-conjugate-gradient.pdf, 1994.

[SMI 96] SMITH B., BJORSTAD P., GROPP W., *Domain Decomposition: Parallel Multilevel Methods for Elliptic Partial Differential Equations*, Cambridge University Press, 1996.

[SNI 98] SNIR M., OTTO S., HUSS-LEDERMAN S. *et al.*, *MPI: The Complete Reference*, The MIT Press, 1998.

[TOS 04] TOSELLI A., WIDLUND O., Domain Decomposition Methods: Algorithms and Theory, vol. 34 of Springer Series in Computational Mathematics, Springer, 2004.

[VER 07] VERSTEEG H., MALALASEKERA W., *An Introduction to Computational Fluid Dynamics: The Finite Volume Method*, Pearson/Prentice Hall, 2007.

[VOS 03] VOSS M. (ed.), *OpenMP Shared Memory Parallel Programming*, vol. 2716 of Lecture Notes in Computer Science, International Workshop on OpenMP Applications and Tools, WOMPAT 2003, Toronto, Canada, 2003, Springer, June 26–27 2003.

[WAL 06] WALSHAW C., JOSTLE: Graph Partitioning Software, Available at: http://staffweb.cms.gre.ac.uk/wc06/jostle, 1995–2006.

Index

Other titles from

in

Computer Engineering

2015

CHEN Ken
Performance Evaluation by Simulation and Analysis with Applications to Computer Networks

CLERC Maurice
Guided Randomness in Optimization

MUNEESAWANG Paisarn, YAMMEN Suchart
Visual Inspection Technology in the Hard Disk Drive Industry

WERTZ Harald
Object-oriented Programming with Smalltalk

2014

BOULANGER Jean-Louis
Formal Methods Applied to Industrial Complex Systems

BOULANGER Jean-Louis
Formal Methods Applied to Complex Systems: Implementation of the B Method

DELAHAYE Daniel, PUECHMOREL Stéphane
Modeling and Optimization of Air Traffic

FRANCOPOULO Gil
LMF — Lexical Markup Framework

GHÉDIRA Khaled
Constraint Satisfaction Problems

ROCHANGE Christine, UHRIG Sascha, SAINRAT Pascal
Time-Predictable Architectures

WAHBI Mohamed
Algorithms and Ordering Heuristics for Distributed Constraint Satisfaction Problems

ZELM Martin *et al.*
Enterprise Interoperability

2012

ARBOLEDA Hugo, ROYER Jean-Claude
Model-Driven and Software Product Line Engineering

BLANCHET Gérard, DUPOUY Bertrand
Computer Architecture

BOULANGER Jean-Louis
Industrial Use of Formal Methods: Formal Verification

BOULANGER Jean-Louis
Formal Method: Industrial Use from Model to the Code

CALVARY Gaëlle, DELOT Thierry, SÈDES Florence, TIGLI Jean-Yves
Computer Science and Ambient Intelligence

MAHOUT Vincent
Assembly Language Programming: ARM Cortex-M3 2.0: Organization, Innovation and Territory

MARLET Renaud
Program Specialization

SOTO Maria, SEVAUX Marc, ROSSI André, LAURENT Johann
Memory Allocation Problems in Embedded Systems: Optimization Methods

2011

BICHOT Charles-Edmond, SIARRY Patrick
Graph Partitioning

BOULANGER Jean-Louis
Static Analysis of Software: The Abstract Interpretation

CAFERRA Ricardo
Logic for Computer Science and Artificial Intelligence

HOMES Bernard
Fundamentals of Software Testing

KORDON Fabrice, HADDAD Serge, PAUTET Laurent, PETRUCCI Laure
Distributed Systems: Design and Algorithms

KORDON Fabrice, HADDAD Serge, PAUTET Laurent, PETRUCCI Laure
Models and Analysis in Distributed Systems

LORCA Xavier
Tree-based Graph Partitioning Constraint

TRUCHET Charlotte, ASSAYAG Gerard
Constraint Programming in Music

VICAT-BLANC PRIMET Pascale *et al.*
Computing Networks: From Cluster to Cloud Computing

2010

AUDIBERT Pierre
Mathematics for Informatics and Computer Science

2005

GÉRARD Sébastien *et al.*
Model Driven Engineering for Distributed Real Time Embedded Systems

PANETTO Hervé
Interoperability of Enterprise Software and Applications 2005

Lightning Source UK Ltd.
Milton Keynes UK
UKOW06n1132231016

285941UK00003B/36/P